FATHER ORSINI'S ITALIAN KITCHEN

Previous books by Father Orsini:

Papa Bear's Favorite Italian Dishes

FATHER ORSINI'S ITALIAN KITCHEN

Father Joe Orsini

Illustrations by Harry Trumbore

*St. Martin's Press * New York*

Design by Chris Welch
Illustrations by Harry Trumbore

Library of Congress Cataloging-in-Publication Data

Orsini, Joseph E.
    Father Orsini's Italian kitchen / Joseph Orsini; introduction by Dom DeLuise.
      p. cm.
    "A Thomas Dunne book."
    ISBN 0-312-06352-0
    1. Cookery, Italian. I. Title. II. Title: Italian kitchen.
TX723.O748 1991
641.5945—dc20
                                                            91-20418
                                                            CIP

First Edition: September 1991
10 9 8 7 6 5 4 3 2 1

To my mother, Carmela Orsini, who now rests in peace with my father, Giuseppe, and my nephew, Dominick. Mamma, you taught me to never give up, to love without counting the cost. I miss you and await the day I will join you at the Feast of the Heavenly Banquet.

FOREWORD

I was co-hosting the "Mike Douglas Show" in Philadelphia when I was told that a priest was going to be one of the guests. Father Orsini had written a cookbook called, *Papa Bear's Favorite Italian Dishes*. He came on the show and cooked eggplant balls and was really terrific, as he substituted eggplant for ground beef in this vegetarian delight. I ended up with a delicious recipe, and more importantly a new friend. That show was over sixteen years ago, and I treasure my friendship with Father Orsini with all my heart. We've had some wonderful times together, and he has been both inspirational and fun. He has now written another cookbook, and I, for one, cannot wait to get my teeth into it. Sit back, relax, and bon appetit. Viva Father Orsini!

All my love,
Dom DeLuise

I WISH TO THANK ANN CONTI WHO STRONGLY
URGED ME TO WRITE A NEW COOKBOOK.
I THANK GOD FOR MY FAMILY, FRIENDS, AND
ASSOCIATES.

CONTENTS

INTRODUCTION

I have been an amateur chef ever since I could reach my mother's kitchen stove. In fact, the first time I reached for the stove was when I was four years old. My mother was preparing *pastina al burro* (tiny macaroni boiled in salted water and seasoned with butter—a typical dish prepared by Italian mothers for their tots) and, as she looked away, I reached up to see what was in the pot. In a second, my first encounter with the stove became a disaster. I spilled the contents all over me and suffered third-degree burns on my left arm.

That didn't discourage me though, for a few years later, I did the same thing, on the same arm, with a pot of hot coffee. You would think I would quit after that, but being a stubborn little Calabrese (the people who come from my parents' region of Italy, Calabria, are famous for being *teste dure*, i.e., hard-headed individuals), I persisted. My career with the stove began in my late teens when I took up the hobby of baking. I baked cookies, cakes, pies, and pizzas at every opportunity I could get. I was getting pretty good at it, but Mamma put a stop to it. I was a great baker but a lousy cleaner-upper. After cleaning up behind me for some time, Mamma decided it was cheaper to buy in the bakery. That ended that.

Some time later, I began cooking in earnest. It was really a matter of survival. I was in the seminary in Little Rock, Arkansas, and this Italian kid just couldn't cope with mustard greens and grits. I went from a 206-pound weakling to a 140-pound weakling in one year. That year, thanks to cornflakes and peanut butter, I barely managed to stay alive. When I arrived home for summer vacation, my mother kept looking for the fat kid she had sent to Arkansas with a supply of dried sausage. Now her kid *looked* like a dried sausage. Mamma made up her mind to formulate a survival plan. During the following years her care packages arrived for me at the seminary at regular intervals. They were filled with familiar Italian foodstuffs. I would carefully unload them when no one was around, and by trial and error, mostly error, I learned to cook. Around my cooking adventures there grew a select "secret" society of fellow seminarians, mostly from the East Coast, who willingly became the guinea pigs for my attempts at Italian cooking. They're all still alive and kicking, and so am I, so I guess it wasn't so bad.

When I was ordained a priest and traveled from parish to parish, I always found a sympathetic family who allowed me to use the kitchen to perfect my expertise. Today I get a lot of kidding from my colleagues about being the "cooking priest," but a lot of them stop kidding when they taste some of the dishes I prepare from these recipes.

This book is an attempt to be an honest-to-goodness cookbook with many fine recipes, but, as you will see, I have tried to make it a little something more. I hope you will laugh at my attempts to be humorous, ponder my attempts to be profound, and enjoy this wonderful life that God has given us while eating some of the best food this side of heaven.

Italian cooking has great simplicity, considerable originality, and flexibility. You can enjoy inexpensive dishes or, with some prices today, take out a bank loan to make the more elegant ones.

Italian housewives, many with large families and limited means, have for generations concentrated on making the best use of fresh local produce. The result is a tradition of practical dishes with distinctive flavors. Herbs, cheese, olive oil, tomatoes, and vegetables are used generously because they are readily available. It is from homespun recipes that the fabric of traditional Italian cooking has been woven.

The hallmarks of Italian cooking are quality of ingredients and freshness of flavor. A restaurant serving overcooked, lukewarm spaghetti or pizza smothered in a heavy blanket of reheated sauce does *not* represent the best of Italian cooking.

Italian cooking has strong regional character. Only a hundred years ago Italy was a collection of individual states, each with its own people, customs, traditions, and foods. What is represented in this book, for the most part, is the style of southern Italy.

Most of the ingredients in these recipes are available at local supermarkets; a few will have to be purchased from Italian specialty shops. It should be noted that the flavor of Parmesan cheese is much finer, and the cost much less, when it is bought by the chunk and then *freshly* grated for soups, pasta, and rice.

About ten years ago, at the insistence of many friends, I wrote and had published a cookbook of Italian dishes called *Papa Bear's Favorite Italian Dishes*. I could not believe its success, perhaps because it was a cookbook written by a Catholic priest or because the recipes were really good. Allow me to explain the title of my previous cookbook, *Papa Bear's Favorite Italian Dishes*. My last name, Orsini, literally translates into "bear cubs" or "little bears." When I was teaching Latin to my students years ago, they came to realize that my name was derived from the Latin word for bear, *ursus*. It took them little time from then on to call me Papa Bear and, of course, my mother became Mama Bear. Thus the title of my first volume on Italian cooking.

As the years have rolled on, I have continued to cook, and, if the people who eat my meals aren't telling white lies in order to not hurt this priest's feelings, I have gotten better at it. Not only that, but I have expanded my repertoire of dishes quite a bit.

I really enjoy cooking, but I enjoy even more the sharing of the results of my labor with family and friends. When I cook now, I remember Mamma, who rests in peace, for it was she who taught me how to cook with love.

Maybe that's it. The magical ingredient. *Love*.

Now, you don't have to do what I do—it helps me when I'm cooking— but I listen to happy Italian music or hum my favorite Italian songs. But remember that special ingredient in all these dishes, love. Without it, life and food would lose their savor and flavor.

As you cook along with me and Mamma, we wish you

Good Food!
Warm Friends!
Long Life!

Love,
Father Joe Orsini

1

THE REGIONS OF ITALY

There are twenty geographical regions of Italy. You will find recipes in this book from every region. I want you to be able to cook and taste the tremendous variety of Italian cooking, and though I have emphasized the cooking of Calabria and Sicily because my roots are there, I certainly do not intend to alienate Italians from the rest of Italy. (I may look stupid, but I'm really not.) The regional dishes in this chapter are indicated at the beginning of each recipe.

Fettuccine all'Albese

(Fettuccine from Alba)

YIELD: *4 Servings*

14 ounces fettuccine
3/4 cup grated Parmesan cheese
5 tablespoons softened butter

Pinch of nutmeg
Salt and freshly ground pepper to taste
1/4 cup thin-sliced raw mushrooms

Cook the fettuccine in plenty of boiling salted water until al dente. Drain thoroughly, then pile in a warmer serving dish. Add the cheese, butter, nutmeg, salt, and pepper. Fold gently to mix. Top with mushrooms and serve immediately.

2 * VALLE D'AOSTA

Costolette alla Valdostana

(Veal Chops, Valle d'Aosta Style)

YIELD: *4 Servings*

4 veal chops
4 slices fontina or mozzarella cheese
Salt and freshly ground pepper
All-purpose flour, for coating

1 or 2 eggs, beaten
1 cup plain bread crumbs
1/3 cup butter

Cut the chops horizontally through the center towards the bone. Place a slice of cheese inside each pocket and press well to flatten slightly. Salt and pepper both sides, then coat with flour. Dip the chops in the beaten egg, then coat with bread crumbs.

Melt the butter in a large frying pan, add the chops, and fry gently about 8 minutes on each side, until chops are golden and tender. Serve immediately.

Pizzoccheri

(Fettuccini with Cabbage and Cheese)

YIELD: *6 Servings*

2¹/₃ *cups raw diced potatoes*
1 pound cabbage, diced
1 pound fettuccine
³/₄ *cup butter*

2 garlic cloves, peeled
1 teaspoon sage
1 cup of diced Pecorino Romano cheese
Freshly ground pepper

Cook potatoes and cabbage in a large pan of boiling salted water for 15 minutes, add the pasta, and cook until al dente (about 5 minutes), then drain.

Melt butter in a small pan, add garlic and sage, and fry until the garlic is browned. Remove garlic and sage from butter. In a warmed serving dish, pile the pasta, cabbage, and potato mixture. Pour flavored butter over the top, add cheese, and sprinkle liberally with pepper. Serve immediately.

Canderli

(Dumplings with Salami and Bacon)

YIELD: *4 to 6 Servings*

3/4 pound dry crumbly bread, diced	*1 tablespoon chopped fresh parsley*
2/3 cup milk	*1 egg, beaten*
2 tablespoons olive oil	*1 egg yolk*
1/2 cup chopped smoked bacon	*Salt*
1/4 cup chopped salami	*61/4 cups beef stock*
1/2 cup all-purpose flour	*Tomato sauce (page 41)*

Put the bread in a bowl, cover with milk, and leave to soften for 1½ hours.

Heat the oil in a small pan, add the bacon and salami, and fry gently for 5 minutes. Remove the meat with a slotted spoon and transfer to a bowl.

Squeeze dry the bread, then add it to the meat mixture. Add the flour, parsley, egg, egg yolk, and salt. Mix until thoroughly combined, then shape the mixture into dumplings the size of walnuts.

Bring the stock to a boil in a large pan. Add the dumplings a few at a time and simmer until they rise to the surface. Remove with a slotted spoon and place in a warmed serving dish. Serve hot with Tomato Sauce.

5 * VENETO

Fegato di Vitello alla Veneziana

(Veal Liver, Venetian Style)

YIELD: *4 Servings*

If you are like me and don't care for liver, this next recipe that I tasted in a restaurant in Venice will change your mind.

4 tablespoons olive oil
2 tablespoons butter
1 pound onions, peeled and thinly sliced
1/2 cup chopped fresh parsley

1 pound veal liver, sliced wafer thin
1/4 cup beef stock
Salt and freshly ground pepper to taste

Heat oil and butter in a frying pan, add the onions and parsley, cover and cook gently for 20 to 30 minutes, until softened.

Add the liver, increase the heat, and stir in the stock. Cook for 5 minutes, then remove from heat and season with salt and pepper. Serve immediately.

6 * FRIULI-VENEZIA GIULIA

Jota

(Bean and Cabbage Soup)

YIELD: 4 to 6 Servings

2 cups dried navy beans, soaked in
   lukewarm water overnight
1/2 cup fatty bacon, diced
2 small heads cabbage, quartered
2 tablespoons cumin seeds
1 bay leaf

Salt
1/4 cup olive oil
2 garlic cloves, minced
2 tablespoons plain flour
1 cup yellow or white cornmeal

Place the beans and bacon in a saucepan and add water to cover. Bring to a boil, lower heat, add cornmeal, stir, and cook at a simmer for 1 1/2 hours, adding more water as necessary.

Meanwhile, combine in a pan the cabbage, cumin seeds, bay leaf, pinch of salt, and 1/4 cup water. Cook for 2 minutes, shaking pan constantly. Set aside.

Heat half the oil in another pan, add garlic, and fry until brown. Stir plain flour into hot oil. Cook for 2 minutes, stirring constantly. Add cabbage mixture and cook 5 more minutes. Add to beans, stir, then serve.

Cima alla Genovese
(Cold Stuffed Breast of Veal)

YIELD: *6 Servings*

6 ounces ground veal
1½ cups ground pork, 12 ounces
½ cup finely chopped fatty bacon
2 cups fresh bread crumbs, soaked in
    milk and squeezed dry
2 cups cooked peas
½ cup grated Parmesan cheese
½ cup pistachio nuts, shelled and
    blanched
2 teaspoons marjoram

Pinch of nutmeg
Salt and freshly ground pepper to taste
1 egg, beaten
2½-pound breast of veal
3 hard-boiled eggs, sliced
1 onion, peeled and chopped
1 carrot, peeled and chopped
½ bay leaf
A few black peppercorns

In a bowl combine the ground veal, pork, bacon, bread crumbs, peas, cheese, nuts, marjoram, nutmeg, and salt and pepper. Stir in the beaten egg.

Place the breast of veal on a cutting board. Take a long sharp knife and make a wide deep slice across the breast just under the bone to create a pocket.

Spread a quarter of the mixture over the meat (the pocket), then arrange egg slices on top. Continue these layers until all the stuffing and eggs are used, finishing with a layer of stuffing. Close the pocket and tie the whole thing with kitchen string.

Place the meat in an ovenproof casserole and sprinkle with salt and pepper. Add cold salted water to cover the meat, then add onion, carrot, bay leaf, and peppercorns. Bring to a boil, lower heat, cover, and simmer for 1½ to 2 hours, until meat is tender.

Drain the meat and place in a snug dish. Cover with a plate, place a weight on top, and leave to cool. Slice neatly before serving.

Ragù Bolognese
(Tomato-meat Sauce, Bologna Style)

YIELD: *4 Servings*

1/4 cup mushrooms
1 onion, peeled
1 carrot, peeled
1 celery stalk
1 thick slice bacon
5 tablespoons butter
1/4 cup olive oil
2/3 cup beef stock

1/3 cup ground beef
1/3 cup ground pork
7 tablespoons red wine
1 3/4 cups skinned and mashed tomatoes
Salt and freshly ground pepper to taste
1 cup frozen or fresh peas
3/4 cup Parmesan cheese

Mince the mushrooms with the onion, carrot, celery, and bacon. Heat 4 tablespoons of the butter and the oil in a heavy pan, add the minced mixture, and simmer for 10 minutes, gradually adding almost all of the stock.

Add the ground meats and cook over high heat for 5 minutes. Stir in the wine, cover, and simmer gently for 15 minutes.

Add the tomatoes, a little more stock, and salt and pepper. Cover again and simmer for 30 more minutes, adding more stock or water if necessary.

Melt the remaining butter in a separate pan, add peas, and cook for 5 minutes. Stir this into the sauce and cook 5 more minutes.

Cook pasta until al dente. Drain and pile into a warmed serving dish. Top with sauce and Parmesan. Serve immediately.

Fagioli all'Uccelletto
(Lima Beans in Tomato Sauce)

YIELD: *4 to 6 Servings*

The small white beans of Tuscany are featured at almost every meal in this region—so much so that the Tuscans are often given the disparaging name *mangiafagioli* (bean eaters) by Italians from other regions. But from my own experience, these beans cooked and served with just salt, pepper, and a splash of Tuscan virgin olive oil are unforgettable.

6 tablespoons olive oil
2 garlic cloves, peeled and chopped
2 sage sprigs
Freshly ground pepper to taste

2 pounds fresh or frozen lima beans, shelled
1½ cups skinned and chopped tomatoes

Heat the oil in a large saucepan; add garlic, sage, and pepper; fry gently for 5 minutes. Remove from heat, add the beans and a pinch of salt, and let rest for 3 to 4 minutes.

Add the tomatoes, cover, and simmer for about 20 minutes, until beans are tender, stirring occasionally. Remove sage sprigs and serve.

Spaghetti alla Nursina

(Spaghetti with Mushrooms)

YIELD: *4 Servings*

6 tablespoons olive oil
½ cup sliced mushrooms (preferably
  porcini, *morels, shiitaki, or other*
  unusual type of mushroom)

1 garlic clove, peeled and crushed
2 anchovies, washed and chopped
14 ounces spaghetti

Heat the oil in a heavy pan, add mushrooms, and cook gently for 5 minutes. Remove from heat and add garlic and anchovies. Return to heat and cook gently for 5 minutes, stirring constantly. Remove from heat and set aside.

Cook spaghetti in plenty of salted boiling water until al dente. Drain thoroughly and pile in warmed serving dish. Cover with sauce, fold gently to mix, and serve.

Vincisgrassi

(Lasagne with Ragù Marchegiano)

YIELD: *6 Servings*

I have a very dear friend, Ray Viviani, of Collingswood, New Jersey, whose parents come from the lovely city of Ascoli Piceno in this region. Ray works for another famous Italian-American, Lee Iacocca, at least indirectly. Ray owns a Chrysler dealership in Collingswood.

He always kids me about where the best Italian food has its origin, but we always agree to disagree. He insists it comes from the Marches and I insist it comes from Calabria. In Ray Viviani's honor, I include this next recipe from the Marches.

4 tablespoons olive oil
¼ pound of butter, use half stick for
*   sauce and other half to grease dish*
1 onion, peeled and chopped
1½ cups ground beef
½ cup diced bacon
¾ pound ground veal

¼ cup white wine
4 tomatoes, skinned and chopped
Pinch of nutmeg
Salt and freshly ground pepper to taste
1 pound lasagne, cooked
½ cup Parmesan cheese, grated
½ pound Mozzarella, sliced

To make the ragu, heat the oil and butter in a heavy pan. Add the onion, beef, bacon, and veal, and stir over moderate heat for 10 minutes. Add the wine, tomatoes, nutmeg, and salt and pepper. Lower heat and simmer one hour.

Cook lasagne until al dente. Drain thoroughly. Preheat oven to 400°F.

Put a layer of prepared lasagne in the bottom of a buttered, deep, oven-proof dish. Cover with a layer of sauce, sprinkle with Parmesan and top with a few slices of mozzarella. Continue these layers until all the ingredients are used, finishing with a layer of cheese. Melt remaining butter and sprinkle over top. Bake for 20 minutes. Serve hot.

Carciofi alla Giudea

(Fried Artichokes, Jewish Style)

YIELD: *4 Servings*

Rome is the center of this region and every time I find myself in a Roman restaurant I try to order this recipe if artichokes are in season.

One Easter season when I was in Rome with my dear friend and "adopted" son, Dan Hughes of Pine Hill, we ate these beauties twice a day. Try them and you will see why.

4 young artichokes
Olive oil
4 small garlic cloves, peeled and chopped

½ cup fresh chopped parsley
Salt and freshly ground pepper to taste

From the artichokes remove the hard outer leaves, the chokes, and tips. Flatten the artichokes slightly by holding them upside down and pressing against a work surface.

Cover the base of a large frying pan with olive oil. Heat slightly, then add the artichokes, stem downwards. Fry over moderate heat for 10 minutes, then turn over, increase the heat, and fry for 10 more minutes, turning frequently until golden brown and crunchy on all sides. Remove the artichokes with a slotted spoon and keep warm.

In the pan, sauté the garlic and parsley for 5 minutes on gentle heat, add salt and pepper. Pour over artichokes and serve.

13 * ABRUZZO

Fettuccine Abruzzesi
(Fettuccine with Herbs and Bacon)

YIELD: *4 Servings*

Another dear friend, Frank Di Mauro, who happens to be my barber, hails from this region, Abruzzo and Molise. Frank keeps me supplied with garlic and sweet basil from his garden behind his shop in Landisville, New Jersey. I dedicate these next dishes to him and his wife, Bruna, and his beautiful children, Lisa and Frank.

3 tablespoons olive oil
1/2 cup chopped fatty bacon
1 onion, peeled and chopped
2/3 cup chicken stock
1 tablespoon chopped fresh parsley

6 fresh basil leaves, chopped
Salt and hot pepper seeds or flakes to taste
14 ounces fettuccine
2/3 cup grated Pecorino Romano cheese

Heat the oil in a heavy pan, add bacon and onion, and fry gently for 5 minutes. Add stock, parsley, basil, and salt and hot pepper. Cook gently, stirring occasionally, until stock is reduced and slightly thickened.

Meanwhile, cook fettuccine until al dente. Drain thoroughly and pile into a warmed serving dish. Add sauce and cheese, fold gently, and serve.

14 * MOLISE

Calzoni alla Molisana
(Fried Dough Pockets)

YIELD: *4 servings*

Dough

3 1/2 cups all-purpose flour
Pinch of salt
1/2 cup shortening

2 eggs, beaten
Freshly squeezed juice of 1 lemon

Filling

1 cup ricotta cheese, firmly packed
½ cup diced ham
½ cup diced provolone cheese

2 egg yolks
Salt and freshly ground pepper to taste

Assembly

1 egg white, lightly whisked
Vegetable oil, for deep-frying. Oil must
  be heated to 120°.

To test oil, drop in a piece of white
  bread, when it turns brown, oil is
  ready for frying the calzoni.

To make dough: Sift flour and salt onto a work surface and make a well in the center. Add the shortening, eggs, and lemon juice; then work all together to make a smooth dough.

To make filling: Press ricotta through a strainer into a bowl. Add ham, provolone, egg yolks, salt, and pepper. Mix thoroughly until well combined.

To assemble: Flatten dough with a rolling pin into a large, fairly thin sheet. Cut out 4 circles, each about 8 inches in diameter. Divide the filling among the circles, placing it in the center of each. Brush the edges of the circles with egg white, then fold dough over filling and press the edges.

Deep-fry one at a time in a deep frying pan until golden brown. Drain on paper towels. Serve hot.

15 * CAMPANIA

Pasta e Ceci alla Napoletana
(Chick-peas and Pasta)

YIELD: *4 Servings*

1 can chick-peas with their liquid,
   19 ounces
½ can water
7 tablespoons olive oil
4 tomatoes, skinned, cored, and chopped

2 garlic cloves, peeled and crushed
12 ounces green fettuccine
1 tablespoon chopped fresh parsley
6 fresh basil leaves, chopped
Salt and freshly ground pepper to taste

In a large saucepan place chick-peas, water, 3 tablespoons of the oil, the tomatoes, and half the garlic. Bring to a boil, lower heat, and simmer for 1 hour.

    Add the fettuccine and cook for 15 minutes. Add parsley, basil, remaining garlic and oil, and salt and pepper. Serve hot.

16 * APULIA

Calzone alla Pugliese
(Onion Pie)

YIELD: *6 to 8 Servings*

⅔ cup seedless raisins
4 tablespoons olive oil
5 cups sliced onions
1 stalk chopped celery
1 cup pitted black olives, finely chopped
1 teaspoon fennel seeds
5 canned anchovies, drained and finely
   chopped

4 tomatoes, skinned, cored, and chopped
Freshly ground pepper to taste
½ cup grated Pecorino Romano cheese
½ cup grated Parmesan cheese
1 recipe pizza dough (page 252)

Soak the raisins in lukewarm water for 15 minutes. Meanwhile, heat 2 table-spoons of the oil in a pan, add onions, celery, and fennel seeds and fry gently for 5 minutes. Add olives, anchovies, and tomatoes. Drain the raisins and dry thoroughly, then add with pepper to onion mixture. Cook for 15 more minutes, remove from heat, and stir in grated cheeses.

Divide the dough in two, making one piece slightly larger than the other. Flatten the larger piece of dough and roll out to fit an oiled 9-inch springform pan. Line the base and sides of the pan with the rolled-out dough. Spread the filling on top.

Flatten remaining dough and roll out to make a top crust. Place over the filling and press edges together to seal. Allow to rise in a warm place for 30 minutes. Sprinkle with remaining oil. Bake at 400°F for 15 minutes, then lower temperature to 375°F and bake for 25 minutes. Slice and serve hot.

17 * BASILICATA

Pasta col Cavolfiore
(Pasta with Cauliflower)

YIELD: *4 Servings*

Basilicata is the region of my dear friend Dom De Luise's parents. I dedicate this dish to Dom and his parents.

9 cups water
Salt
1½ pounds cauliflower, divided into
* flowerets*
14 ounces mezze ziti or any other short
* tubular macaroni*

7 tablespoons olive oil
1 slice stale bread, crumbled
Freshly ground pepper to taste

Bring water and a little salt to a boil in a large pan. Add cauliflower and cook for 3 minutes. Add pasta and cook for 12 more minutes, or until al dente.

Drain the cauliflower and pasta. Keep hot in a warmed serving dish. Heat the oil in a small pan; add bread crumbs and fry over brisk heat until well browned. Sprinkle over the cauliflower and pasta, add pepper, and fold gently to mix. Serve hot.

Millecosedde

(Thick Bean Soup)

YIELD: *6 to 8 Servings*

This recipe I dedicate to another extraordinary friend, Mr. Nicholas Sestito. Nick and I grew up in Bayonne, New Jersey. While we were going to college, I at Seton Hall, he at Villanova, we had regular meetings on my mother's front porch, where we discussed philosophy and theology.

Nick has his roots in the town of San Vito (Province of Catanzaro) in Calabria. Nick exemplifies in his life the sterling qualities of undying loyalty in friendship and love of family. He is an example of excellence in a sea of mediocrity. With love to Nick, his wife, Dee, his children, Donna, Lisa, and Nick, Jr., here is Millecosedde.

½ cup dried red kidney beans
½ cup dried navy beans
½ cup chick-peas
½ cup dried lentils
7 tablespoons olive oil
½ cup chopped bacon
1 carrot, peeled and diced
1 onion, peeled and chopped

5 cloves garlic, peeled and crushed
9 cups clear chicken stock
½ small green cabbage, shredded
1½ cups sliced mushrooms
Salt and freshly ground pepper, to taste
½ pound small-sized pasta (ditali, ditalini, *or elbows*)
1 cup grated Pecorino Romano cheese

Soak the kidney beans, navy beans, chick-peas, and lentils in water overnight. Drain and place in a large pot.

Cover with water and bring to a boil. Lower heat, cover, and simmer for 1¼ hours.

Heat the oil in a large, heavy pan. Add the bacon, carrot, onion, and garlic; fry gently for 5 minutes. Add stock and bring to a boil. Lower the heat, add cabbage, and simmer for 5 minutes.

Drain the beans and add to the stock along with mushrooms and salt and pepper. Stir well, add pasta, and cook another 15 minutes. Sprinkle with cheese and serve hot.

Pasta col Broccolo

(Macaroni with Broccoli)

YIELD: *4 Servings*

This recipe I dedicate to a friend of more than thirty years, Dr. Salvatore Cerniglia of Moorestown, New Jersey. I was eleven years old when I met Dr. Sal; he was eight years old and newly emigrated from his home town of Villa Frati (Province of Palermo) in Sicily. When I spoke to him in Sicilian, I saw a frightened eight-year-old kid transform into a comfortable, confident, and gutsy Sicilian. I was the priest at his wedding and have baptized his children, Daniele and Marcello.

Most Sundays now, I am a guest for dinner prepared by his beautiful and talented wife, Rosemarie. Rosemarie is a noted interior designer and an old-fashioned Italian-American girl who, like me, was born and raised in Bayonne.

3/4 pound broccoli, chopped
1/4 cup olive oil
1 onion, peeled and sliced
2 cups crushed skinned tomatoes
Salt and freshly ground pepper to taste
1 garlic clove, peeled and crushed
6 canned anchovies, drained and soaked
  in milk

4 1/2 tablespoons raisins soaked in
  lukewarm water for 15 minutes
4 1/2 tablespoons pine nuts (pignoli)
3/4 pound short macaroni
4 basil leaves, chopped
3/4 cup grated Pecorino Romano cheese

Boil the broccoli in salted water for 15 minutes. Drain thoroughly.

In a separate pan heat half the oil, add the onions, and fry gently for 5 minutes. Add the tomatoes and salt and pepper. Cover and simmer for 30 minutes.

In a separate pan, heat the remaining oil, add garlic, and fry gently until browned. Add the anchovies and cook, stirring, until broken down. Add the anchovies, raisins, broccoli, and pine nuts to the tomato sauce. Cook 5 more minutes, stirring frequently.

Cook macaroni until al dente, drain, and pile in a warmed serving dish. Cover with the sauce, add basil and cheese, fold gently to mix, and serve hot.

Favata

(Bean and Sausage Stew)

YIELD: *4 to 6 Servings*

1½ cups dried white kidney or navy
   beans
1½ cups diced fatback or smoked bacon
1½ cups skinned Italian sausage
¼ pound Italian salami, diced

1 whole canned roasted red pepper (sweet
   bell)
2 garlic cloves, peeled
Salt to taste
8 to 12 slices stale Italian bread

Soak the beans overnight. Drain, then place in a large saucepan and cover with cold water. Bring to a boil, lower heat, and simmer for 40 minutes.

Add remaining ingredients except the bread. Cover and simmer for 2 hours, stirring frequently.

Place 2 slices of bread in each soup bowl. Discard the garlic and roasted red pepper and spoon the stew over the bread. Serve hot.

2

A STOP IN SPAIN

I am convinced that unconditional love makes us whole and real. That is the kind of love that Jesus taught and urges us to show one another. I have written about that in my other books, and from the response I have received, I know that thousands of others are convinced of the same fact.

When I wrote my other books, I tried to recall certain individuals who had a lasting influence on me. Of course, when you start to name people, there's always the chance that you'll unintentionally leave out someone. I remember vividly that when those books hit the bookstores, not only a few of my friends and relatives asked with hopeful gleams in their eyes, "Hey, Joe, is *my* name in your book?" My brother-in-law Joe Varela was one who wanted to ask that question, but was too humble to do so. One night recently in pleasant conversation over good coffee at his house, we were discussing my writing this book. I told my brother-in-law that, although all of the other recipes would be Italian, I would include a few of his, which would be Spanish. My brother-in-law is a warm and earnest Christian and I love him more as a blood brother than as a mere in-law. So to honor him and his Spanish heritage, we divert our fantastic culinary journey with some of his great native dishes. (I must confess, however, that I tampered a bit with some of the ingredients, so if they taste a little Italian, blame me.)

Meatballs alla Spagnola

YIELD: *4 to 5 servings*

Meatballs

2 pounds chopped chuck
1 large onion, chopped
1 teaspoon salt
1/2 teaspoon freshly ground pepper

1 cup plain bread crumbs
3 garlic cloves, diced fine, OR 1 teaspoon
   garlic powder
1 green bell pepper, chopped fine
1 egg

Sauce

1 teaspoon vegetable oil
1 onion, chopped
2 garlic cloves or 3/4 teaspoon garlic
   powder
1 cup hot water mixed with enough flour
   to make a runny paste

1/2 teaspoon salt
Freshly ground pepper
Paprika to taste

2 potatoes, peeled and quartered

To make meatballs: In a bowl, mix all ingredients. Form meatballs and fry in a heavy pan until browned. Set aside.

To make sauce: In the same frying pan, add oil and sauté onions and garlic. Add flour mixture and seasonings, simmer, and stir for 10 minutes.

Add the meatballs and potatoes, cover, and simmer over low heat till potatoes are done, about ½ hour.

Caldo Gallego, Spanish Soup

YIELD: *4 to 5 Servings*

3 quarts cold water
1½ pounds smoked pork hocks
4 cups chopped green cabbage, washed
2 medium-sized carrots, diced
2 medium-sized potatoes, scalloped
1 pound chorizo, skinned and diced

1 can (1 pound) small white beans,
  rinsed and drained
⅛ teaspoon salt
⅛ teaspoon white pepper
1 bay leaf
⅛ teaspoon Spanish paprika

In a small pot, bring the cold water to a boil and add the pork hocks. Boil for 3 minutes to clean and remove excess smoked flavor.

In a large soup pot, bring all ingredients to a boil. Cover pot, reduce heat, and simmer for 3 hours. After 2 hours, remove hocks. Remove meat and dice. Return all to soup. To serve, remove bone and skin; salt and pepper to taste.

Variation: Replace 2 cups of the cabbage with 2 cups of broccoli raab (stems removed), washed and chopped.

Arroz con Pollo

YIELD: *4 to 5 Servings*

1 large (3–4 pounds) frying chicken, quartered
¼ cup olive oil
1 pound chorizo, sliced
1 medium-sized onion, chopped
2 green bell peppers, diced
1 fresh tomato, diced, or 2 canned plum tomatoes, crushed
3 garlic cloves, minced
1 teaspoon salt

½ teaspoon freshly ground black pepper
⅛ teaspoon Spanish paprika
1 or 2 bay leaves
.2 grams Spanish saffron
Pinch of oregano
1 packet Goya Sazon (Goya seasoning)
4 cups cold water, boiled
2 cups washed rice
1 or 2 real pimientos, strips
3 or 4 green stuffed olives, sliced

Dust chicken pieces with black pepper. In a large sauce pot in hot oil, brown pieces on both sides. Add chorizo and sauté 2 to 3 minutes until browned. Add remaining ingredients except the cold water, rice, pimientos, and olives. Mix, cover, and simmer for 5 minutes. Add the water and mix thoroughly. When it begins to boil, add rice and stir. Allow to set, lay pimiento slices and olives on top. Cover and simmer on low heat for 20 to 25 minutes, until rice is done.

Meatloaf alla Varela

YIELD: *4 to 5 Servings*

1½ to 1¾ pounds lean ground beef
¾ pound ground veal
1 medium onion, chopped fine
1 jar (7 ounces) pimientos with juice, chopped fine
1 can (7 ounces) tomato sauce
1 egg

1 cup fine-ground bread crumbs
2 tablespoons flour
1 teaspoon Worcestershire sauce
Salt and freshly ground pepper to taste
¼ cup of water
1 hard-boiled egg

Preheat oven to 350°F. In a large bowl mix all ingredients except hard-boiled egg. Add a ¼ cup water if needed. Form a loaf, placing the hard-boiled egg in the center. Grease a meatloaf pan, fill with formed meat, and bake for 1 hour.

Mushroom Gravy Coruña

YIELD: *4 to 5 Servings*

1 small onion, sliced
3 tablespoons olive oil
1/8 teaspoon paprika
2 tablespoons flour
*1 can (4 ounces) mushroom stems and
  pieces*

1 tablespoon butter
1 cup boiling water
1 cup chicken broth
1/2 teaspoon Worcestershire sauce
1/8 teaspoon Gravy Master
Salt and pepper to taste

In a skillet sauté onion in olive oil; when transparent, add paprika and flour. Once flour is blended in, add mushrooms, stirring constantly to avoid sticking. Add butter. As flour browns, add 1 cup of the boiling water, the broth, Worcestershire sauce, Gravy Master, and salt and pepper. Bring to a boil, lower heat, simmer, and continue stirring until gravy thickens to a velvetlike consistency, about 5 minutes. If the gravy becomes too thick, add more water a little at a time. Continue to cook for at least another 5 minutes.

Chicken alla Spagnola

YIELD: *4 to 5 Servings*

1 large frying chicken, quartered
1/4 cup olive oil
1 onion, chopped
4 potatoes, peeled and quartered
3 green bell peppers, diced

2 garlic cloves, minced
1 teaspoon salt
1/2 teaspoon freshly ground pepper
Pinch of saffron

Dust chicken pieces with black pepper. Heat the oil in a frying pan. Add the chicken and brown on both sides. Remove chicken and set aside. Then in the same pan sauté the onion, potatoes, bell peppers, garlic cloves, and salt and pepper. Add chicken pieces and saffron and simmer covered over low heat till potatoes and chicken are done, about 1/2 hour.

Flan

YIELD: *4 to 6 Servings*

Butter, for mold
1 cup sugar
2 tablespoons water
4 eggs

1 can (14 ounces) sweetened condensed
milk
1 cup water
1/2 teaspoon cinnamon
1/2 teaspoon grated lemon rind

Preheat oven to 350°F.

Butter a 4-cup mold; keep warm.

Combine sugar and the 2 tablespoons water in a heavy, small skillet. Cook, stirring constantly, until caramelized and syrupy. Immediately pour into prepared mold; tilt to coat bottom and sides of container while sugar is still hot.

Beat eggs well. Add milk, the 1 cup water, cinnamon, and lemon rind; mix well. Pour into prepared mold. Place mold in a larger pan containing hot water to level of custard. Bake for 1 hour, or until knife inserted in center comes out clean. Cool completely.

Loosen custard with knife; invert on serving platter. Spoon caramel over top.

*   *   *

The next recipe is very special to my family because of its history. About thirty years ago, my sister Evelyn tried to learn it from her mother-in-law Trina Varela. But Grandma-Mamma Varela was the typical European mom who cooks from experience and not rigid recipes. When my sister tried to duplicate Grandma-Mamma's instructions of "a handful of this and a little of that," it just didn't come out right. One day, my sister and brother-in-law's son Frank, who was just a sophomore in high school at the time, had the day off from school; he found a recipe in a magazine that sounded like Brazo Gitano to him and so he proceeded to bake it. When my sister and her husband returned home from shopping, they found a perfect Brazo Gitano on their kitchen table. Now you can make it for yourself and see why it's one of my family's favorites.

Brazo Gitano
(Gypsy's Arm)

YIELD: *8 to 10 Servings*

Cake

4 eggs
1 teaspoon baking powder
1/4 teaspoon salt
3/4 cup sugar

1 teaspoon vanilla
3/4 cup sifted Presto or Bisquick
Confectioner's sugar

Cream Filling

1 cup heavy cream
1 cup milk

1 package (3 1/2 ounces) French Vanilla
Jell-o Instant Pudding

Preheat oven to 400°F. Grease bottom and sides of a 15 × 10 × 1-inch pan; line with waxed paper and grease lightly.

To make cake: Beat eggs until foamy. Add baking powder and salt; beat until very light. Add sugar, about 1 tablespoon at a time; continue beating until very thick. Fold in vanilla and Presto a little at a time. Pour into prepared pan. Bake for 13 minutes, or until slightly browned.

While cake bakes, sift confectioners' sugar lightly over a towel. When cake is done, loosen from pan with the point of a paring knife. Invert cake onto towel and remove pan. Quickly peel off paper and trim off crisp edges. Roll up cake starting at narrow side. Wrap tightly into a roll. Cool and then unroll cake carefully.

To make cream filling: Follow package instructions.

Spread cake with filling and roll up again.

3

LET'S BEGIN

Antipasto, meaning "before the meal," is the first course of an Italian meal. Since Italian-Americans are becoming these days as weight conscious as the rest of society and there is a trend towards lighter meals and less starchy foods, an antipasto is often served instead of pasta. The antipasto can be extremely simple, or as elaborate as you like—anything from a crisp tomato salad to a dozen different ingredients artistically combined, such as Insalata Suprema (p. 211). The point to remember is that the antipasto should complement the rest of the meal. Following is a recipe for vegetable fritters northern Italian style, a great beginning to any meal.

Fritto Misto di Verdure

Batter

½ cup flour
½ teaspoon salt
2 tablespoons olive oil

10 tablespoons warm water
1 large egg white

Vegetables

Cauliflower, parboiled
Broccoli, parboiled
Fennel, sliced and parboiled
Celery, slice and parboiled
Beets, sliced and boiled
Potatoes, sliced and parboiled

Mushrooms, thin sliced
Eggplant, thin sliced
Zucchini, thin sliced
Tomatoes, thin sliced
Onions, thin sliced

To make batter: Sift the flour and salt into a bowl. Stir in the oil and warm water, forming a smooth, fairly stiff batter. Beat well and let stand in refrigerator for 1 hour. Just before using, whisk the egg white to a light foam and fold gently into the batter.

Coat the vegetables with frying batter and fry in olive oil until crisp and golden. Drain on absorbent paper and serve immediately.

Mozzarella in Carrozza
(Italian Fried Cheese Sandwich)

1 1/2 -ounce-slice mozzarella
2 square slices firm bread
Flour

1 egg, lightly beaten with a dash of salt
Oil, for frying

Remove crusts from bread. Sandwich the mozzarella between the slices of bread and cut into halves or quarters. Dip each minisandwich in flour, then in salted egg, allowing bread to soak up egg. Turn once. Drain, press sandwich firmly together, and fry in hot oil until golden on both sides. Serve immediately (it makes a great lunch or hot antipasto).

Antipasto di Uova Sode, Fave e Pecorino

(Hard-boiled Egg, Fava Bean, and Pecorino Appetizer)

12 hard-boiled eggs
Parsley sprigs, for garnish
Salt and freshly ground pepper to taste

1 pound fresh fava beans
½ pound pecorino cheese, broken into
   small pieces

Just before serving, shell eggs and slice them. Arrange on a serving platter and decorate with parsley sprigs. Season with salt and pepper.

On another platter arrange the fava beans with the cheese. The beans are shelled at the table.

Tramezzino Fantasia

("Fantasy" Sandwich)

2 tablespoons mayonnaise
1 teaspoon mustard
2 tablespoons Gorgonzola
5 slices white bread, buttered
4 slices ham
4 slices salami

4 pickles, sliced
4 slices provolone cheese, cut into strips
3 tablespoons tuna packed in oil, mashed
4 lettuce leaves
1 hard-boiled egg, sliced

Blend mayonnaise, mustard, and Gorgonzola using a fork. Spread mixture on buttered bread slices. Top with remaining ingredients to taste, pressing well. Cut into triangles, if desired.

Pane con Mozzarella Olive Nere

(Mozzarella and Black Olive Sandwiches)

1 pound mozzarella
8 tablespoons olive oil
2 ounces black olives, pitted and chopped
1 heaping tablespoon capers in vinegar, chopped

½ cup chopped fresh parsley
Salt to taste
8 slices bread, toasted and buttered

Slice mozzarella and set aside.

Add olive oil, capers, and parsley to chopped olives, mixing well. Add salt. Pour mixture on mozzarella and let rest for 30 minutes.

Top 4 bread slices with dressed mozzarella, and assemble sandwiches.

Olive Repiene Marchigiane

(Stuffed Olives, Marche Style)

YIELD: *12 Servings*

1/4 onion, chopped
1 celery stalk, chopped
1 baby carrot, chopped
4 ounces lean pork
2 ounces lean beef
2 ounces chicken breast
A dash of dry white wine
Salt and freshly ground pepper to taste
2 tablespoons butter or margarine

1 tablespoon Italian parsley, chopped
3 eggs, beaten
2 heaping tablespoons Parmesan cheese
Dash of nutmeg
Rind of 1 lemon
48 Spanish olives, pitted
Flour, for dredging
2 eggs, beaten
Seasoned bread crumbs
Oil, for frying

Saute onion, celery and carrot in a large pan with oil until water evaporates. Add meats and sprinkle with wine, salt, and pepper to taste. Add butter or margarine and parsley, cover and cook for 30 minutes over a low flame. Place mixture into an electric blender. Add 3 eggs, cheese, nutmeg, lemon rind, and additional salt and pepper. Blend until smooth. Fill the olives with the mixture, then dredge in flour. Dip into beaten eggs and coat with bread crumbs. Heat oil in a large frying pan and fry olives until golden. Drain well on paper towels; serve hot.

Torta Primavera

(Springtime Torte)

YIELD: *12 Servings*

Crêpes

2 cups all-purpose flour
1/2 teaspoon salt
4 eggs

3 cups milk
1 cup water
2 tablespoons oil

Assembly

12 tablespoons mayonnaise
8 thin slices mortadella
8 thin slices salami
8 thin slices provolone
8 slices tomato

6 thin slices cooked veal pâté
1 cup cooked spinach, well-drained
1 thin omelet
3 green roasted peppers, peeled and split
    lengthwise

Glaze

1 tablespoon unflavored gelatin
1 cup chicken broth, heated

1¼ cups mayonnaise
2 tablespoons dry white wine

To make crepes: Combine all ingredients in a mixing bowl. Chill for 1 hour. Ladle batter onto a hot, buttered, 9-inch non-stick skillet and cook each crêpe until golden on both sides. Make 12 crepes and set aside.

To assemble: Spread 1 teaspoon mayonnaise on each crêpe. Place 1 crêpe, mayonnaise side up, on a serving platter. Proceed to layer the following: ½ roasted green pepper, 4 slices of mortadella, 1 crêpe mayonnaise side up, ½ roasted green pepper, 4 slices of the salami, 1 crêpe, 4 slices of the provolone, 1 crêpe, tomatoes, 1 crêpe, ½ roasted green pepper, veal pâté slices, 1 crêpe, remaining 4 slices mortadella, 1 crêpe, remaining 4 slices provolone, ½ roasted green pepper, 1 crêpe, remaining 4 slices salami, 1 crêpe, spinach, 1 crêpe, remaining roasted green pepper, omelet, 1 crêpe.

Refrigerate stack of crêpes and fillings until cool.

To make glaze: Dissolve gelatin in chicken broth, and blend in mayonnaise. Stir in white wine, and chill until mixture begins to harden. Glaze torte with mixture.

If desired, decorate rim of torte with Boston lettuce leaves and top with sliced black olives.

Caponata
(Cold Eggplant Appetizer)

YIELD: *4 Cups*

1 small eggplant (about 1 pound), cut into 1/2-inch cubes

2 teaspoons coarse salt

1 large red or green bell pepper, seeded and cut into 1-inch pieces

1 large yellow bell pepper, seeded and cut into 1 inch pieces

1/2 cup coarsely chopped onion

1/4 cup coarsely chopped celery

1/4 cup olive oil

1 can (1-pound) Italian plum tomatoes, drained and seeded

2 medium zucchini, cut into 1/4-inch slices

2 tablespoons pine nuts (pignoli)

2 tablespoons tomato paste

1 to 2 tablespoons capers, drained

2 tablespoons white wine vinegar

1 tablespoon sugar

6 large green olives, pitted and thinly sliced

1 fresh or dried bay leaf

1/8 teaspoon freshly ground pepper

Place eggplant cubes in a colander and sprinkle with the salt. Cover with a plate and drain 30 minutes.

Sauté bell peppers, onion, and celery in 2 tablespoons of the oil in a large skillet over medium heat, stirring frequently, until onions are soft, 5 to 8 minutes. Remove from skillet and set aside. Add remaining oil to skillet.

Squeeze excess liquid from eggplant. Sauté in skillet over medium heat, stirring frequently, until light brown, 5 to 8 minutes. Return pepper-onion mixture to skillet and stir in all remaining ingredients. Cook over medium-low heat, stirring frequently, until most of the liquid has evaporated, 10 to 15 minutes.

Cover and cool to room temperature. Refrigerate at least 2 hours. Remove bay leaf before serving.

Malfatti

(Unevenly Shaped Dumplings)

YIELD: *6 Servings*

*1 cup (10-ounce package) finely chopped
    cooked spinach*
1½ cups ricotta cheese
¼ cup grated Parmesan cheese
1 cup bread crumbs
2 eggs, beaten

1 teaspoon salt
1 teaspoon fresh or dry basil
½ teaspoon nutmeg
1 garlic clove, pressed
Flour, to roll the cylinders

Mix together all ingredients except the flour in a large bowl.

Form the mixture into cordlike cylinders the thickness of your index finger and about 2 inches long. Roll each cylinder in flour. Place cylinders on a baking sheet and refrigerate for at least 2 hours.

In a wide saucepan heat 2 inches of water with 1 teaspoon of salt to boiling. Drop the *malfatti* in several at a time. They will sink to the bottom, then will rise to the surface when cooked. Remove with a slotted spoon and place on a baking sheet in a 200°F oven. Bake for 20 minutes. Serve hot.

Macaroni Shell
Hors d'Oeuvres

Cook and drain #21 macaroni shells according to package directions. Spread on absorbent paper in a single layer and allow to dry completely. Then fill each shell with one of the following fillings. Stick a toothpick through the filled shell, arrange on a serving tray, garnish as desired, and serve.

Egg Spread

YIELD: *Enough Filling for 36 Shells*

1 hard-cooked egg
¼ cup finely diced parsley
1 teaspoon lemon juice

1 teaspoon mayonnaise
Dash of salt and freshly ground pepper
Paprika

Mince the egg. Add the other ingredients except the paprika. Fill shells, sprinkle with paprika, and serve.

Sausage Filling

YIELD: *Enough Filling for 36 Shells*

½ pound Italian sausage, without casing
   and crumbled
¼ cup bread crumbs

Dash of powdered garlic or 1 clove fresh
   garlic, minced
Dash of salt and freshly ground pepper

Fry sausage with 3 tablespoons of water until browned. Cover and steam for 10 minutes. Remove cover, add bread crumbs, garlic, and salt and pepper, and sauté for 3 minutes. Fill shells with stuffing and serve.

Blue-Cheese Spread

YIELD: *Enough Filling for 24 Shells*

2 ounces blue cheese
1 tablespoon evaporated milk or cream

⅛ teaspoon Worcestershire sauce
¼ teaspoon paprika

Crumble cheese into a bowl. Add milk, Worchestershire, and paprika. Mix thoroughly. Fill shells with stuffing and serve.

Shrimp Paste

YIELD: *Enough Filling for 48 Shells*

1 cup cooked shrimp, shelled
1 tablespoon lemon juice

1 tablespoon ketchup
1 tablespoon mayonnaise

Mince shrimp fine, add lemon juice, ketchup, and mayonnaise, and mix well. Fill shells with stuffing and serve.

Melanzane 'a Scapici'
(Marinated Eggplant)

YIELD: *6 Servings*

5 eggplants, peeled
Salt
7 tablespoons minced onion
1 cup olive oil
2 tablespoons white vinegar

4 cups tomato sauce
1 handful fresh mint leaves, chopped
2 ounces seasoned caciocavallo cheese,
    cut into small pieces

Cut eggplant into ¾-inch-thick slices. Place them in a sieve and sprinkle with salt. Let sit for at least 1 hour to remove bitterness.

In the meantime, cut onions into large slices.

Wash eggplant under running water, pat dry, and halve each slice.

Heat olive oil in a large skillet, add eggplants and onion, and fry over medium-high heat.

When cooked, pour excess oil into a cup. Add vinegar and tomato sauce to eggplant mixture and simmer over low flame for 10 minutes.

Remove from heat and stir in mint leaves and caciocavallo. Serve cold.

4

SORRY FOLKS, BUT THIS TOMATO SAUCE YOU CAN'T BUY!

The most important feature of Italian-American cooking is the indispensable tomato sauce. Without a tomato sauce that is correctly spiced, most Italian recipes will taste like gruel prepared for patients with severe digestive problems. The secret is in the sauce. In my haphazard career as an amateur cook, I've found that if you've spoiled the sauce, it's better to throw the whole thing away and start all over again.

During my years as a priest, I have lived in many "Homes for Unwed Fathers," more commonly known as rectories. With one or two exceptions, the meals served in those rectories were nothing to write home about. Usually it was meat and potatoes; sometimes, for variety, it was potatoes and meat. But there always came a point when I just couldn't stand it anymore and would invade the rectory kitchen (almost always to the delight of the housekeeper) to prepare a huge pot of tomato sauce. Well, from then on I was caught—making sauce became a weekly assignment, unofficial, of course, but a duty nonetheless. Now we can share, dear reader, the magic and mystery of my mamma's famous tomato sauce.

Mamma Bear's
Basic Tomato Sauce

YIELD: *10 Cups*

2 *large cans (5 pounds total) Italian*
   plum tomatoes
⅓ cup olive oil
2 *large onions, peeled and thinly sliced*
5 *garlic cloves, finely minced, or* 1
   tablespoon garlic powder

1½ *tablespoons salt*
1 *teaspon freshly ground pepper*
1 *teaspoon oregano*
1 *teaspoon sweet basil*
1½ *cups water*
1 *tablespoon sugar*

Run the tomatoes through a food mill or chop them in a blender for a few seconds and reserve.

In a large saucepan, sauté in olive oil the onions and garlic till soft. Add salt, pepper, oregano, and basil; stir. Add the water and simmer for 10 minutes. Add reserved tomatoes and sugar. Slowly bring to a boil, then simmer over low heat for 2½ to 3 hours, stirring occasionally.

Variation: Add browned sausage, meatballs, chunks of beef, chicken pieces, or pork chunks in any combination for the last hour of cooking the tomato sauce. Serve along with the pasta for a complete and hearty meal.

Salsa Pizzaiola

YIELD: *4 Cups*

The recipe for this distinctive sauce is Neapolitan in origin, and may be used to make pizza, steak *pizzaiola*, or spaghetti.

2 garlic cloves, peeled and crushed
2 tablespoons olive oil
1 pound fresh or canned tomatoes, peeled
1 teaspoon salt

1/2 teaspoon freshly ground pepper
1 teaspoon oregano
1 teaspoon chopped parsley

In a saucepan over low heat, cook the garlic in the olive oil for several minutes. Chop the tomatoes into fairly large pieces and add to saucepan with salt and pepper. Cook briskly for 5 minutes, or until the ingredients have softened. Stir in oregano and parsley.

People sometimes avoid the previous dishes because they find that tomato sauce is hard on the digestive system. There is a solution for these unfortunate people in the next recipe from Northern Italy. With this easy-to-prepare sauce, they can have their pasta and eat it too!

Béchamel Sauce
(White Sauce for Macaroni)

YIELD: *2 Cups*

4 tablespoons butter
1/4 cup flour
2 1/2 cups milk (boiling hot)

Salt and freshly ground pepper to taste
Nutmeg (optional)

In a small saucepan melt the butter over gentle heat. Add the flour, and, using a wooden spoon, stir and cook without browning for several minutes. Remove from heat, and stir in the milk, little by little, mixing to a smooth sauce. Return to heat and stir until boiling, then simmer for 10 minutes. Season with salt and pepper (a little nutmeg wouldn't hurt either).

Tuna and Tomato Sauce for Pasta

YIELD: *2½ Cups (Ten ¼-Cup Servings)*

1 can (7 ounces) water-packed tuna
3 tablespoons grated lemon rind
½ pound fresh plum tomatoes
2 tablespoons olive oil

6 large shallots, peeled
¼ cup chopped fresh Italian parsley
1 medium avocado (optional)

Drain tuna and mash it in a bowl. Sprinkle with lemon rind.

Wash and core tomatoes, then chop (there should be about 1 cup).

Heat oil in a frying pan and chop shallots directly into the pan. Sauté until shallots are translucent. Add tomatoes and parsley and cook for 5 minutes, stirring. Add tuna and cook for 2 minutes. Serve over green or white fettuccine. If desired, garnish with sliced avocado.

Artichoke Sauce for Pasta

YIELD: *2 Cups (6 Servings)*

6 fresh baby artichokes
⅓ cup virgin olive oil
4 garlic cloves, peeled, and crushed
1 tablespoon fresh parsley, chopped

4 fresh tomatoes, cored, peeled, and diced
¼ cup grated Pecorino Romano cheese
Freshly ground pepper to taste

Cut away the outer leaves of the artichokes. Cut hearts into small pieces.

Heat oil in a saucepan and sauté the garlic for 2 minutes. Add the artichokes, parsley, and tomatoes, and cook 8 minutes, covered, stirring often. Serve hot artichoke sauce over cooked rigatoni or *penne* pasta, and top with Pecorino and pepper.

Simple Pesto for Pasta, Fish, and Eggs

YIELD: *1 Cup (Five or Six 3-Tablespoon Servings)*

2 cups large fresh basil leaves
3 tablespoons freshly grated Pecorino
   Romano cheese

3 tablespoons olive oil
1/4 cup chopped fresh Italian parsley

Wash basil thoroughly in cold water, then dry.

Place basil in a blender with cheese, oil, and parsley. Blend for 5 seconds, or until smooth and creamy. Serve with hot or cold pasta. You may store pesto sauce in the refrigerator for a week.

Caper Sauce

YIELD: *1 1/2 cup (Eight 3-Tablespoon Servings)*

2 hard-boiled eggs
1/4 cup red wine vinegar
3 tablespoons extra-virgin olive oil

2 tablespoons drained chopped capers
1 garlic clove, peeled and crushed
Pinch of cayenne pepper

Mash eggs and place them in a blender with remaining ingredients. Blend for 2 seconds, or until well mixed and smooth. Cover and chill. Serve over salads, fish, veal, cold vegetables, and pasta salads.

Ragù
(Meat Sauce)

1 medium onion, chopped
2 tablespoons olive oil
3/4 pound lean ground beef
1/4 pound lean ground pork
1/4 pound ground veal
1 small carrot, pared and finely chopped
1 small stalk celery, finely chopped
1 cup dry white wine
1/2 cup milk
1/8 teaspoon ground nutmeg
1 can (1 pound) Italian plum tomatoes, drained, seeded and chopped

1 cup tomato puree
1 cup homemade beef broth
1/4 cup tomato paste
2 tablespoons chopped fresh parsley
1 tablespoon finely chopped fresh basil or 1/4 teaspoon dried
1 teaspoon finely chopped fresh thyme or 1/4 teaspoon dried
1/4 teaspoon freshly ground pepper
2 bay leaves
1/2 pound mushrooms, cleaned and sliced

Sauté onion in oil in a large skillet over medium heat until soft, about 5 minutes. Add meats and cook, breaking them into fine pieces with a fork, until cooked but not brown, about 5 minutes. Stir in carrot and celery and cook 2 minutes. Stir in wine and cook until wine evaporates, 8 to 10 minutes. Stir in milk and nutmeg and cook until milk evaporates, about 5 minutes. Remove from heat.

Add remaining ingredients except mushrooms. Return to medium heat and bring to a boil. Reduce heat to low and simmer, uncovered, stirring frequently, until sauce is thick, about 45 minutes. Stir in mushrooms and cook 15 minutes longer. Remove and discard bay leaves. Serve with your favorite pasta.

Porcini Sauce

YIELD: *1½ Cups*

1 cup water
1 cup dried porcini mushrooms
2 tablespoons vegetable oil
½ cup chopped onions

1 tablespoon chopped pancetta
1 tablespoon butter
1 tablespoon tomato sauce

In a saucepan boil the water. Add mushrooms and simmer until soft. Set aside.

In a skillet heat vegetable oil and brown onions and *pancetta*. Drain oil. Add softened mushrooms with their water, the butter, and tomato sauce; simmer until sauce thickens. Serve with your choice of pasta.

*　　　　　*　　　　　*

My maternal grandfather, Letterio Amore, was a Sicilian from the beautiful city of Messina. I believe that fact drew me to explore this fantastic island and to experience its language and its food more intensely. Oh, its cooking! To taste Sicilian food is to taste the ages, to sense nature, to feel the people, and to begin to know and love the land.

Sicilian cooking is sumptuous and spicy, not subtle or delicate like that of northern Italy. Basically the cuisine is composed of foods cultivated in the rich but dry soil, nurtured in the almost-constantly warm sun, and abounding in the clear waters of the Tyrrhenian and Ionian seas surrounding the island.

I was privileged on my last trip to speak with many Sicilian chefs; they gladly gave me their recipes. Whenever a recipe is Sicilian, it will be so indicated.

Salsa al Pomodoro—Sicilian
(Red Sauce)

YIELD: *1½ Quarts*

This Sicilian sauce is ruby red in color, thick and pulpy in texture, and sweet in taste. It's excellent over fresh or commercially made pastas, fish dishes, and poultry.

2 tablespoons olive oil
1 medium onion, chopped
2 garlic cloves, halved
1 2½ pound can plum or whole
  tomatoes

1 can (16 ounces) tomato paste
3 sprigs fresh basil or 1 tablespoon dried
5 sprigs fresh parsley
1 teaspoon salt
¼ teaspoon freshly ground pepper

Heat oil in a saucepan and sauté onion and garlic until golden, about 3 minutes. Add tomatoes, tomato paste, basil, parsley, salt, and pepper. Bring to a boil. Cover and simmer slowly for 1 hour. Correct seasoning if necessary. Discard garlic and parsley before serving.

Salsa di Conserva di Pomodori—Sicilian
(Quick Tomato Sauce)

YIELD: *About 1½ Quarts*

Quick Tomato Sauce is economical during the winter months, when fresh tomatoes are expensive, but actually it is an ideal sauce all year round. It's so simple to prepare, and basic enough to be served with meat or fish dishes and over pasta, rice, and pizza.

3 tablespoons olive oil
1 large onion, chopped fine
3 garlic cloves, cut in half
2 cans (7 ounces each) tomato paste

3 cups water
3 sprigs fresh basil or 1 tablespoon dried
1 teaspoon salt
¼ teaspoon freshly ground pepper

In a large saucepan heat oil and sauté onions and garlic until onion is soft. Add tomato paste and sauté for 3 minutes. Pour in the water; season with basil, salt, and pepper. Bring to a boil; cover and simmer slowly for 30 minutes, discard garlic and correct seasoning if necessary.

Salsa di Funghi e Pomodori— Sicilian

(Mushroom and Tomato Sauce)

YIELD: *About 2 Quarts*

Mushroom and tomato sauce may be teamed with fish, poultry, spaghetti, and rice dishes.

2 tablespoons olive oil
1 medium onion, chopped
2 garlic cloves, cut in half
1 No. 3 can (2 pounds 3 ounces) plum
*   tomatoes in puree or 2 pounds fresh*
*   plum tomatoes cored, peeled, and diced*

¼ cup chopped fresh Italian parsley
1 teaspoon salt
¼ teaspoon freshly ground pepper
½ pound mushrooms, sliced lengthwise

In a large saucepan heat oil and sauté onion and garlic until golden, about 3 minutes. Add tomatoes, parsley, salt, and pepper and bring to a boil. Cover, lower heat, and simmer slowly for 30 minutes. Add mushrooms and simmer 10 minutes longer. Correct seasoning if necessary and discard garlic before serving.

Salsa Marinara—Sicilian

(Sailor-Style Sauce)

YIELD: *About 2 Quarts*

Quick and *easy* superlatively describe Salsa Marinara. Its fresh flavor adds a touch of spring and summer to pasta, fish, and poultry dishes.

2 tablespoons olive oil
1 bunch scallions, chopped fine
1 No. 3 can (2 pounds 3 ounces) whole
*   tomatoes or 2 pounds fresh, cored,*
*   peeled (see Tip), and diced*

4 sprigs fresh basil or 1 tablespoon dried
*   basil*
1 teaspoon salt
¼ teaspoon freshly ground pepper

In a large saucepan heat oil and sauté scallions for 3 to 5 minutes. Stir in whole tomatoes, basil, salt, and pepper. Bring to a boil; cover and simmer slowly for 30 minutes. Correct seasoning if necessary.

Tip: If fresh tomatoes are used, plunge them into boiling water for 1 to 2 minutes to facilitate removal of skins and stems.

Sugo di Carne e Pomodori— Sicilian
(Meat and Tomato Sauce)

YIELD: *About 2 Quarts*

Time-saving recipes are essential to every busy homemaker, but the proof of the pudding is in the eating. Meat and Tomato Sauce satisfies both these principles; it saves time and produces thick sauce that is excellent over ravioli, pizza, spaghetti, and lasagne.

2 tablespoons olive oil
1 medium onion, chopped fine
2 garlic cloves, halved
1½ pounds ground beef
1 2½ pound can tomato puree

1 cup water
1 tablespoon dried oregano or basil
1 teaspoon salt
¼ teaspoon frehsly ground pepper

In a large saucepan heat oil and sauté onion and garlic until golden. Add ground beef and brown for 5 minutes stirring frequently with spatula to separate meat and to brown evenly.

Pour in tomato puree, the water, oregano, salt, and pepper. Bring to a boil, cover, and simmer slowly for 1 hour. Discard garlic before serving.

5

PASTA GOES WITH ANYTHING

For the Southern Italian, pasta (macaroni products), rather than bread, is the staff of life. Pasta goes with just about anything—meat, fish, or vegetables. Pasta all by itself is a good source of belly-filling carbohydrates. Pasta is to the Italian what the potato is to the Irishman.

Many civilizations have claimed to have originated it. Once simple peasant fare, it's now a *must* on the most elegant menus. It is healthful, hearty, and surprisingly low in calories—and probably the most thoroughly adaptable of foods.

Pasta is considered by many to be a meal fit for a king. Some "authorities" even go so far as to claim that it began at the court of Federico II, the Holy Roman Emperor and King of Sicily, in 1220—a contradiction to the more popular notion that spaghetti found its way to Italy from China thanks to Marco Polo in 1279. Some maintain it first took shape with the Etruscans, others say it started with the Arabs, and then there are those who claim that it was introduced into Europe during the Mongol invasions of the thirteenth century. Although pasta may have had its beginnings in many different countries, and dates of origin are hard to pinpoint, it is, of course, most often associated with Italy.

Not too long ago, people ate spaghetti mainly because they were unable to afford anything else. But through the years, the low-priced staple has won over the most sophisticated diners; many now select fettuccine over filet mignon. In fact, it has acquired such snob appeal that many restaurants can and do charge too much for just a sampling of these al dente delicacies.

In the sports community, pasta has been called the food of champions. Because of the complex carbohydrates it contains, it is a high-energy food, whereas sugar and candy, which contain simple carbohydrates, give quick, short-lived boosts. Today, many athletes fill up on pasta before going into competition in order to build up the level of carbohydrates that will be burned off during the event.

Low in protein, pasta is easier to digest than foods such as red meat and enables the body to concentrate on breaking records rather than on breaking down protein.

Pasta also contains B-vitamins, riboflavin, niacin, and iron, and is—contrary to popular belief—low in calories. An average serving (five ounces) has only 210 to 220 calories, and some pastas in today's market are even lower in calories. The sauce that tops the dish is what adds on the pounds. Pasta is also low in cholesterol: One study showed that Southern Italians, who eat more pasta than their Northern counterparts, had lower levels of cholesterol in their blood and suffered from fewer coronary diseases.

Although pasta is not usually a part of most weight-reduction diets, it can be worked in as a substitute depending on the quantity and the manner in which it is served. Think of it this way: The word *diet* originated from the Greek word *diaita*, which was originally defined as "a way of living well," and later came to mean "health-giving nourishment." Perhaps the Italians understand the first definition better. According to the National Pasta Association, Italians consume about sixty pounds of pasta per capita per year. Yet Italy does not suffer from an obesity problem because pasta is a low-fat, low-sodium, easily digested food. The conclusion is that a diet rich in carbohydrates and low in protein develops more energy within the body, burning off more calories.

Perhaps the best thing about pasta is that it can be found in over one hundred shapes and sizes. There is pasta *lunga,* or long pasta, such as spaghetti, spaghettini, *cappellini, bucatini, mezzanelle,* ziti, linguine, and *fresine.* Pasta *corta,* or short pasta, includes such fun shapes as rigatoni, *ditalini, tortiglioni, gemelli, penne, tofette*—and the list goes on and on and on. There is even a special category of the pale yellow delectables called *paste speciali,* and it includes lasagne, *mafaldine, tripoline,* and *farfalle,* as well as *farfalline, fusilli lunghi,* and *tagliatelle.* Remember, each region in Italy has its own special varieties; this listing is only a sampling.

The next best thing about pasta is the sauce with which it is served. The preparation can be as easy as adding butter and cheese and serving. You can eat just about anything with pasta. If you have a craving for fish, there are sauces made with tuna or salmon; a desire for meat can be satisfied with a

Bolognese sauce; while vegetarians can get their fill with any number of sauces—the most popular being *salsa primavera*—made with broccoli, artichokes, eggplant, mushrooms, peas, and even cauliflower.

To obtain the tastiest results, remember that certain pasta shapes best accompany certain sauces. Spaghetti is the most adaptable to the greatest variety of sauces, and spaghettini is best served with seafood sauces or olive oil–based sauces. Meat sauces and other chunky sauces go with stubby pasta, such as rigatoni and shells, which trap bits of the sauce in their openings and ridges. A creamy sauce goes great with *fusilli* since it can cling to the twists.

In Italy pasta is eaten as a *primo piatto* and never as a side dish as is sometimes done in America. Along with the variety of shapes, there is also the choice of buying fresh or dry pasta. Specialty food stores do sell fresh pasta, but most often it is made at home with the help of one of the many new pasta machines on the market.

Directions for making and cooking pasta can be found in most Italian cookbooks and, if dried, on the packaging. As far as cooking goes, all food experts agree on the following dos and don'ts:

- Do have the water boiling rapidly when you add the pasta.
- Do not overcook, since the pasta should be firm to the bite, or al dente.
- Do not rinse the pasta to stop the cooking; merely drain it in a colander and serve immediately.

So, take your choice from the many varieties—fresh or dry—pick a topping, pour a glass of wine, and *mangia*.

There is a custom in many Italian-American families of making fresh pasta to go along with the fresh sauces. It takes a little more work and time, but the results are well worth the effort.

Try the following recipes for yourself and then you can decide whether you will take the time or run down to your local store and depend upon the commercial products.

Basic Pasta
(Homemade Macaroni)

YIELD: *½ Pound*

1 cup plain flour (see Note)
2 large eggs
A little cold water

To make pasta is really very simple once you have done it a few times and know the "feel" of it.

Sift the flour into a mound on a working surface and make a hole in the center. Crack the eggs into the hole and using your fingertips mix the yolks and the whites and then start drawing in the flour a little at a time. Add a very little bit of cold water as necessary and continue mixing until a very firm but elastic dough is formed. Using the palm of your hand, knead the dough strongly for about 10 minutes, until smooth and silky, dusting with flour now and then to prevent sticking.

With a rolling pin, roll out the dough first in one direction, then in the other, until the pasta is so thin that the work surface can just be seen through it. It takes patience and a strong arm but this quantity should roll out to about 2 feet by 2 feet. Drape a clean cloth over the back of a kitchen chair and hang the pasta to dry for about 20 to 30 minutes, not longer. Then cut into desired shapes and lengths.

To cook pasta, in a large pot bring 3 quarts of water, 1 tablespoon each of salt and olive oil to a rapid boil. Add pasta, bring back to boiling and cook uncovered, stirring occasionally, for 3 to 5 minutes, until pasta rises to surface. (Do not overcook.)

For fettucine: Roll the sheet of pasta up loosely. With a thin, sharp knife cut across into ¼-inch strips. Unwind and hang the ribbons over the back of a chair to dry. Then drop in boiling salted water until the pasta rises to the surface.

For lasagne: Cut the pasta into large enough rectangles or squares to fit your baking dish or pan and dry flat. Then proceed with the recipe for lasagne. You must, of course, cook the pasta first in boiling salted water until they rise to the surface.

For ravioli: After the sheet has dried according to instructions given above, divide in half and roll into tissue-thin pieces, each about 12 inches square. Trim the edges. Prepare the filling (see page 58).

Lay one sheet of pasta flat on a working surface and with the side of a ruler lightly impress the dough at 1½-inch intervals going along both sides to make 1½ inch squares (or you can make them as small or as large as you wish). Put one small teaspoon of filling in the center of each square. Using a small brush, dampen with water the dividing marks in each direction (to help the edges stick firmly when the pasta is cut). Lay the second sheet of pasta lightly over the top and press together firmly along the marks in each direction. With a fluted edged cutter, or a sharp knife, cut along the marks and divide the ravioli into separate squares.

Cover the ravioli with a floured cloth until ready to cook. Bring a large saucepan of salted water to a boil, lower the ravioli one by one gently into the water, cooking in batches of fours to avoid overcrowding. As the ravioli rise to the top, give them another minute, then remove with a perforated spoon. Serve very hot with a generous covering of Mamma Bear's Basic Tomato Sauce (page 41) or with Carbonara sauce (page 72).

Egg Pasta

YIELD: *1½ Pounds*

3 cups unsifted all-purpose flour
½ teaspoon salt
4 eggs

1 tablespoon salad or olive oil
2 to 3 tablespoons lukewarm water

Sift the flour with the salt into a medium bowl. Make a well in the center and add eggs and oil. Pour water in gradually and, using a fork, mix until well combined. The dough will be stiff. Form into a ball. Turn out onto a lightly floured wooden board. Knead dough until it is smooth and elastic, about 15 minutes. Cover with the bowl and let rest at least 30 minutes (this makes it easier to roll out).

On a lightly floured pastry cloth or board, roll each part into a rectangle about 16 by 14 inches and about 1/16-inch thick. With a thin sharp knife, cut roll cross-wise, 1/8-inch wide for fettuccine. For lasagne, cut the rolled dough into strips 2 inches wide, 6 inches long. For wide noodles cut into strips 3/4-inch wide. For narrow noodles, cut 1/4-inch wide.

Spinach or Broccoli Pasta

YIELD: *1½ Pounds*

1 package (10 ounces) frozen chopped
 spinach or broccoli
3 cups unsifted all-purpose flour
½ teaspoon salt

2 eggs
1 tablespoon vegetable or olive oil

Cook spinach according to package directions; drain well. Puree in food processor or blender. Follow directions for making Egg Pasta (above), adding pureed spinach along with eggs and oil and omitting water. (If dough seems sticky, add more flour to board during kneading.)

Tomato Pasta

YIELD: *1½ Pounds*

3 cups unsifted all-purpose flour
½ teaspoon salt
2 eggs

1 tablespoon vegetable or olive oil
1 can (8 ounces) tomato sauce
2 teaspoons dried basil leaves

Follow directions for Egg Pasta, adding tomato sauce and basil with eggs and oil and omitting water. (If dough is sticky, add more flour to board during kneading.)

Whole Wheat Pasta

2 cups whole wheat flour
1 cup unsifted all-purpose flour
½ teaspoon salt

4 eggs
1 tablespoon vegetable or olive oil
3 to 4 tablespoons lukewarm water

Follow directions for Egg Pasta.

Parmesan-Cheese Pasta

YIELD: *1½ Pounds*

3 cups unsifted all-purpose flour
½ teaspoon salt
¼ cup grated Parmesan cheese

3 eggs
1 tablespoon vegetable or olive oil
5 to 6 tablespoons lukewarm water

Follow directions for Egg Pasta. Add Parmesan with flour and salt.

Carrot Pasta

YIELD: *1½ Pounds*

2 cups sliced carrots
3 cups unsifted all-purpose flour
½ teaspoon salt

2 eggs
1 tablespoon vegetable or olive oil

In a small saucepan, cook carrots covered in 2 inches boiling water until tender. Drain and puree in a food processor or blender. Cool completely. Use 1 cup of the pureed carrots and add with eggs. Follow directions for Egg Pasta.

Asparagus Pasta

YIELD: *Makes 1⅔ Pounds*

1 package (10 ounces) frozen asparagus
3 cups unsifted all-purpose flour
½ teaspoon salt

3 eggs
1 tablespoon vegetable or olive oil

Cook asparagus according to package directions and then drain well. Puree in a food processor or blender. Follow directions for making Egg Pasta, adding pureed asparagus along with the eggs and oil and omitting the water. (If dough seems sticky, add more flour to board during kneading.)

Orange Pasta

YIELD: *1¼ Pounds*

3 cups unsifted all-purpose flour
½ teaspoon salt
3 eggs

1 tablespoon vegetable or olive oil
2 tablespoons grated orange peel
3 to 4 tablespoons orange juice

Follow directions for making Egg Pasta, substituting orange juice and peel for water. (If dough seems sticky, add more flour to board during kneading.)

Potato Gnocchi

*1 pound potatoes, peeled, cooked, and
  mashed*
3/4 cup regular flour

1 egg
1 tablespoon grated Parmesan cheese
Salt and freshly ground pepper to taste

In a bowl mix together all ingredients thoroughly, forming a dough. Roll into 1-inch finger shapes with your hands. Drop a few gnocchi at a time into boiling salted water and cook till they rise to the surface. Remove with a perforated spoon. Serve hot with Mamma Bear's Basic Tomato Sauce (page 41).

Cannelloni

I have traveled by air to Italy seven times in the last ten years with Alitalia, the Italian Airlines. Almost every time, I was served a delicious dish of cannelloni. I think it was the cannelloni that prompted me to use the same airline time after time. So you won't have to take a trip to Italy just to taste them, I include my recipe for them.

Basic Pasta (page 52)
Ravioli Filling (page 58)

1/4 cup Parmesan cheese
*Mamma Bear's Basic Tomato Sauce
  (page 41)*

Prepare one recipe for Basic Pasta and cut the rolled dough with a sharp knife into four 9 × 6-inch squares. Cook in boiling salted water until they rise to the surface. Remove and cool. Then fill generously with Ravioli Filling. Roll the pasta carefully around the filling and make a stovepipe shape with each. Arrange side by side in a shallow oven dish and sprinkle with grated Parmesan cheese. Cover with tomato sauce and bake in a preheated 350°F oven for 15 minutes.

Filling Variations for Cannelloni or Ravioli

YIELD: *Yields will vary according to how many you wish to make*

Ham Filling

2 tablespoons butter
6 ounces minced cooked ham
1/4 cup chopped parsley
2 ounces grated Parmesan cheese

1 egg, beaten
2 slices bread soaked in 4 tablespoons milk
Salt and freshly ground pepper to taste

In a skillet, melt the butter and fry the ham. Add the soaked bread, parsley, cheese, egg, and salt and pepper to the ham. Mix well, fill pasta, and cook as directed.

Cheese Filling

8 ounces ricotta
1 large egg
2 heaping teaspoons grated Parmesan cheese

Salt and freshly ground pepper to taste
Sprinkling of chopped fresh parsley

Mix together all ingredients. Fill pasta and cook as directed.

Spinach and Cheese Filling

5 ounces (1/2 of a 10-ounce package) frozen chopped spinach
8 ounces ricotta

1 ounce grated Parmesan cheese
1 egg
Salt and freshly ground pepper to taste

Allow the spinach to defrost; drain and squeeze very dry. Mix thoroughly with the remaining ingredients. Fill pasta and cook as directed.

Stuffed Shells or Manicotti

YIELD: *Serves 6*

One of the reasons that you don't find too many skinny Italians is because they love to eat dishes like this one. When in the supermarket, select either large-shell macaroni or manicotti. Cook them according to the directions on the package and then fill by spoon with the following:

2 pounds ricotta
2 eggs, lightly beaten
½ cup grated Parmesan cheese
1 cup shredded mozzarella
¼ cup chopped fresh parsley

Salt and freshly ground pepper to taste
1 pound shells, cooked
Mamma Bear's Basic Tomato Sauce
(page 41)

Preheat oven to 350°F.

Mix together ricotta, eggs, cheeses, parsley, and salt and pepper until smooth for cheese filling.

Once the macaroni has been stuffed cover generously with tomato sauce and pop into oven for ½ hour. Serve immediately.

Lasagne

YIELD: *Serves 6*

A generous serving of this popular Italian dish is a meal in itself. It is best appreciated if you starve yourself for a day before sitting down to its delectable aroma and deliciously fattening rich taste. When you taste it, you will know why it is so popular.

1 pound lasagne
1 recipe Mamma Bear's Basic Tomato Sauce (page 41)
1 recipe Mamma's Meatballs (page 138)

1 pound sweet or hot Italian sausage
1 recipe Cheese Filling (preceding recipe)

Cook the lasagne according to the package directions. In the tomato sauce, cook the meatballs. Then in the tomato sauce, cook the Italian sausage. (Remove the sausage from the skin and crumble the meat for easy use.) Cover the bottom of a large pan with some of the tomato sauce. Then cover with strips of cooked lasagne. On top of the lasagne arrange a generous covering of the cheese filling, crumbled sausage and meatballs, and a covering of tomato sauce. Cover this layer with cooked lasagne and follow same procedure as for the first layer. Make as many layers as your ingredients allow, but make sure you have enough lasagne to cover the top and reserve some sauce for serving. Place in 350°F oven for ½ hour. Remove and let set for ½ hour. Then remove and discard the topping of pasta, which will have become dried and crisp from the heat of the oven. Slice lasagne into generous servings. Over each serving pour a piping-hot cover of tomato sauce.

Pasta alla Hughes

YIELD: *Serves 6*

This next recipe was one that I enjoyed many times with my South Jersey family, the Hughes. Even though our parents are no longer with us because they have passed on, we—Patti, Danny, and Papa Bear—continue our beautiful friendship. In this dish Italy meets Ireland and the results are in good taste.

6 beef short ribs
1 can (16 ounces) whole tomatoes, diced
3 stalks of celery with leaves, diced

1 medium onion, diced
Salt and freshly ground pepper to taste
1 pound perciatelli *(#6)*

Fill a 6- to 8-quart pot with cold water ¾ full. Add all ingredients except *perciatelli* and bring to a boil. Cover, reduce heat to a simmer, and cook for 1½ hours.

Right before you want to serve, remove beef and keep it warm in the oven. Bring the broth to a boil and add pasta. Cook pasta until al dente.

Accompany with a bowl of chopped onion, 3 or 4 boiled whole potatoes, the beef ribs, and grated Parmesan.

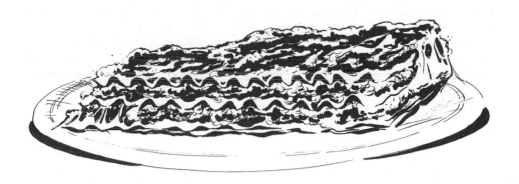

Timballo alla Calabrese
(Macaroni Pie)

YIELD: *4 to 5 servings*

Crust

2 cups all-purpose flour
7 tablespoons butter, cubed

¼ cup sugar

Filling

¼ pound chicken giblets (optional)
1 tablespoon butter
½ pound ground chuck
Pinch of salt
¼ cup dry white wine
2 cups Mamma Bear's Basic Tomato
   Sauce (page 41)

2 cups diced boiled mushrooms
1 cup Béchamel Sauce (page 42)
1 pound cooked macaroni (ziti or
   mezzani)
1 cup grated Parmesan cheese
2 egg yolks beaten with 3 tablespoons
   water

To make crust: Grease a round, deep oven-proof dish and sprinkle it with a little flour. In a bowl combine ingredients for crust, mix well, and let stand for 1 hour. Roll dough out to ¼-inch thick and line the dish; reserve remaining crust for the top.

To make filling: Wash chicken giblets well. Dice. Heat 1 tablespoon butter in a large saucepan. Brown giblets and ground chuck lightly, stirring with a fork to crumble the chopped meat. Add salt and wine. Let wine evaporate almost completely, then add the tomato sauce and mushrooms. Cover and simmer slowly for ½ hour. Add Béchamel, egg yolks, and Parmesan. Blend thoroughly. Toss macaroni with the sauce. Put the mixture into the crust-lined dish, cover with remaining crust. Prick with fork. Bake in 450°F oven for 20 minutes. You won't want to stop eating.

Spaghetti alla Genovese
(Spaghetti with Veal)

YIELD: *4 to 5 Servings*

In my mother's home we have the following dishes once in a while as a pleasant change from macaroni with tomato sauce. The first one, I'm pretty sure, was taught to my mom by my sister's godmother, Grazia Raggio. Grazia Raggio was a wonderful woman who was born in Sardinia, married her husband Carlo, who had come from Genoa, and settled in New York. My parents were befriended by them when they arrived in New York from Italy; and when my sister, Evelyn, was born, Grazia and Carlo Raggia became her godparents. It is in their memory that I have included this recipe.

2 pounds stewing veal
1/4 cup olive oil
3 large potatoes, peeled and quartered
1 large onion, thinly sliced

1 tablespoon salt
1 teaspoon freshly ground pepper
1/4 cup chopped fresh parsley
4 cups water

In a large saucepan, brown veal well in olive oil. Remove veal and add potatoes, browning them and adding more oil if needed. Remove potatoes. Sauté onion in same pan, and add salt, pepper, and parsley. Then return cooked meat and potatoes to pan. Simmer for 5 minutes, add water, bring to a boil over medium heat, then simmer over low heat for 1 hour. Serve with 1 pound of freshly cooked spaghetti.

Pasta with Asparagus

YIELD: *4 Servings*

2 pounds asparagus, cleaned
3 tablespoons butter
4 tablespoons olive oil
1 garlic clove, minced
8 plum tomatoes, peeled and diced

1 pound linguine (see Note)
3 tablespoons heavy cream
Salt and freshly ground pepper to taste
1 tablespoon grated Parmesan cheese

Steam asparagus for about 5 minutes. Drain and cut on the diagonal into 1-inch-long pieces. Sauté asparagus pieces in butter, oil, and garlic for about 6 minutes. Add tomatoes and simmer on low heat for 12 minutes.

While this mixture is simmering, cook the linguine until al dente, 8 to 10 minutes. Drain and place on a warmed serving platter.

Pour cream into asparagus-tomato mixture. Season with salt and pepper. Pour sauce over the pasta and sprinkle with Parmesan cheese.

Note: Almost any style of pasta can be substituted for linguine.

Fettuccini di Spinaci con Salsa di Filetto di Pomodoro— Sicilian

(Spinach Fettuccini with "Beefsteak" Tomato Sauce)

YIELD: *4 to 6 Servings*

Plum tomatoes are referred to as small "beefsteaks" in Italian. Their plump, plum-shaped bodies yield a sweet, light, and savory sauce.

2½ pounds fresh plum tomatoes or 1
    No. 3 can plum tomatoes (2 pounds 3
    ounces)
¼ cup butter
1 small onion, chopped fine
½ pound ham or prosciutto, diced

6 sprigs fresh basil or 1 tablespoon dried
    sweet basil
1 teaspoon salt
¼ teaspoon freshly ground pepper
1 pound spinach fettuccine
¾ cup grated Parmesan cheese

If using fresh tomatoes, plunge in boiling water for 1 to 2 minutes. Then remove stems and skins, slice, and discard seeds. Set aside.

In a large saucepan melt butter and sauté onion until golden. Add ham and sauté 3 minutes longer. Stir in tomatoes, basil, salt, and pepper. Simmer slowly until excess water from tomatoes has been reduced, 20 to 30 minutes.

While sauce is simmering, cook fettuccine according to package directions. Drain and transfer to a warm serving bowl. Cover with some of the sauce and sprinkle with grated cheese. Serve with additional sauce and grated cheese.

Ravioli di Carne e Spinaci— Sicilian

(Meat and Spinach Ravioli)

YIELD: *6 to 8 Servings*

1 recipe Basic Pasta (page 52)
2 packages (10 ounces each) frozen
  chopped spinach
1/4 cup minced onions
2 tablespoons olive oil
1 pound ground beef

1 teaspoon salt
1/4 teaspoon freshly ground pepper
1 egg, slightly beaten
Mamma Bear's Basic Tomato Sauce
  (page 41)
Parmesan cheese, for serving

Prepare Basic Pasta. Cook spinach according to package directions, drain, and squeeze out excess liquid using hands.

In a skillet brown minced onions in hot oil. Add ground beef and sauté for 5 minutes, turning meat with spatula to brown evenly.

In a bowl combine spinach and meat mixtures and season with salt and pepper. Cool for 5 minutes; add egg and mix thoroughly.

Prepare ravioli following directions on page 53. Cook and serve with hot tomato sauce and grated cheese.

Variation: Serve ravioli with Béchamel Sauce (white sauce, page 42) accented with a splash of tomato sauce and grated cheese.

Crosetti—Sicilian

(Zucchini and Meat Pie)

YIELD: *6 to 8 Servings*

¼ cup plus 2 tablespoons olive oil
1½ pounds zucchini, cut into ½-inch
  slices
1 large onion, chopped
2 garlic cloves, minced
2 stalks celery, chopped fine
1½ pounds stewing veal
1 No. 2½ can plum tomatoes in puree
  (28 ounces)

3 sprigs fresh basil or 1 tablespoon dried
2 sprigs fresh parsley, chopped
1 teaspoon salt
¼ teaspoon freshly ground pepper
1 pound mafalda *(broad noodles) or*
  lasagne
1 cup coarsely grated caciocavallo cheese

In a large skillet heat ¼ cup olive oil and brown zucchini lightly. Set aside. In same skillet sauté onions, garlic, and celery until golden, about 5 minutes. Transfer to a large saucepan. Add 2 tablespoons oil to skillet and brown veal lightly on all sides. Transfer to a saucepan. Stir in tomatoes, basil, parsley, salt, and pepper, and simmer slowly until meat is tender, about 1 hour. Remove meat, cool, shred, and return to sauce. Preheat oven to 350°F.

Cook *mafalda* according to package directions. Drain, rinse with cold water, and drain again. Pour a ladleful of sauce into a 10-inch round spring-form pan. Layer *mafalda* (overlapping layers), zucchini, sauce, and cheese. Continue layering; cut top layer of *mafalda* to fit pan. Cover with sauce and cheese and bake for 30 minutes. For easy handling, cool for 10 minutes before serving. Cut in wedges and serve with additional sauce and cheese.

Spaghetti alla Norma— Sicilian

YIELD: *6 Servings*

Spaghetti alla Norma is a culinary accolade to the famous composer Vincenzo Bellini, for his incredibly beautiful opera *Norma*. Bellini, a native son of Catania, Sicily, is remembered and honored with sumptuous gardens, monuments, and Spaghetti alla Norma.

2 tablespoons plus ¼ cup olive oil
2 garlic cloves, halved
1 medium onion, minced
1 No. 2½ can plum tomatoes (28 ounces)
1 can (6 ounces) tomato paste
1 tablespoon dried basil

1 teaspoon salt
¼ teaspoon freshly ground pepper
1 large eggplant (about 2 pounds)
1 pound spaghetti
1 cup grated ricotta salata or Asiago cheese

Heat 2 tablespoons olive oil in a large saucepan and sauté garlic and onion until golden. Add plum tomatoes, tomato paste, basil, 1 teaspoon salt, and pepper. Bring to a boil, cover, and reduce heat and simmer slowly for 1 hour.

Remove stem from eggplant and peel skin from top to bottom. Cut in ½-inch slices, salt liberally, and let stand in a colander for ½ hour. Rinse off salt, pat slices with absorbent paper, and fry in ¼ cup hot oil until crisp. (Add more oil if necessary.) Drain on absorbent paper; keep warm and set aside.

Cook spaghetti according to package directions. Drain. Portion spaghetti in warm serving bowls; layer with eggplant slices, sauce, and grated cheese. Serve immediately.

Pasta Tiano—Sicilian

(Eggplant, Meat, and Macaroni Casserole)

YIELD: *8 to 10 Servings*

Named in dialect after the ceramic dish in which it is baked, this casserole is savory and satisfying and intrigues a crowd.

3 tablespoons olive oil
1½ pounds beef, cut in 2-inch cubes
1 large onion, chopped
3 garlic cloves, halved
1 can (6 ounces) tomato paste
1 can water
1 No. 2½ can whole tomatoes (28 ounces)

3 sprigs fresh basil or 1 tablespoon dried
1½ teaspoons salt
½ teaspoon freshly ground pepper
1 large eggplant (about 2 pounds)
¼ cup olive oil
1 pound elbow macaroni
1 cup grated Romano cheese

In a large skillet heat 3 tablespoons oil and lightly brown beef cubes. Transfer to a large saucepan. Brown onion and garlic in same skillet until onion is soft. Transfer to saucepan and stir in tomato paste, water, tomatoes, basil, salt, and pepper. Bring to a boil, cover, and simmer slowly until meat is very tender, about 1½ hours. Discard garlic and correct seasoning if necessary. Remove meat, cool, shred, and return to sauce.

Remove stem from eggplant and peel skin from top to bottom. Cut in thin slices, salt liberally, and let stand in colander for ½ hour. Rinse off salt, pat slices dry, and fry in ¼ cup oil until crisp. (Add more oil if necessary.) Drain on absorbent paper and set aside. Preheat oven to 400°F.

Cook elbow macaroni according to package directions. Drain. Ladle ½ cup sauce in shallow baking dish (9 × 13 inches); layer pasta, eggplant slices, meat sauce, and grated cheese. Continue layering, ending with cheese on top (and reserving sauce and cheese for serving). Bake for approximately 20 minutes. For easy cutting and handling, let casserole stand for 10 to 15 minutes before serving. Cut in large squares and serve with additional sauce and cheese.

Agli'e Olio
(Garlic, Oil, and Cooked Spaghetti)

YIELD: *Serves 4*

8 garlic cloves, peeled
2 teaspoons chopped fresh parsley
1 teaspoon salt

½ teaspoon freshly ground pepper
½ cup olive oil
1 pound cooked spaghetti

In a skillet sauté garlic, parsley, salt, and pepper in oil over medium heat. When garlic begins to turn brown, remove from heat. Toss entire contents with 1 pound cooked spaghetti. Serve with a sprinkle of Italian bread crumbs (page 97).

Spaghetti alla Carbonara Romana
(Spaghetti with Pancetta and Egg Sauce)

YIELD: *Serves 4*

1¼ pounds spaghetti
6 ounces pancetta or bacon, diced
2 tablespoons olive oil
4 whole eggs

Salt and freshly ground pepper to taste
½ cup heavy cream
1 handful grated Parmesan cheese
½ stick (¼ cup) butter

Cook spaghetti in lightly salted boiling water.
    In a large skillet sauté pancetta in olive oil. Set aside.
    In a large bowl beat eggs, adding salt, pepper, heavy cream, and cheese.
    When the spaghetti is al dente, drain and transfer to skillet. Add egg mixture and butter, and mix very well away from flame. Serve hot.

Pasta con Fagioli e Castagne
(Pasta with Beans and Chestnuts)

YIELD: *6 Servings*

1 cup kidney beans
A generous handful of dried chestnuts
½ pound spaghettini, broken into small pieces

Freshly ground pepper to taste
1 tablespoon olive oil

Soak kidney beans and chestnuts in water to cover overnight.

The next day, cook beans and chestnuts in soaking water until tender.

Cook spaghettini in lightly salted boiling water until almost al dente.

Using a ladle, remove most of the water from the pasta. Add beans, chestnuts, and their liquid to the pasta and return to heat. Pepper to taste and cook until pasta is al dente. Stir in olive oil and serve hot.

Pasta alla Checca
(Pasta with Celery and Fennel)

YIELD: *6 Servings*

1 cup virgin olive oil
8 garlic cloves, lightly crushed
1 stalk celery, cleaned and cut into 2-inch-long strips
1 bulb fennel, cleaned and cut into 2-inch-long strips

3 tablespoons balsamic vinegar
2 tomatoes, peeled and seeded
6 leaves fresh basil
Salt and freshly ground pepper
1 pound spaghetti

Place olive oil and garlic in a skillet over moderate heat. Brown garlic and remove.

Place celery and fennel in oily skillet, and sauté gently until soft. Add vinegar, tomatoes, and basil, and cook for 5 minutes. Salt and pepper to taste; keep sauce warm while preparing pasta.

Cook spaghetti in lightly salted boiling water until al dente. Drain, then toss with sauce. Serve hot.

Ravioli in Walnut-Ricotta Sauce

YIELD: *4 Servings as a main course or 8 Servings as a first course*

1 cup shelled walnuts
½ cup fresh ricotta
⅓ cup toasted pine nuts (pignoli)
¼ cup olive oil
2 tablespoons fresh Italian parsley, minced

½ garlic clove, minced
1 tablespoon fresh basil, minced
Salt and freshly ground pepper to taste
1 pound cheese ravioli, cooked

Combine all ingredients except ravioli in a food processor blender, and mix until smooth. Toss with cooked pasta and serve.

Pasta alla Marietta

YIELD: *Serves 4*

This recipe was given to me by Marietta La Bozzetta, my mother's seventy-three-year-old godchild who still resides in Reggio Calabria, Italy. I suggest you make it *only* when fresh sweet basil is abundant.

1 pound boiled domestic ham (cold cut), chopped
¼ pound butter
1 cup chopped fresh basil
1 recipe Mamma Bear's Basic Tomato Sauce (page 41)

1 cup plain bread crumbs
½ cup grated Parmesan cheese
1 pound spaghetti

Sauté the ham over low heat in melted butter. Add basil, stir, and remove from heat. Warm the tomato sauce. Cook pasta until al dente, drain well, and add to sauce along with ham mixture and remaining ingredients. Toss well and serve hot.

Pasta alla Repice Carbonara Sauce

YIELD: *Serves 4*

I enjoyed this dish when I visited recently with my dear friend and book-keeper Anthony Repice, of Vineland, New Jersey. Tony is an extraordinary young man and this recipe comes from his beautiful mom, Theresa.

4 eggs
1/4 cup butter or margarine
1/4 cup heavy cream
1 pound fettuccini or spaghetti

2 packages (3 1/2 ounces each) sliced
  pepperoni, cut in strips
1 cup grated Parmesan cheese
1/4 cup parsley, chopped
freshly ground pepper, to taste

With eggs and cream at room temperature, beat together until blended.
   Cook pasta 10 to 12 minutes in boiling water, then drain well. Turn pasta into a preheated (in a 250°F oven) ovenproof dish. Toss pasta with room-temperature butter and pepperoni. Pour egg mixture over and toss. Add cheese and parsley, toss, and mix.

Pasta con Salsa di Peperoni
(Pasta with Roasted Pepper Sauce)

YIELD: *8 Servings*

2 large red bell peppers
2 large green bell peppers
1 pound ripe plum tomatoes
1 pound thin pasta
1 onion
2 tablespoons olive oil

1 garlic clove, peeled
1/3 cup chopped fresh Italian parsley
Cayenne pepper to taste
6 marinated artichoke hearts, drained
  and diced (optional)
1/2 cup crumbled Asiago cheese (optional)

Roast the peppers over direct heat or under a broiler until the skin is browned. When they are cool enough to handle, peel off the skins, but do not wash the peppers. (If some blackened specks of peel remain on the peppers, it doesn't matter.) Discard the pepper ribs and seeds and then dice.

Wash and core tomatoes, then chop. Place tomatoes and peppers in a blender and reduce to a puree.

Cook pasta in a large pot of boiling water until al dente.

While pasta is cooking, peel and mince onion. Heat the olive oil in a deep saucepan and push the garlic through a press into the oil. Add the onion and sauté until translucent. Add the pepper-tomato puree, parsley, and cayenne pepper, and cook for 5 to 6 minutes.

When pasta is done, drain and toss with the sauce. If desired, garnish with artichoke hearts and Asiago cheese.

Pasta con Salsa di Melanzane

(Spaghetti with Eggplant Sauce)

YIELD: *6 Servings*

5 small eggplants or 1 medium eggplant (about 1 pound)
2 tablespoons olive oil
2 garlic cloves, crushed
3 shallots or ¼ cup diced yellow onion, minced
¼ teaspoon crushed hot red pepper flakes

2 cups canned imported plum tomatoes with juice, coarsely chopped
¼ cup chopped fresh Italian parsley
1 pound green fettuccine or linguini
3 tablespoons freshly grated Parmesan cheese

Peel and dice eggplant, then soak in salted cold water for 15 minutes. Rinse and pat dry.

Place oil, garlic, shallots, red pepper flakes, and eggplant in a large frying pan. Sauté, stirring often, for 8 to 10 minutes. Add tomatoes and parsley and cook for another 10 to 15 minutes.

Meanwhile, cook pasta in boiling water until al dente, then drain.

Pour some of the sauce into a warmed serving bowl and add the pasta. Sprinkle with Parmesan cheese and toss. Add the rest of the sauce, toss again, and serve.

Variation: Add ½ cup sliced fresh mushrooms and sauté with the shallots. The sauce can be made without the tomatoes, using just the eggplant, shallots, garlic, and mushroom mixture with lots of parsley.

Fettuccine al Formaggio

(Green Fettuccine with Cheese Sauce)

YIELD: *Eight 3-ounce servings*

1 pound green fettuccine
2 cups part-skim ricotta
1/2 cup skim milk

3 tablespoons freshly grated Parmesan
cheese
1/4 cup chopped fresh basil leaves

Cook fettuccine in lightly salted boiling water until al dente, then drain.

While pasta is cooking, mix ricotta with milk and Parmesan cheese. Add basil and stir until smooth and creamy.

Place cheese mixture in a large saucepan and stir for 5 minutes over low heat. When warm and smooth, remove from heat, add drained fettuccine, and toss. Top with additional grated Parmesan cheese, if desired.

Pasta alla Napoletana con Pepperoni Freschi

(Macaroni from Naples with Roasted Peppers)

YIELD: *Serves 6*

5 red bell peppers
2 tablespoons butter
3 tablespoons olive oil
4 garlic cloves, chopped

Salt to taste
1 pound ziti
2 1/2 ounces (1/4 cup) Parmesan cheese
grated
2 ounces (1/4) cup large fresh basil leaves

Roast the red peppers in a 350°F oven until pepper is soft, turning frequently. Remove from oven, place in a large bowl, and cover for 15 minutes. Peel loosened outer skin. Cut into thin slices, put into a bowl with olive oil, garlic, and salt.

Bring 9 pints of water to a boil, add salt, put in the pasta, and boil according to package directions.

Drain pasta well, place in a large bowl with butter and roasted-pepper mixture, and top with grated cheese and fresh pieces of basil.

Vermicelli with Chicken Tetrazzini

1/4 cup butter
1 tablespoon olive oil
1/4 pound mushrooms, washed and sliced
1/4 cup flour
1/2 teaspoon salt
1/8 teaspoon freshly ground pepper
1/4 teaspoon paprika

1 1/2 cups milk
1/2 cup rich chicken stock or 1 bouillon
  cube in 1/2 cup milk
1/2 pound vermicelli
2 cups cooked chicken tenders
Grated Parmesan cheese
1 tablespoon chopped fresh parsley

In a large saucepan heat butter, oil, mushrooms. Add flour to thicken, salt, pepper, paprika, milk, and chicken stock. Stir constantly until sauce thickens, about 10 minutes. Remove from heat.

Boil vermicelli until al dente and drain. Preheat oven to 350°F.

Blend sauce and vermicelli in the saucepan. Spread in a buttered baking dish, add chicken, and sprinkle with Parmesan cheese. Brown in oven for 20 minutes.

Ricotta Cavatelli, or Gnocchi

4 cups all-purpose flour
Pinch of salt

1 pound ricotta
Grated Parmesan cheese

Combine flour, salt, and ricotta; mix thoroughly. Knead on a lightly floured board until dough is smooth. Set dough aside on one corner of floured board. Cut small pieces from dough, roll quickly into finger-thin rolls about 1/2 inch in diameter and cut into 1/2-inch long pieces. Flatten each piece gently and bring long sides together to form a hollow tube. Arrange separately on a floured board and sprinkle with flour.

Drop gnocchi gently into rapidly boiling salted water. Cook 12 to 15 minutes, stirring occasionally to prevent sticking. Remove from water with a slotted spoon and drain well. Serve with tomato sauce and a generous sprinkling of Parmesan cheese.

Perciatelli alla Napoletana

(Perciatelli Naples Style)

YIELD: *Serves 6*

*½ pound lean ground beef or Italian
  sausage*
1 can (14 ounces) tomatoes, crushed
½ pound frozen peas
½ teaspoon salt

1 pound perciatelli
½ pound mozzarella, shredded
*¼ cup grated Parmesan or Romano
  cheese*

Brown meat in a large skillet; drain off fat. Add tomatoes, peas, and salt.
Cook briskly over high heat about 5 minutes. Lower heat and simmer 20 to
30 minutes, until peas are tender and sauce thickens. Cook macaroni as directed on package. Drain and combine with meat sauce and mozzarella in a
bowl. Toss to blend. Serve grated cheese separately for individual helpings.

Lasagne Imbottite

(Baked Lasagne, Another Version)

YIELD: *6 Servings*

Sauce

1/4 cup olive oil
1 small onion
1 garlic clove
1 No. 2 1/2 can Italian tomatoes

1 tablespoon chopped fresh parsley
3 basil leaves, chopped
Salt and freshly ground pepper to taste
1 can tomato paste (8 ounces)

Meatballs

1/2 pound chopped round steak
1/4 cup bread crumbs
2 tablespoons chopped fresh parsley
2 tablespoons milk

1 egg, beaten
3 tablespoons grated Parmesan cheese
Salt and freshly ground pepper

Assembly

3 tablespoons salt
1 tablespoon olive oil
1 pound lasagne
1 pound ricotta

1 egg, beaten
2 tablespoons grated Parmesan cheese
    plus
1 small mozzarella, sliced 1/2 pound

To make sauce: In a skillet over medium heat, lightly brown the onion and garlic in oil. Add tomatoes, parsley, basil, salt, pepper, and tomato paste. Simmer for 15 minutes.

To make meatballs: In a bowl thoroughly mix all ingredients. Shape into tiny meatballs. Brown the meatballs in an oiled frying pan, then add to the sauce and simmer for an additional 30 minutes.

Assembly: While sauce is simmering, boil 6 quarts of water. Add the salt and oil. When boiling rapidly, slowly add lasagne. Cook about 25 minutes. Drain well.

In a bowl mix ricotta, egg, and Parmesan cheese. Preheat oven to 350°F.

Arrange casserole with several spoonfuls sauce on bottom, a layer of lasagne, several slices of mozzarella, then 4 or 5 tablespoons of ricotta mixture. Sprinkle with some grated cheese and top with about 1/4 of the sauce. Repeat layers, ending with a layer of lasagne and sauce. Bake 20 minutes in preheated oven, or until cheese bubbles over.

Pasta al Rosmarino

(Egg Noodles with Butter and Rosemary)

YIELD: *Serves 4*

3 tablespoons salt
1 pound large egg noodles
1/4 cup butter or margarine
3 large garlic cloves, crushed

3 sprigs fresh rosemary or *2 teaspoons dried leaves*
1 beef bouillon cube, crushed
1 tablespoon freshly grated Parmesan cheese

Bring 7 pints of water to a boil and add salt and noddles when water boils. Cook as directed on package.

In a small saucepan melt the butter and add the garlic and rosemary. Cook over medium heat for 4 or 5 minutes, stirring frequently. Add the bouillon cube. Stir and cook until bouillon cube has completely dissolved.

When noodles are cooked, drain and put into a serving bowl. Pour sauce through a strainer onto the noodles and toss. Serve with Parmesan cheese sprinkled on top.

* 6 *

PASTA GOES WITH EVERYTHING

When my mother was living, Fridays had always been special for me since I was ordained. On Fridays I had always taken the trek up the New Jersey Turnpike to see my mom and family for a few hours. On Saturday mornings the rides back down to South Jersey had always been made more pleasant because of my evening visits home and the warm memories of solid family love and the taste of the following recipe still on my tongue.

Almost every Friday I would arrive home to the warm embraces and kisses that my mom showered on me just before my brother John's daily visit to her. My brother John's daily visits usually lasted about ten minutes, but on Friday he would stay about a half hour. I had never figured out why he stayed longer on Fridays. Either it was because I was there or because he waited for Mamma's Friday question: *"Vuoi 'nu piattu di fagioli, Gianni?"* ("Would you like a dish of beans, John?") John would smile and say, "Yeah, Ma!" I loved to watch him dipping a piece of Italian bread into his meal and wiping the dish clean.

Then followed the wait for my brother Oreste to arrive home before we sat down to supper. After about five minutes into the meal, the back door would open and in would step our regular Friday night visitor, my brother Toto (Anthony). My brother Oreste and I would join in a chant: *"Ma, u bordante è cca!"* ("Ma, the boarder is here!") Mom would smile and hurry to fill a dish while saying, *"Toto, figliu bellu, giust'a tempu, ancora c'è."* ("Toto, beautiful son, just in time, there's still some left.") Toto would join us in the wonderful sharing of family love and Mamma's Pasta e Fagioli. A little later, my brothers Mimi and Leo would show up, and strangely enough there would always be enough for them, too.

Pasta e Fagioli
(Macaroni and Beans—the Famous Pastafazool!)

YIELD: *Serves 6*

5 garlic cloves, whole or minced
1/4 cup olive oil
1 1/2 teaspoons salt
1 teaspoon freshly ground pepper

4 cups water
1 teaspoon tomato paste (optional)
2 small potatoes, peeled and diced

Wash the beans in cold water in a colander, then soak overnight covered in cold water.

Place beans in a large saucepan and cover with cold water. Bring to a boil over medium heat, then add the remaining ingredients. Simmer over low heat for 1 hour.

Serve mixed with 1 pound of cooked macaroni, such as *ditali* or *ditalini*, or with cooked rice.

Pasta e Ceci
(Macaroni and Chick-peas)

YIELD: *Serves 4*

There is a story told about the main ingredient of this next recipe, chick-peas, or *ceci*. When Sicily was held by France, the Sicilians were terribly abused by their French masters. Finally the proud Sicilians couldn't take any more and began a bloody, ultimately successful revolt, and rid their island of the hated French. In fact, some historians report that the infamous Mafia was formed at this time as a part of this revolt against foreign oppression. They say that the word *Mafia* is an abbreviation of the following war cry: *"Morte alla Francia*

Italia annella!" (Death to France Italy cries). In the cleanup operation that followed this Sicilian revolt, bands of Sicilian patriots would confront suspected Frenchmen with a handful of chick-peas and ask: *"Quisti chi sunu?"* (What are these?). The Frenchmen had mastered the Sicilian dialect except for the distinctive *chi* sound in the word *ciceri*. They would often pronounce the sound as *ki*. If they did, they were executed on the spot. As with many stories in Italian tradition, we don't really know if they are true or not, so we say *"Se non è vero, è ben trovato"* (if it's not true, it's still a good story). We hope this rather gruesome story doesn't prevent you from enjoying the following dish.

2 garlic cloves, finely minced	1/2 cup chopped fresh parsley
1/4 cup olive oil	Salt and freshly ground pepper to taste
2 (1 pound, 3 ounce) cans of chick-peas	1 pound cooked ditali or ditalini

Sauté the garlic in the olive oil, and then add the chick-peas. Add the parsley and salt and pepper. Simmer over low heat for 1/2 hour, and serve with cooked macaroni.

Faggiolini con Spaghetti
(Pasta with Vegetables)

YIELD: *Serves 6*

2 garlic cloves, finely minced	2 cups water
2 tablespoons olive oil	1 tablespoon salt
1 pound fresh string beans, washed, and ends snapped off	1/2 teaspoon freshly ground pepper
2 medium potatoes, diced	1 pound spaghetti, cooked

In a large saucepan sauté the garlic in oil. Add string beans. Stir and simmer for 5 minutes. Add the potatoes, water, salt, and pepper. Bring to a boil, then simmer on low heat for 1 hour. Mix with the cooked spaghetti and serve.

Pasta e Cavolifiore

(Pasta with Cauliflower)

YIELD: *Serves 6*

3 garlic cloves, minced
1/4 cup olive oil
1 cup crushed tomatoes
1/2 teaspoon crushed hot red pepper flakes
1 large head cauliflower, broken into bite-sized pieces

1 tablespoon salt
Dash of freshly ground black pepper
1 pound cooked ziti or rigatoni

In a large saucepan sauté the garlic in oil. Add the tomatoes and red pepper. Bring to an easy boil and add cauliflower, salt, and pepper. Simmer for 1 hour, adding just enough water to cover cauliflower. Mix with the cooked macaroni and serve.

Broccoli e Pasta

(Broccoli with Spaghetti)

YIELD: *Serves 6*

1 or 2 bunches broccoli (about 1 1/2 pounds)
2 garlic cloves, finely minced
1/4 cup olive oil

1 cup water
1 teaspoon crushed hot red pepper flakes
1 1/2 teaspoons salt
1 pound cooked spaghetti

Wash broccoli and cut off the tough stalks.

In a large saucepan sauté garlic in oil. Add the water. Bring to an easy boil and add broccoli, red pepper, and salt. Simmer for 1 hour, or until broccoli is fork-tender, adding water if needed. Mix with the cooked spaghetti or serve as a vegetable. (If you like broccoli, this will become one of your favorite dishes.)

Ziti alla Siciliana

(Baked Macaroni, Sicilian Style)

YIELD: *Serves 6*

*1 large eggplant (about 2 pounds),
    peeled*
¼ cup olive oil
*3 cups Mamma Bear's Basic Tomato
    Sauce (page 41)*

1 pound ziti or mezzani, *cooked*
1 pound mozzarella, grated
1 cup grated Parmesan cheese

Preheat oven to 350°F. Cut the eggplant into thin slices and sauté in a skillet in olive oil till soft.

Cover the bottom of an ovenproof pan with 1 cup of the sauce; follow with a layer of macaroni, then mozzarella, then cooked eggplant sprinkled with Parmesan, then more sauce. Repeat layers, covering top with remainder of sauce. Bake for ½ hour. Serve immediately.

Spaghetti con Salsa Verde

(Spaghetti with Green Sauce)

YIELD: *Serves 6*

1 cup olive oil
1 garlic clove, finely chopped
*1 tablespoon pine nuts (pignoli), finely
    chopped*
2 cups basil leaves, freshly washed

½ teaspoon salt
1 cup grated Parmesan cheese
Pinch of cayenne pepper
¼ cup boiling chicken stock
1 pound spaghetti or fettuccine, cooked

In an electric blender, combine half the olive oil with remaining ingredients except pasta and blend on low speed until the consistency of a paste. Continue blending on low speed, adding gradually the remaining ½ cup oil.

Pour green sauce over freshly cooked spaghetti or fettuccine. This would be a terrific dish to serve on St. Patrick's Day.

Spaghetti con Salsa di Funghi

(Spaghetti with Mushroom Sauce)

YIELD: *Serves 6*

*1 pound small mushrooms, washed and
  drained*
3 tablespoons butter
1/4 cup grated Parmesan cheese

1/2 cup dry white wine
*2 cups Mamma Bear's Basic Tomato
  Sauce (page 41)*
1 pound spaghetti or linguini, cooked

Parboil and mushrooms in boiling salted water for 10 minutes, drain.

In a large saucepan, sauté the mushrooms in the butter until light brown. Add the cheese and stir. Add the wine and simmer briskly until the wine evaporates. Add the tomato sauce and simmer until heated through. Pour over freshly cooked spaghetti or linguini.

Spaghetti alla Giardiniera

(Spaghetti Gardener's Style)

YIELD: *Serves 6*

1 onion, chopped
1 garlic clove, minced
7 tablespoons butter
1/2 cup olive oil
2 green bell peppers, cut into strips
*1 package (10 ounces) frozen artichoke
  hearts, defrosted*
1/2 pound fresh mushrooms, diced
1/2 pound fresh lima beans, shelled

1 pound fresh green peas, shelled
1 teaspoon salt
1/2 teaspoon freshly ground black pepper
1/2 cup dry red wine
*1 pound tomatoes, peeled, or 1 1/2 cups
  Mamma Bear's Basic Tomato Sauce
  (page 41)*
1 pound spaghetti, cooked
3/4 cup grated Parmesan cheese

Sauté onion and garlic until golden brown in a large saucepan with butter and oil. Add peppers, artichoke hearts, mushrooms, beans, and peas. Season with salt and pepper and add the wine. When wine has partially evaporated, add tomatoes. Cover the pan and simmer for 1/2 hour. Pour over cooked spaghetti and top with cheese. A vegetarian's delight!

Fettuccini Verdi al Quattro Stagioni

(Pasta Four Seasons Style)

YIELD: *Serves 4*

1/4 pound Swiss cheese, cubed
1/4 pound Muenster cheese, cubed
1/4 pound mozzarella cheese, cubed
1 cup heated milk

1 pound green (spinach) noodles
1/3 cup melted butter
1 cup grated Parmesan cheese

Soak the cubed cheeses in the heated milk for 1 hour. The cheeses should soften but not melt.

Preheat oven to 450°F. Cook the noodles according to package directions, drain, and turn into a hot, ovenproof casserole dish. Sprinkle with butter and add 3 tablespoons of the Parmesan. Pour half of the cheese sauce onto the noodles and toss gently. Pour onto the noodles the remaining sauce and top with a heavy sprinkling of the Parmesan. Place in oven for 10 minutes. Remove, sprinkle rest of Parmesan, and serve. Protein rich and savory!

Pasta ai Asparagi

(Pasta with Asparagus)

YIELD: *Serves 4*

2 pounds asparagus, cleaned
3 tablespoons butter
4 tablespoons olive oil
1 garlic clove, minced
8 plum tomatoes, peeled and diced

1 pound linguini or pasta of choice
3 tablespoons heavy cream
Salt and freshly ground pepper to taste
1 tablespoon grated Parmesan cheese

Steam asparagus for about 5 minutes. Drain and cut on the diagonal into 1-inch-long pieces. Sauté pieces in butter, oil, and garlic for about 6 minutes. Add tomatoes and simmer on low heat for 12 minutes.

While this mixture is simmering, cook the linguini until al dente, 8 to 10 minutes. Drain and place on a warmed serving platter.

Pour cream into asparagus-tomato mixture. Season with salt and pepper. Pour sauce over the pasta. Sprinkle with Parmesan cheese and serve.

* 7 *

A CHANGE FROM PASTA: RISOTTO

Northern Italy is as well known for its rice casseroles and cornmeal dishes as southern Italy is for its pasta specialties. We give this fact a nod by the addition of the following dishes typical of the North but made tastier through southern interpretation. I think you will find them a nice change from pasta. Strangely enough, rice was first introduced to European gastronomy by the Sicilians. In the ninth century the Arabs brought rice fields to Sicily. Unfortunately, the methods of cultivation in those times were rudimentary and the terrain produced sparse crops. Hence, the price was high and rice was served only on the tables of the wealthy. In the centuries following, the situation became progressively worse and the planting of rice was completely abandoned.

However, as soon as any foreigner arrives in Sicily, his first encounter with the cuisine will be with rice croquettes, called *arancini*. They are sold everywhere, in fry stands on the beach, in cafes, and in bars serving hot food (*tavola calda*). This contradiction is easy to explain: The love of this particular dish remained even though the product was not readily available, and today most of the rice comes from the mainland of Italy.

When people from the provinces came to the city on daily business, rather than buying dinner and in order to save money, they would buy several *arancini* to appease their hunger and reserve their appetite for a large plate of pasta awaiting them at home.

Sicilian rice dishes are not many in number, but they are very different in composition and flavor.

Risotto fra Giuliano

(Father Julian's Special Rice Casserole)

This is one of my favorite dishes. The recipe was given to me by Italian Cistercian monk, Father Giuliano Bruni. The dish takes a lot of time and preparation but is well worth the effort.

Sauce

1 large can (2½ pounds) Italian peeled tomatoes
3 garlic cloves, finely minced
2 medium onions, peeled and thinly sliced
¼ cup olive oil

1 pound mushrooms, washed and chopped
1 teaspoon saslt
½ teaspoon freshly ground pepper
½ teaspoon sugar
1 pound chopped meat (chuck)

Rice

2 cups rice
5 cups chicken stock (see Note)
3 eggs
½ cup grated Parmesan cheese

Salt and freshly ground pepper to taste
1 pound mozzarella cheese, grated

To make sauce: Run the tomatoes quickly through a food mill or chop them in a blender. In a large saucepan sauté garlic and onions in the olive oil until soft. Add mushrooms and sauté for about 10 minutes. Add salt, pepper, sugar, and chopped meat, crumbling it into pan, and stir with a fork until the meat begins to brown. Stir in crushed tomatoes, and simmer over low heat for 1 hour. Sauce should be very thick. Set aside.

To make rice: Boil the rice in the chicken stock. Cook the rice until all the liquid is absorbed, about 20 minutes. Set aside to cool.

In a bowl beat together eggs, Parmesan, and salt and pepper.

Mix half of the cooled rice with half of the mozzarella. Pack this mixture into the bottom half of a well-greased springform pan. Wet with three tablespoons of the egg mixture. Press down with a spoon to form a trench in the middle of the packed rice. Pour in meat-mushroom sauce, saving about ½ cup. Add the remaining rice and mozzarella. Pack down. Pour remainder of egg mixture over rice. Top with the rest of the sauce. Bake for 45 minutes. Allow to cool for 1 hour, then remove sides of pan, cut in large wedges, and serve.

Note: If you don't want to go through the bother of making fresh chicken soup, you may use chicken-broth powder or cubes, or clear canned chicken broth.

Risotto alla Milanese
(Rice, Milan Style)

YIELD: *8 Servings*

The classic rice dish comes from the beautiful city of Milan.

1 pound fresh asparagus
Salt to taste
4 1/2 cups chicken broth
1 cup chopped onion
4 tablespoons unsalted butter
1 pound raw Arborio rice

1 cup dry white wine
1/8 teaspoon powdered saffron
1/8 teaspoon freshly ground pepper
1/3 cup freshly grated Parmesan cheese
  plus additional for serving

Wash asparagus and cut off tough ends. Cook in boiling, salted water until tender-crisp. Drain. Cut into ½-inch lengths and set aside.

Heat broth in a 2-quart saucepan over medium-high heat to a simmer and set aside.

Sauté onion in 2 tablespoons of the butter in a large skillet over medium heat until soft, about 5 minutes. Stir in rice and cook, stirring for 3 minutes. Stir in wine and cook until wine evaporates, about 3 minutes.

Dissolve saffron in about 2 tablespoons of the warm broth. Set aside. Gradually stir remaining broth into rice mixture. Stir in saffron mixture and pepper. Continue cooking, uncovered, until rice is tender but al dente, 15 to 20 minutes. Stir in asparagus and Parmesan during last 5 minutes of cooking time. Serve with Parmesan.

Arancini—Sicilian Variation
(Rice Croquettes)

YIELD: *8 Servings*

Rice

2 cups uncooked long-grain rice
1 quart chicken stock or bouillon
1 teaspoon saffron

3 tablespoons softened butter
4 egg yolks
1 cup grated Parmesan cheese

Filling

1/4 cup olive oil
1/4 cup chopped onion
1/4 teaspoon chopped celery
1/2 pound veal, beef, or pork
1 can (6 ounces) tomato paste

1 can water
1/2 teaspoon salt
1/4 teaspoon freshly ground pepper
1/3 cup canned or frozen peas

Frying

1 quart vegetable oil, for deep frying
4 egg whites, slightly beaten

2 cups bread crumbs

To prepare rice: Combine rice, chicken stock, and saffron in a large kettle. When chicken stock begins to boil, turn heat to low, stir rice once, cover kettle tightly, and simmer until all liquid is absorbed, about 15 minutes. (Rice should be soft and slightly sticky so that it will hold together.) Allow rice to cool, then add softened butter, egg yolks, and Parmesan. Stir well and refrigerate.

To make filling: In a saucepan heat oil and sauté onion and celery until golden, about 5 minutes. Add meat and brown. Stir in tomato paste, water, salt, and pepper. Cover and simmer until meat is tender, about 1 hour. Add peas and cook for 5 minutes longer. Remove meat and cool. When cool enough to handle, shred the meat and return to sauce. Set aside.

Heat oil in a deep-fat fryer to 370°F (a 1-inch bread cube should brown evenly in 1 minute).

Shape rice mixture into round balls (about 1/2 cup each). Using your index finger, make a hole in each rice ball; add 1 tablespoon of the filling and fill hole with more rice.

Dip croquettes in egg whites and roll in bread crumbs until thoroughly coated. Drop carefully into heated oil, a few at a time, and fry until golden, turning once. Remove with a slotted spoon and drain on absorbent paper. Serve warm or at room temperature.

Variation: Shape croquettes into a triangular form and fill centers with béchamel (page 52) instead.

Insalata di Riso con Pomodori e Olive—Sicilian

(Cold Rice Ring)

YIELD: *6 to 8 Servings*

2 cups uncooked long-grain rice
4 cups water
2 teaspoons salt
2 tablespoons butter
¼ cup olive oil

2 fresh or canned tomatoes, skinned,
   seeded, and chopped
½ cup black olives, pitted and sliced
1 tablespoon minced sweet basil
Fresh parsley, chopped for garnish

In a saucepan cover rice with the water; add the salt and butter and bring to a boil. Stir with fork; lower heat and cover. Simmer until the water has been absorbed, 25 to 30 minutes.

Stir in oil, tomatoes, olives, and basil and mix well. Pour into a 2-quart ring mold and press down lightly with fork. Let stand at room temperature, up to 1 hour, until ready to serve. Unmold by reversing onto a serving plate, shaking mold to loosen rice. Garnish with parsley.

Variation: Substitute tomatoes with one 6-ounce jar roasted red peppers, chopped. Garnish with lemon wedges and parsley.

Riso e Melanzane alla Palermitana—Sicilian

(Rice and Eggplants, Palermo Style)

YIELD: *4 to 6 Servings*

2 large eggplants, peeled
Salt
1/2 cup olive oil
2 cups uncooked long-grain rice
1 quart chicken stock or bouillon
2 large green bell peppers, cut in strips
1 medium onion, chopped

1 No. 2 1/2 can tomato puree
1 tablespoon fresh minced basil or 1
    teaspoon dried
1 teaspoon salt
1/4 teaspoon freshly ground black pepper
1 cup grated caciocavallo cheese (reserve
    1/3 cup for serving)

Destem eggplants and cube. Sprinkle liberally with salt and let drain in colander for 30 minutes. Then rinse with cold water, drain, and dry with absorbent paper. Set aside.

Heat 2 tablespoons of the olive oil in a saucepan; pour in rice and toast lightly for 3 to 5 minutes. Pour in chicken stock and bring to a boil. Stir with fork, cover, and simmer slowly for 20 minutes. (Rice should be slightly undercooked.) Drain and set aside. Preheat oven to 350°F.

In a large skillet heat 1/4 cup of olive oil. Sauté peppers and cubed eggplant until lightly browned, about 10 minutes. (Add more oil if necessary.) Set aside.

Sauté onions in remaining 2 tablespoons oil until golden. Add tomato puree, basil, salt, and pepper. Stir and simmer for 15 minutes.

In a large oiled casserole, layer rice, eggplant-pepper mixture, tomato sauce, and grated cheese alternately until eggplant-pepper mixture and tomato sauce are used up, ending with rice, sauce, and cheese on top. Bake for approximately 20 minutes. Serve with additional rice and cheese.

Riso ai Carciofini e Olive— Sicilian

(Rice with Artichokes and Olives)

YIELD: *Serves 6*

2 tablespoons olive oil
1 medium onion, chopped
1 package (10 ounces) frozen artichoke
  hearts, thawed and halved
2 cups whole tomatoes, chopped
2 teaspoons marjoram
1/2 teaspoon salt
1/4 teaspoon freshly ground pepper
2 anchovies, chopped (optional)
6 black olives, pitted and chopped
1 cup uncooked long-grain rice
1/2 cup grated Romano cheese

In a saucepan heat oil and brown onion for 2 minutes. Add artichoke hearts and sauté for 5 minutes. Stir in tomatoes, marjoram, salt, and pepper and simmer for 15 minutes. Add anchovies and olives and simmer for 5 minutes.

Cook rice according to package directions. Drain rice and place in a serving bowl. Cover with sauce and sprinkle with grated cheese. Serve hot.

Risotto alla Pescatora— Sicilian

(Fisherman-Style Rice)

2 tablespoons olive oil
2 medium onions, chopped
2 garlic cloves, halved
2 pounds squid, cleaned and sliced
1 No. 2½ can tomato puree (28 ounces)
½ cup clam juice, bottled
½ cup water

4 sprigs fresh parsley
1 pound fresh shrimp, shelled
2 dozen fresh clams, scrubbed
Salt
2 cups uncooked long-grain rice
3 tablespoons minced fresh parsley

In a saucepan heat oil and brown onion and garlic with squid for 5 minutes. Pour in tomato puree, clam juice, water, and parsley. Stir and simmer until squid is tender, 20 to 25 minutes. Add shrimp and clams and simmer until clams steam open, 5 to 8 minutes. Salt to taste. Discard garlic and parsley.

Cook rice according to package directions. Drain and place in a serving bowl. Cover with fisherman's sauce and sprinkle with minced parsley. Serve hot.

Pasticcio di Riso

(Rice, Cheese, and Meat Torte)

YIELD: *6 to 8 Servings*

Tomato sauce

1 medium onion, chopped
2 garlic cloves, crushed
4 tablespoons olive oil
2 No. 2½ cans tomato puree (28 ounces)
1 tablespoon dried basil
4 sprigs fresh parsley

1 teaspoon salt
¼ teaspoon freshly ground pepper
3 cups water
1 whole frying chicken (2 pounds) with giblets
1 recipe meatballs (page 132)

Rice

2½ cups uncooked long-grain rice
3½ cups chicken stock or bouillon
3 tablespoons butter

3 eggs, slightly beaten
1 cup Parmesan cheese

Cheese Filling

1 pound ricotta
8 ounces mozzarella cheese, chopped
2 tablespoons fresh basil or 1 tablespoon dried

½ teaspoon ssalt
¼ teaspoon freshly ground pepper

To make tomato sauce: Sauté onion and garlic in 2 tablespoons of the oil for 3 to 5 minutes. Stir in tomato puree, basil, parsley, salt, pepper, and water. Bring to a boil, add chicken and giblets, cover, and boil gently. Prepare and shape meatballs. Brown in remaining 2 tablespoons hot oil for 3 to 5 minutes. Add meatballs to sauce and simmer until chicken is tender, about 45 minutes. Remove chicken and cool. When cool enough to handle, remove and discard skin and bones. Shred chicken and set aside. Discard garlic and parsley.

To make rice: In a saucepan cover rice with chicken stock, 1 cup of the tomato sauce, and butter. Bring to a boil, stir with a fork, lower heat, cover, and simmer slowly for 20 to 25 minutes. (Rice should be slightly undercooked.) Drain rice, then combine with eggs and cheese. Cool. Preheat oven to 350°F.

To make cheese filling: Combine ricotta, mozzarella, basil, salt, and pepper; mix well.

Brush a 10-inch springform pan with oil; spread with 1 layer of rice. Cover with layers of cheese filling, shredded chicken, and meatballs and sauce. Continue layering until rice and chicken are used up, ending with rice and sauce on top. Bake for 30 to 40 minutes. Let stand at room temperature 10 minutes before removing from springform. Slice cake-style and serve with additional sauce and cheese.

Risotto Calabrese

(Hearty Rice Main Dish)

YIELD: *Serves 4*

1 large onion, finely sliced
1 small garlic clove, finely minced
1 teaspoon salt
1 teaspoon crushed hot red pepper flakes
⅛ cup olive oil

2 cans (8 ounces each) tomato sauce or
*   2 cups Basic Tomato Sauce (page 41)*
2 raw potatoes, peeled and diced
4 cups cooked rice
Parmesan cheese, for serving

Sauté onion and garlic with salt and red pepper in olive oil over low heat. Add tomato sauce and potatoes and simmer over low heat for 1 hour. Mix with cooked rice and serve hot sprinkled with grated Parmesan cheese.

Polenta Calabrese

(Cornmeal with a Zip)

Again from Reggio Calabria comes its interpretation of a dish typical in northern Italy.

2 onions, thinly sliced
1/4 cup olive oil
1 teaspoon crushed hot red pepper flakes
1 tablespoon salt
2 cans (8 ounces each) tomato sauce or 2 cups Basic Tomato Sauce (page 41)

2 cups warm water
3/4 cup yellow cornmeal
2 links Italian sausage, skinned and browned
Parmesan cheese, for serving

In a saucepan sauté onions in olive oil. Stir in red pepper and salt. Add tomato sauce and simmer slowly in covered pan for ½ hour. Add the warm water and the cornmeal. Cook, stirring constantly for 30 minutes over low heat.

Add Italian sausage. Crumble the meat and stir into cornmeal mixture. Serve hot topped with grated Parmesan cheese.

Polenta Mozzarella

YIELD: *4 Servings*

1 cup yellow cornmeal
1/2 teaspoon salt
1 cup cold water
2 cups chicken stock

2 tablespoons butter
1 cup grated mozzarella
1/4 cup grated Parmesan cheese
1 cup meat sauce (page 45)

Combine cornmeal, salt, and cold water; mix well. Heat chicken stock in a saucepan to boiling. Add cornmeal slowly and cook over direct heat for 2 minutes, stirring constantly. Reduce heat and add butter, mozzarella, and Parmesan cheese. Cook for 1 hour, stirring constantly. Serve and top with meat sauce or eat plain.

* 8 *

CRUMBS AND STUFFING

Italian Bread Crumbs

You will notice that many of the recipes in this chapter call for Italian bread crumbs. You'll find they are tasty and can transform many simple items into culinary masterpieces.

1 pound dry bread crumbs
½ cup chopped fresh parsley
3 garlic cloves, finely minced or *1 tablespoon garlic powder*

1½ teaspoons salt
1 teaspoon freshly ground pepper
1 cup grated Parmesan cheese

In a bowl mix together all ingredients. These basic bread crumbs are used as coatings and stuffings in a variety of dishes such as the following:

Veal cutlets: Dip cutlets in slightly beaten egg, coat with bread crumbs, and fry to golden brown in olive oil.

Tomato cutlets: Cut slightly green tomatoes into ¼-inch slices. Dip in slightly beaten egg, coat with bread crumbs, and fry to golden brown in olive oil.

Pork chops; Dip chops in slightly beaten egg, coat with bread crumbs, and fry to golden brown in olive oil.

Ricotta cutlets: Ricotta must be the slicable dry type. Slice into 1-inch-thick pieces. Dip in slightly beaten egg, coat with bread crumbs, and fry to brown in olive oil.

Eggplant cutlets: Wash, peel, and cut peeled eggplant into ¼-inch slices. Salt slices and place in a colander to drain liquid for ½ hour. Pat slices dry, dip in lightly beaten egg, cover with bread crumbs, and fry in olive oil till golden brown.

Inflation Meatless Balls

In these days of economic inflation, most of us find it difficult to keep up with the rise in food prices. Though we are unwilling to cut down on the quality and quantity of food on our family tables, at the same time we don't want to wind up on welfare either. This recipe is my own recent invention and may help us in our current situation.

1 Italian Bread Crumbs (page 97)
1 pound mozzarella cheese, grated

2 eggs, lightly beaten
Oil, for frying

In a bowl mix together all ingredients to form a thick mixture. If you find when you try to roll spoonfuls of the mixture into balls that it does not hold together, add water. Form mixture into small balls using your hands. Fry in hot oil until golden brown. They may be eaten as is, or served in tomato sauce.

Stuffed Peppers

Frying peppers: Wash, slice off tops, and remove core and seeds. Stuff with Italian Bread Crumbs (page 97), and sauté in ¼ olive oil in a skillet until bottoms become soft. Then carefully turn over and sauté covered until tender. Serve hot or cold. These are good also as an antipasto.

Bell peppers: Wash, slice off tops, and remove core and seeds. Stuff with Italian Bread Crumbs, place in a baking pan, drizzle with olive oil, and bake in a 350°F oven till tender. Serve hot or cold.

Stuffed Tomatoes

Choose as many large ripe tomatoes as you wish. Wash, remove dark core and slice about ¼ inch off top and reserve. Scoop out tomato meat and seeds (reserve for tomato sauce). Stuff tomatoes with Italian Bread Crumbs and place in a baking pan. Drizzle with olive oil and place sliced tops back on tomatoes. Bake in a 350°F oven until tender. Serve hot or cold. These are good also as an antipasto.

Stuffed Artichokes

Wash artichokes and remove tough outer leaves. Remove choke using an apple corer. Turn artichokes upside down onto a flat surface and press down hard to open. Turn right side up and, using a spoon, fill with Italian Bread Crumbs to which chopped green or black olives have been added. Place stuffed artichokes in a heavy pot, drizzle with olive oil, and add enough water to cover bottoms of artichokes. Cover and simmer over low heat for about 1 hour, until outer leaves can be easily torn off. One eats these by taking leaves in hand, one at a time, and scraping them against lower and upper teeth when biting them.

Stuffed Mushrooms

1 pound fresh mushrooms   *Olive oil*
Italian Bread Crumbs (page 97)

Wash mushrooms and boil for ½ hour. Drain and wash again in cold water. Remove stems and chop the stems fine; add them to the bread crumbs. Stuff the mushroom caps with the stem–bread crumb mixture. Place stuffed caps in an oiled pan. Drizzle with olive oil and bake at 350°F for ½ hour. Serve hot.

9

VEGETABLES WORTH EATING

Many vegetables served in the American style are usually overcooked, bland, and tasteless affairs served with a pat of butter. In fact if it weren't for Popeye, most kids wouldn't touch vegetables with a ten-foot pole. Italians, on the other hand, consume vegetables by the ton. I'm sure it's not because they're vitamin and mineral conscious, but because the way in which Italians prepare their vegetables tickles the palate. What follows are a few ways to make vegetables very popular to your family and friends.

Giambotto
(Vegetable Stew Featuring Zucchini)

YIELD: *Serves 4*

¼ cup olive oil
1 medium onion, thinly sliced
3 garlic cloves, finely minced, or 1 teaspoon garlic powder

1 medium eggplant, washed, peeled, and diced
1 tablespoon salt

2 cans tomato sauce (8 ounces each) or
  2 cups freshly crushed tomatoes
2 medium potatoes, washed, peeled, and
  diced
½ pound fresh string beans, washed and
  diced

1 tablespoon freshly ground black pepper
  or crushed hot red pepper flakes
5 medium unpeeled zucchini, washed,
  ends sliced off, and diced

In a large saucepan sauté in olive oil the onion and garlic. Then add the tomato sauce, potatoes, string beans, eggplant, salt, and pepper and allow to simmer for 1 hour. Add the zucchini and allow to simmer for another ½ hour. Serve hot in soup bowls with hot buttered Italian bread.

Stuffed Eggplant

YIELD: *Serves 4*

1 large eggplant (2 pounds)
¼ cup finely chopped onion
2 tablespoons olive oil
1 cup fresh diced, peeled tomatoes

1 cup ground cooked meat
½ teaspoon salt
½ cup tubettini, cooked and drained
2 tablespoons grated parmesan cheese

Preheat oven to 375°F.

Cut eggplant in half lengthwise. Scoop out pulp, leaving shell intact, and dice. Sauté onion and diced eggplant in olive oil in a skillet.

Add tomatoes, cover, and cook 5 minutes. Add meat and salt. Add cooked *tubettini.* Place mixture in the eggplant shell, piling it high. Sprinkle cheese on top. Place stuffed eggplant halves in a baking pan, and add hot water about ⅛ inch deep. Bake for about 20 minutes, or until cheese is brown.

Stuffed Tomatoes

YIELD: *Serves 4*

4 *large ripe tomatoes*
1/4 *cup chopped onion*
1/4 *cup chopped celery*
2 *tablespoons olive oil*

1 *cup orzo, cooked and drained*
1/2 *cup chopped cooked ground beef*
1/2 *teaspoon salt*
Pinch of pepper

Preheat oven to 375°F.

From the top of each tomato cut a slice 1/2 inch thick. Scoop out center and dice tomato pulp.

In a large skillet, sauté onion and celery in olive oil. Add cooked orzo, tomato pulp, meat, and salt. Remove from heat.

Fill tomato cups with mixture, top with the 1/2-inch tomato slice. Place in a shallow baking dish with 1/4 inch of hot water. Bake for about 25 minutes, or until tender.

Egg Noodles with Broccoli

YIELD: *Serves 4 to 6*

1/4 *cup diced onion*
1 *garlic clove, diced*
1/4 *cup olive oil*
1/2 *cup canned tomato paste*
1 *cup hot water*

3/4 *teaspoon salt*
Pinch of pepper
2 *pounds broccoli (one bunch), cleaned*
1 *pound medium egg noodles, cooked*
   and drained

In a skillet sauté onion and garlic in olive oil until translucent. Add tomato paste, the hot water, salt, and pepper. Bring to a boil, then reduce heat to simmer.

Cut broccoli into 2-inch pieces. Cook in salted water for 5 minutes. Drain and add to the sauce. Cook 10 minutes, or until broccoli is tender.

Place noodles on a serving dish, add tomato sauce, toss lightly, and arrange broccoli on top.

Cheese-Baked Macaroni with Broccoli

YIELD: *Serves 4*

*1 bunch fresh broccoli or 2 packages of
  frozen*
3 tablespoons butter
1 tablespoon olive oil

½ cup grated Parmesan cheese
1 pound ziti, cooked and drained
1 pound mozzarella, diced
2 eggs

Preheat oven to 375°F.

Cook broccoli in a small amount of boiling salted water. Drain, cool, and cut into small spears.

Sauté broccoli in butter and olive oil in a medium-sized skillet until well saturated, stirring constantly.

Sprinkle the bottom of a 3-quart buttered casserole with Parmesan cheese; cover with a layer of macaroni, then a layer of broccoli. Top with a layer of mozzarella. Sprinkle with Parmesan cheese. Continue alternating layers, finishing with a layer of macaroni.

Break eggs into a bowl, add 2 tablespoons grated Parmesan cheese, and beat well. Pour over macaroni, dot with butter, and bake, uncovered, for 20 minutes, or until macaroni has a golden crust.

Polpetti di Melanzane

(Mamma's Own Original Mock Meatballs
Made from Eggplant)

2 large eggplants (4 pounds)
2 cups Italian Bread Crumbs (page 97)
¼ cup chopped fresh parsley
3 garlic cloves, finely minced, or *1*
*   teaspoon garlic powder*

2 eggs
1½ cups grated Parmesan cheese
Olive oil, for frying

Wash eggplant, cut off ends, peel, then slice into quarters and boil in salted water until soft. Place in a colander to drain and cool. Once cooled, remove most water from eggplant by carefully squeezing.

In a large mixing bowl combine the eggplant with the remaining ingredients. Mix well and add more bread crumbs as needed until you can form mixture into 1-inch balls. Roll the balls in bread crumbs and fry in olive oil until very brown. You can serve these as a vegetable side dish; in our Basic Tomato Sauce (page 41)—add them during the last fifteen minutes of cooking the sauce and serve as a meat substitute with spaghetti; or they may be used as a hot antipasto.

Asparagus al Prosciutto

4 slices prosciutto
1 tablespoon olive oil
1 pound cooked asparagus spears

½ cup grated Parmesan cheese
3 tablespoons butter
¼ cup chopped fresh parsley, for garnish

Preheat oven to 375°F. Frizzle ham in oil for 3 minutes. Then arrange ham slices in a baking dish. Place equal number of asparagus spears on each slice, sprinkle with cheese, and dot with butter. Bake for 15 minutes. Serve hot garnished with parsley.

Sformato di Cardoni
(Baked Cardoons)

YIELD: *6 Servings*

¾ pound cardoons
2 tablespoons butter
Salt to taste
1 cup milk

1 tablespoon flour
3 eggs
1 ounce grated Parmesan cheese plus
  additional for topping

Preheat oven to 350°F.

Clean cardoons, cut into small pieces, and parboil. Then lightly fry them in 1 tablespoon butter. Add salt to taste. When butter has been absorbed, add ½ cup of the milk and continue cooking over very low flame for 15 minutes.

Combine remaining 1 tablespoon butter and ½ cup milk. Add flour and mix well.

In a separate bowl beat together eggs and 1 tablespoon of the cheese. Stir into the butter mixture to form a béchamel.

Place contents of frying pan into a lightly buttered baking dish. Top with béchamel and generously sprinkle with grated Parmesan cheese. Bake at 350°F for 20 minutes, or until golden. Serve hot.

Asparagi alla Parmigiana
(Parmesan-Style Asparagus)

YIELD: *6 Servings*

24 asparagus spears
3 tablespoons butter, melted

1 cup grated Parmesan cheese

Preheat oven to 350°F.

Using a sharp knife, gently scrape the white part off the asparagus. Place asparagus in lightly salted boiling water and cook until al dente. Remove asparagus from hot water and immediately place in a bowl of cold water. Let sit for 3 to 4 minutes.

Arrange asparagus in a lightly buttered baking dish. Drizzel with melted butter and sprinkle with cheese. Bake for 20 minutes, or until golden. Serve hot.

Gâteau

Another prizewinner is this recipe for a potato casserole. It comes from my relatives in Italy—although it has a French name, the taste is definitely Italian.

YIELD: *6 Servings*

5 pounds mashed skinned potatoes
1½ cups grated Parmesan or Romano
  cheese
1 cup milk
2 eggs, beaten
½ cup chopped fresh parsley

½ pound butter, in pats
1 garlic clove, finely minced
6 slices mortadella, ham, or salami
6 hard-boiled eggs, sliced
2 cups grated mozzarella cheese

Preheat oven to 400°F.
   Mix together the potatoes, cheese, milk, eggs, parsley, butter, and garlic.
   Grease well with butter or olive oil an ovenproof deep casserole. Spoon in half of the potato mixture. Cover with mortadella slices. Add hard-boiled eggs and mozzarella. Spoon in rest of potato mixture. Bake for 25 minutes. Let the *gâteau* set for ½ hour, then slice and serve.

Patate alla Laziale
(Lazio-Style Potatoes)

YIELD: *8 Servings*

3 pounds brown potatoes
1 onion, finely sliced
½ cup virgin olive oil
2 packages powdered saffron dissolved in
  3 ounces chicken stock

¼ teaspoon fresh rosemary, chopped
Salt and pepper to taste

Preheat oven to 400°F.
   Wash and peel the potatoes, dice into ½-inch cubes, and transfer to a bowl. In a skillet sauté onions in olive oil. Let cool.
   Add onions, saffron-stock mixture, rosemary, and salt and pepper to potatoes. Place in a small baking pan, cover, and bake for about 25 minutes. Serve hot.

Pomodori Ripieni
(Stuffed Tomatoes)

YIELD: *8 Servings*

*4 large tomatoes, halved and seeds
   removed*
*1 small green apple, peeled, cored, and
   finely diced*
3 tablespoons Gruyere cheese, diced
1 skinless frankfurter, finely sliced
3 tablespoons mayonnaise

*1 teaspoon finely chopped fresh Italian
   parsley*
1/2 teaspoon mustard
Dash of Worcestershire sauce
Salt and pepper to taste
Parsley sprigs, for garnish (optional)

Place tomato halves flat side down on a large plate covered with absorbent paper and refrigerate for half an hour.

Combine remaining ingredients in a bowl, and fill tomatoes with the mixture. If desired, decorate with parsley sprigs before serving.

Carciofi alla Romana

(Roman-Style Artichokes)

YIELD: *10 Servings*

2 lemons, halved
10 large artichokes
10 garlic cloves, finely chopped
1/2 cup plus 3 tablespoons extra-virgin olive oil
1 cup seasoned bread crumbs

1 cup chopped fresh Italian parsley
1 teaspoon salt plus to taste
1/2 teaspoon freshly ground pepper plus to taste
1 cup grated Pecorino Romano cheese

Squeeze the juice of the lemons into a large bowl of cold water big enough to contain all the artichokes; place the lemon halves in the water.

Cut the bottoms of the artichokes flat and cut 1 inch off the tops. Using scissors, cut the points off all the outer leaves. With a metal spoon remove the choke from the center, and place the artichokes in the cold water.

Gently sauté the garlic in 3 tablespoons of olive oil. Mix bread crumbs, 1 teaspoon salt, 1/2 teaspoon black pepper, and cheese with the garlic-oil mixture and set aside.

Rub the artichokes, top side down, back and forth on a wooden cutting board to open them up a bit. Place your fingers in the center to widen the opening. Stuff the bread crumb mixture into each artichoke, then fit them tightly in a baking pan.

Add the remaining 1/2-cup olive oil to the pan, cover the artichokes halfway with water, sprinkle with salt and pepper, and bake at 350°F for about 1 hour, basting them every 10 minutes with their sauce. Serve warm or cold.

Melanzane in Carrozza

(Eggplant Surprises)

2 pounds eggplant
Salt to taste
3 eggs
Flour, for dredging

1 pound mozzarella or melting cheese of choice, sliced as thinly as the eggplant
2 cups bread crumbs

Peel the eggplants, cut into thin slices, and salt. Place in a colander under a weight for 30 minutes to drain off bitterness, then wash in cold water and dry as much as possible, squeezing them carefully with paper towels.

In a bowl lightly beat the eggs with a little salt. In plain flour, dredge eggplant slices and mozzarella slices, shake off excess flour.

Dip the eggplant and mozzarella slices in eggs.

Make sandwiches of 1 slice of eggplant, 1 slice of mozzarella, and 1 slice of eggplant. Press together. Dip the sandwiches in bread crumbs.

Fry the sandwiches until golden brown (both sides) in plenty of hot oil. Drain them in paper towels. Serve immediately or warm them in your oven right before serving them. They're best when hot.

Cannellini al Diavolicchio
(Devilish White Kidney Beans)

YIELD: *6 Servings*

These beans can be used as a zippy side dish or mixed with 1 pound of your favorite cooked pasta as a main dish.

2 cans (1 pound each) cannellini (white kidney) beans
1 garlic clove, peeled
1/4 cup olive oil
1 medium onion, chopped
1 tablespoon crushed hot red pepper flakes
1 1/4 cups chopped fresh parsley
Salt to taste
1 cup (8 ounces) tomato sauce

Place the canned beans into a colander and wash with cold water. Let the beans drain, then dry off.

In a saucepan sauté garlic in olive oil until golden. Add the onion, pepper flakes, parsley, and salt. Sauté for 1 minute. Remove the garlic, add the tomato sauce, and boil for 3 minutes. Turn off the heat. Add the beans and mix well. Cover and let stand for 6 minutes.

Fette di Melanzane Ripiene
—Sicilian

(Breaded Eggplant Sandwiches)

YIELD: *4 to 6 Servings*

1 large eggplant (about 2 pounds)
Salt
1½ cups bread crumbs
⅓ cup grated Parmesan cheese
¼ teaspoon salt

⅓ cup chopped fresh parsley
½ pound mortadella, thinly sliced
½ pound provolone cheese, thinly sliced
2 eggs, slightly beaten
¼ cup olive oil

Remove and discard stem from eggplant; cut into ½-inch slices and place in a colander. Salt liberally, weight down with heavy plate, and drain for 1 hour. Rinse salt off slices and dry with absorbent paper. Set aside. Preheat oven to 350°F.

Combine bread crumbs, Parmesan, salt, and parsley. Set aside. Put 1 or 2 slices mortadella and 1 slice provolone between 2 eggplant slices. Dip eggplant sandwiches in beaten eggs, then in bread crumb mixture.

Pour olive oil in a shallow baking pan; heat in oven for 5 minutes. Place eggplant sandwiches in pan and bake for 15 minutes on each side. Serve hot or at room temperature.

Panelle—Sicilian

(Chick-pea Croquettes)

YIELD: *4 to 6 Servings*

Panelle, sold in Palermo exclusively, are shouted from fry stands like outbursts of joy. These flat and crispy croquettes are made with chick-pea flour, water, and salt. They require skill and are rather time consuming to make, but a tasty facsimile can be made easily with canned chick-peas and seasonings. In Palermo, *panelle* are sold sandwiched between crusty rolls, but I like to serve them as hors d'oeuvre or as accompaniment to fish and meat dishes.

1 No. 2 can chick-peas (1 pound 3
  ounces)
1 small onion, chopped fine
4 sprigs parsley, minced
½ teaspoon salt

2 tablespoons flour
¼ cup olive oil
1 lemon
Freshly ground pepper

Drain chick-peas, reserving 2 tablespoons of the liquid. Blend or mash chick-peas with liquid until smooth. Add onion, parsley, salt, and flour and stir until well mixed.

Heat the olive oil in a large skillet; slip rounded tablespoons of chick pea mixture into hot oil (push mixture off spoon with a spatula). Fry until golden, about 3 minutes on each side. Drain on absorbent paper and keep warm while remainder are frying. Squeeze lemon over croquettes and season with pepper. Serve hot or at room temperature.

Zucchini con Formaggio al Forno—Sicilian

(Baked Cheese Zucchini)

YIELD: *6 Servings*

3 small zucchini
6 tablespoons softened butter

6 tablespoons grated Parmesan cheese
Salt and freshly ground pepper

Preheat oven to 400°F.

Remove and discard stems from zucchini. Wash with cold water and drain. Slice zucchini in half lengthwise and place in a baking pan. With a palate knife, spread 1 tablespoon butter on each half. Sprinkle with cheese (about 1 tablespoon per half), salt lightly, and add pepper to taste.

Bake until zucchini are tender, 15 to 20 minutes.

Fagiolini Casalinghi al Pomodoro—Sicilian

(Home-Style String Beans and Tomatoes)

YIELD: *4 to 6 Servings*

1½ pounds fresh string beans
1 medium onion, chopped
¼ cup olive oil
2 cups fresh or canned tomatoes, chopped

1 tablespoon fresh minced basil or 1
    teaspoon dried
1 teaspoon salt
¼ teaspoon freshly ground pepper

Snap off and discard string bean stems. Rinse beans well with cold water and drain.

In a saucepan sauté onion in hot olive oil for 5 minutes. Add string beans, tomatoes, basil, salt, and pepper; stir. Bring to a boil, cover, lower heat, and simmer slowly until beans are tender but firm, 25 to 30 minutes. Serve hot or at room temperature.

Crocchette di Cavoli— Sicilian

(Cabbage Croquettes)

YIELD: *6 Servings*

1 medium head cabbage
1 egg
6 sprigs fresh parsley, minced
1 small onion, minced
⅓ cup grated Parmesan cheese

2 tablespoons flour
½ teaspoon salt
¼ teaspoon freshly ground pepper
¼ cup olive oil

Cut cabbage into quarters and remove core from each piece. Wash quarters with cold water, place in a kettle, and cover with water. Bring to a gentle boil and cook, uncovered, until cabbage is tender, 20 to 30 minutes. Drain, cool, and chop.

Combine chopped cabbage with egg, parsley, onion, cheese, flour, salt, and pepper. Heat olive oil in a skillet and slip rounded tablespoons of cabbage mixture into hot oil. Flatten croquettes slightly with spatula and fry until golden, 3 to 5 minutes on each side. Add more oil to skillet if necessary. Serve hot.

Frittura di Carciofini— Sicilian

(Crisp-Fried Artichoke Hearts)

YIELD: *6 to 8 Servings*

1½ cups bread crumbs
⅓ cup grated Parmesan cheese
2 tablespoons minced fresh parsley
⅛ teaspoon onion salt
¼ teaspoon garlic salt
Freshly ground pepper to taste

2 packages (10 ounces each) frozen artichoke hearts, thawed, or 2 No. 2 cans artichoke hearts, drained (12 ounces)
2 or 3 eggs, slightly beaten
1½ quarts vegetable oil, for deep-frying

Combine bread crumbs, cheese, parsley, onion salt, garlic salt, and pepper. Dip artichoke hearts in eggs, then in bread crumb mixture, coating well on both sides.

Heat oil in a deep fryer to 370°F. (a small piece of bread will brown evenly in 1 minute). Add artichoke hearts, a few at a time, and fry until golden, 3 to 5 minutes on each side. Remove with a slotted spoon and drain on absorbent paper. Serve hot (see Tip).

Tip: Deep-fried foods should always be served hot; keep food in a warm oven (250°F) until all pieces are fried.

Zucchine al Formaggio— Sicilian

(Cheesed Zucchini)

YIELD: *4 Servings*

2 tablespoons olive oil
1 small onion, minced
1½ pounds zucchini, thinly sliced

2 ounces Romano cheese, cut in slivers
Salt and freshly ground pepper to taste
2 tablespoons water

In a large skillet heat oil and sauté onion until golden. Add zucchini and brown lightly on both sides. Sprinkle cheese slivers over slices; season with salt and pepper. Add the water, cover, and simmer until zucchini is tender and translucent, about 10 minutes.

Biede e Pomodori in Padella— Sicilian

(Swiss Chard and Tomato)

YIELD: *4 Servings*

1 large Swiss chard (about 1½ pounds)
Salt
1 small onion, chopped

2 tablespoons olive oil
1 cup canned tomatoes, chopped
Freshly ground pepper

Remove and discard core and bruised and tough outer leaves of Swiss chard. Wash Swiss chard with cold water and drain. With a sharp knife, separate stalks from leaves and cut stalks into 2-inch pieces. Place stalks in a small pot; cover with salted water and boil gently until stalks are tender, about 10 minutes. Add leaves and cook 5 minutes longer. Drain.

In a saucepan sauté onion in oil for 3 minutes. Pour in tomatoes and simmer for 5 minutes. Add Swiss chard and salt and pepper to taste, and simmer for 5 minutes longer.

Pomodori alla Piana Degli Albanesi—Sicilian

(Grecian Tomatoes)

YIELD: *6 Servings*

1 cup rice
2 cups water
Salt
1 tablespoon butter
6 large, ripe tomatoes

3 tablespoons pine nuts (pignoli)
1 tablespoon minced basil (fresh or
*   dried)*
Olive oil

In a saucepan combine rice, the water, 1 teaspoon of salt, and butter. Bring to a boil, stir well, cover, lower heat, and simmer slowly until water has been absorbed—15 to 20 minutes. Set aside.

Preheat oven to 400°F.

Cut a ½-inch slice from the top of each tomato and discard. Hollow tomato centers using a grapefruit knife and spoon, reserving pulp and leaving ½-inch-thick shells. Chop pulp and mix with cooked rice, pine nuts, basil, 2 tablespoons of olive oil, and salt to taste. Place shells in an oiled casserole and brush shells with oil. Bake for 10 to 15 minutes, basting once or twice with drippings during baking. Serve warm or at room temperature.

Melanzane ai Quattro Formaggi—Sicilian

(Eggplant-Cheese Quartet)

YIELD: *6 to 8 Servings*

This savory casserole alternates eggplant slices, tomato sauce, and a quartet of cheeses into a rich, sharp and "meaty" combination.

4 medium eggplants (about 4 pounds)	*¼ teaspoon freshly ground pepper*
Salt	*¼ pound provolone cheese, sliced*
Olive oil	*¼ pound mozzarella cheese, diced*
1 medium onion, chopped	*¼ pound natural Gruyère or Swiss*
1 garlic clove, minced	*cheese, chopped*
2 cups fresh or canned tomatoes, skinned	*¼ pound grated Parmesan cheese*
and chopped	*¼ cup butter*
4 sprigs fresh basil or 1 tablespoon dried	

Remove stems and peel from eggplants and cut into ½-inch slices. Salt liberally on both sides and place in a colander, weighted with a heavy platter or board. Drain for 1 hour. Rinse salt off and dry slices with absorbent paper.

In a saucepan heat 2 tablespoons olive oil and sauté onion and garlic for 3 minutes. Pour in tomatoes, basil, and pepper; simmer for 10 to 15 minutes.

Preheat oven to 350°F.

In a large skillet heat ¼ cup oil and brown eggplant slices on both sides. (Add more oil during browning, if necessary.) Drain on absorbent paper.

In a buttered casserole spread one ladle of sauce, then one layer of eggplant slices; spoon sauce over the eggplant and cover with provolone slices. Add a second layer of eggplant slices, sauce, and mozzarella cubes. Cover with a third layer of eggplant slices, sauce, and Gruyère. End with a layer of eggplant slices, sauce, and grated Parmesan; dot with butter.

Bake for 30 to 40 minutes. Serve hot or at room temperature as an appetizer, entree, or side vegetable.

Broccoli fra Diavolo—Sicilian
(Deviled Broccoli)

YIELD: *6 to 8 Servings*

2 tablespoons olive oil
2 garlic cloves, minced
2 packages (10 ounces each) frozen
  broccoli, thawed

Flour
1/2 teaspoon crushed hot red pepper flakes
Salt

In a skillet heat the olive oil and sauté garlic for 2 minutes.

Dredge broccoli in flour and fry in the hot oil until lightly browned on both sides. Sprinkle on pepper and salt and serve.

Panicolo Italiano
(Italian Corn)

YIELD: *4 Servings*

3 garlic cloves, finely chopped
6 tablespoons olive oil
1 can (12 ounces) whole kernel corn,
  drained
1 teaspoon dried sweet basil

1/2 teaspoon salt
1/2 teaspoon freshly ground pepper
1/4 cup chopped fresh parsley
1/3 cup grated Parmesan cheese

In a skillet sauté garlic in oil, add remaining ingredients except cheese. Toss well. Sprinkle mixture with cheese, cook till cheese is melted, and serve hot.

Minestra Calabrese
(Vegetable Stew)

YIELD: *Serves 6*

1 large onion, thinly sliced
2 garlic cloves, finely minced, or 1
  teaspoon garlic powder
1/4 cup olive oil
2 celery stalks, washed and chopped
1 small head green cabbage, cored and
  cut into small pieces
2 large heads escarole, washed
  thoroughly and torn in pieces

1 pound fresh spinach, washed and torn
  into pieces
1 large tomato, peeled, cored, and
  quartered
1 tablespoon salt
1 teaspoon crushed hot red pepper flakes

In a large, deep saucepan, sauté the onion and garlic in oil. Add each vegetable, one at a time, and sauté until tender-crisp. Add salt and red pepper and just enough water to cover. Simmer for 1 hour and serve.

Variation: You may add a can or two of white cannellini beans near the end of cooking time and serve the stew in bowls sprinkled with grated Parmesan cheese for a hearty and healthy dish.

Funghi alla Casa Nostra
(Tasty Fried Mushrooms)

YIELD: *Serves 4*

1 pound fresh white mushrooms
1 cup all-purpose flour
1 teaspoon salt
1/2 teaspoon freshly ground pepper

3 small garlic cloves, finely minced, or 1
  teaspoon garlic powder
1/4 cup olive oil

Boil the mushrooms in salted water for ½ hour, then drain.

Season the flour with salt, pepper, and garlic. Dredge the mushrooms with the mixture.

In a hot skillet, fry the mushrooms in the olive oil until golden and toasty brown.

*   *   *

I have one sister-in-law who is not of Italian descent: May, the wife of my brother Mimi (short for Dominick). I can remember that when they were courting and she was over at my house for dinner, we always had to have boiled ham and mayonnaise on hand. We would all sit down to one of Mamma's masterpieces and poor May would timidly ask, "Could I have a ham sandwich?"

Over the years she has become Italian in taste by the process of absorption. Now from her kitchen wafts the soul-stirring aromas of garlic and grated Italian cheese. I don't think she's had a ham sandwich in years. I dedicate these next two recipes to her because when she tasted them, she insisted that Mamma teach her how to make them.

Cavoli e Riso
(Cabbage and Rice)

YIELD: *4 Servings*

¼ cup olive oil
1 medium onion, thinly sliced
1 garlic clove, finely minced
1 teaspoon salt

1 teaspoon crushed hot red pepper flakes
1 large head green cabbage, chopped
1 cup cooked rice
Parmesan cheese, grated

In a large saucepan sauté in oil the onion, garlic, salt, and pepper. Add chopped cabbage and stir. Cover and simmer over low heat for 1 hour.

Combine with 1 cup of cooked rice and serve hot sprinkled lightly with grated Parmesan cheese.

Cavoli Estivi

(Summer Cabbage)

YIELD: *4 Servings*

1 small garlic clove, minced
¼ cup olive oil
2 links Italian sausage, sliced or
   crumbled
2 large fresh ripe tomatoes, peeled, cored,
   and crushed

2 small heads green Savoy cabbage,
   coarsely chopped
1 teaspoon salt
½ teaspoon crushed hot red pepper flakes

In a large saucepan lightly sauté garlic in olive oil. Add sausage and brown. Add tomatoes and simmer for 5 minutes. Add cabbage, salt, and pepper. Cover and simmer over low heat for ½ hour, stirring occasionally. Serve hot as a main dish or side dish.

Frittelli Calabresi

We had a beautiful family custom in my house. Every one of my brothers stopped in every day to pay a visit to Mamma, even if it were only for ten minutes. When Mamma had a plateful of these delightful little delicacies on the table, my brothers usually stayed a little longer. When you taste them you'll know why.

Basic Flour Paste

1 cup all-purpose flour
1 garlic clove, finely minced
1 teaspoon salt

½ teaspoon freshly ground pepper
1 teaspoon chopped fresh parsley
Water

Olive oil, for frying
Potatoes, cauliflower, zucchini and
   pumpkin flowers, mushrooms, and/or
   beets

To make flour paste: In a large bowl combine all paste ingredients, adding water gradually until you have a thin paste. Use this basic paste for dipping the following items.

Potatoes: Boil in skin until tender. Cool, peel, and cut into ¼-inch slices. Dip in paste and fry in oil in a hot skillet till golden brown.

Cauliflower: Boil flowerettes in salted water until tender. Cool, dip in paste, and fry in oil in a hot skillet till golden brown.

Zucchini and Pumpkin flowers: Wash carefully, squeeze dry, dip in paste, and fry in oil in a hot skillet till golden brown.

Mushrooms: Boil 5 minutes in salted water. Drain, add to paste, and spoon into oiled skillet. Fry till golden brown.

Beets: Boil in salted water until tender. Drain, slice in ¼ inch pieces, dip in paste, and fry in a hot skillet till golden brown.

I'm sure you'll enjoy the next two recipes. I owe them to my sister in-law Marie, the wife of my brother John.

Panserotti
(Potato Croquettes)

YIELD: *6 Servings*

*5 large raw potatoes, peeled and
    quartered*
*1½ cups Italian Bread Crumbs (page
    97)*
¾ cup grated Parmesan cheese
¼ cup chopped fresh parsley

3 garlic cloves, finely minced, or *1½
    teaspoons garlic powder*
¼ pound Italian salami, chopped
1 egg, beaten

Boil potatoes in salted water until soft. Drain, allow to cool, then mash. In a bowl combine potatoes with remaining ingredients except oil. Mix together well and form into oblong croquettes. Fry until golden brown in hot olive oil.

Calzoni

(Delightful Hot Appetizers)

½ pound Italian salami or pepperoni,
   chopped
½ pound grated mozzarella, Swiss, or
   Muenster cheese

½ pound of grated Parmesan cheese
2 cans (10 ounces each) refrigerated
   biscuits

Preheat oven to 375°F.

In a bowl combine salami and cheeses.

Roll out biscuits and fill the center of each with a generous spoonful of the meat-cheese mixture. Fold biscuits to center and pinch closed. Place each calzoni pinched side down on an oiled cookie sheet and bake until very brown about 10 minutes. Serve immediately.

* 10 *

ZUPPA!

Zuppa di Lenticchie
(Papa Bear's Own Lentil Soup)

YIELD: *Serves 6*

Many biblical scholars say that the next dish is the "mess of pottage" for which Esau sold his birthright. When you taste it, you can hardly blame Esau. Mamma Orsini's own recipe for this dish has many times evoked the comment: "*Questu piattu fa resuscitare i morti!*" which means, "This dish would bring back the dead!" Of course we know that the dead will rise again, not due to this lentil soup, as delicious as it is, but because of the power of Jesus' Resurrection. Here it is now! This recipe alone is worth the price of this whole book ...

2 quarts water
1 pound dried lentils, washed
2 medium onions, diced
3 garlic cloves, minced
2 fresh tomatoes, peeled, cored, and
   quartered

2 carrots, peeled and diced
2 potatoes, peeled and diced
1½ teaspoons salt
½ teaspoon freshly ground pepper
1 teaspoon oregano
½ cup olive oil

In a large pot bring water to a boil. Add all ingredients at once (just throw them in together). Boil for 15 minutes, then simmer on low heat for ½ hour. Cooked rice or macaroni may be added for a stick-to-the-ribs dish. Nothing like it.

Zuppa di Zucchini

(Zucchini and Rice Soup)

YIELD: *Serves 6*

1 pound zucchini, chopped	*6 cups chicken broth*
1 medium onion, chopped	*1/2 cup raw rice*
4 tablespoons olive oil	*1 teaspoon chopped fresh parsley*

In a soup pot sauté zucchini and onion in oil.

Add broth, bring to a boil, and cook zucchini until barely tender. Remove zucchini from broth and mash it using a large fork.

Add rice to broth and cook until tender. Return the mashed zucchini to the soup and simmer another 10 minutes. Sprinkle with parsley and serve.

Brodo di Pollo

(Mamma's Chicken Broth)

YIELD: *Serves 6*

1 large soup or stewing chicken	*1 tablespoon salt*
1/2 cup chopped fresh parsley	

Wash chicken well. Place chicken in a large pot and cover with water. Bring to a rolling boil for about 5 minutes. Remove chicken and discard water. Return chicken to pot, add fresh water, and bring to a slow boil. Add parsley and salt. Simmer for 1½ hours over low heat, or until chicken begins to fall apart.

Serve hot with cooked rice or soup macaroni and sprinkle with grated Parmesan cheese to taste.

Variation: For a holiday first course this soup may be made special by the addition of marble-sized meatballs (page 000) with one exception: Don't fry these little meatballs, just drop them in the simmering soup for the last half hour of cooking.

There is nothing like a bowl of good hot soup to warm one's body and lift one's dropping spirits. If you were to travel south from Calabria you would reach the wonderful island of Sicily. I may be partial to Sicily and Sicilians because my mother's father was born there, try the following two recipes for Sicilian condiments for chicken soup, and you will appreciate Sicily as much as I do.

I owe thanks for these two recipes to the grandmother of a Sicilian-American family, the Bottino family of Lindenwold, New Jersey, whose food and love I am privileged to share on many occasions.

Sicilian Soup Condiments

Scapelli

2 eggs
1/2 teaspoon salt
Dash of freshly ground pepper

1/4 cup grated Parmesan cheese
About 1 tablespoon all-purpose flour

Quadrati d'Uova (Egg Squares)

6 eggs
1/2 cup grated Parmesan cheese
1 1/2 teaspoons salt

1 teaspoon freshly ground pepper
1 cup chopped fresh parsley

To make scapelli: Mix eggs, salt, pepper, and cheese in a bowl and beat well, then gradually add flour, a little at a time, to make an easy-to-pour batter (about the consistency of pancake batter).

Oil or grease lightly a large skillet and place over a high flame. Pour batter into skillet and cook as if a pancake. When bottom is turning brown, flip quickly, and brown the other side. Remove from skillet, allow to cool, then roll tightly. With a sharp knife, cut into narrow (1/8-inch) slices.

Drop rolled slices into bottoms of soup bowls, pour on piping hot chicken broth (page 124), sprinkle with grated Parmesan, and serve.

To make egg squares: Beat all ingredients together well, pour into a well-oiled or greased, shallow (1/2- to 1-inch) oven pan. Place in a 350°F oven for approximately 15 minutes, or until egg mixture is hard-cooked (dry and firm). Remove and let get cold. Then cut into 1-inch squares. Drop generous amounts of these squares into bottoms of soup bowls, pour on piping hot chicken broth (page 124), sprinkle with grated Parmesan, and serve.

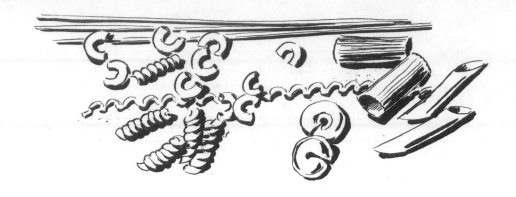

Passatelli in Brodo

(Cheese Noodles in Broth)

YIELD: *Serves 4*

Another favorite of mine is the following recipe I tasted in Bologna, Italy. You begin by using the recipe for Mamma's Chicken Broth.

2 ½ cups chicken broth (page 124)   *3 tablespoons fine plain bread crumbs*
1 egg   *2 level teaspoons flour*
3 tablespoons grated Parmesan cheese   *Piece of butter the size of a walnut*

Bring the broth to a boil in a saucepan.

 Break the egg into a large bowl, add the cheese, bread crumbs, flour, and butter. Work into a stiff paste with a wooden spoon, adding, if necessary, more bread crumbs. Press the pasta through a coarse-holed colander into the fast boiling soup. When the noodles rise to the surface, in 1 to 2 minutes, remove pot from the heat and let stand for 5 minutes before serving.

Zuppa Pavese
(Soup from Pavia)

YIELD: *6 Servings*

There is one more variation for satisfying bowls of soup that can easily be considered as the main course in these days of penny pinching. It comes from the medieval city of Pavia and features protein-rich eggs combined with filling toasted Italian bread.

2 tablespoons butter	*7 cups chicken broth (page 124)*
6 large slices Italian bread	*½ cup grated Parmesan cheese*
6 eggs	*Freshly ground pepper*

Preheat oven to 450°F.

Melt butter over low heat in a frying pan. Toast the slices of bread in the hot butter until golden brown. Place the slices in the center of 6 ovenproof soup dishes and break an egg carefully over each slice of bread. Bake until the whites of the eggs set lightly, about 5 minutes. Remove from oven and pour hot chicken stock over the contents of the dishes to fill them. Sprinkle generously with cheese, add a dash of black pepper, and serve immediately. Mmm . . . mmm good!

Zuppa di Pesce

(Fish Soup)

YIELD: *6 servings*

6 cups of water

2 tablespoons fresh lemon juice

2 teaspoons salt

1 whole, uncooked lobster or crab (about 1 pound)

1 pound medium shrimp, in the shell

1 pound mussels or clams, in the shell, well scrubbed

1 cup coarsely chopped onion

1 cup coarsely chopped celery, including tops

1 cup dry white wine

2 bay leaves

1/2 cup finely chopped onion

3 garlic cloves, finely chopped

2 tablespoons olive oil

2 pounds ripe tomatoes, peeled, cored, seeded, and chopped

2 tablespoons finely chopped fresh parsley

2 tablespoons tomato paste

2 teaspoons dried basil, crumbled

1 teaspoon dried oregano, crumbled

1 teaspoon dried thyme, crumbled

1/2 teaspoon freshly ground pepper

1/8 teaspoon powdered saffron

1 1/2 pounds assorted fresh fish fillets, cleaned, scaled, and cut into 1 1/2-inch chunks (use a combination of at least 3 different kinds: halibut, cod, flounder, haddock, snapper, sole, etc.)

1 lemon, cut into 6 wedges for garnish

Heat 6 cups of water, lemon juice, and 1 teaspoon of the salt to boiling in a 5-quart Dutch oven. Drop in lobster and cook for 5 minutes. Remove from pot and reserve. Add shrimp to boiling water and cook for 1½ minutes. Remove shrimp using a slotted spoon, cool with running water, and reserve. Add mussels to water and cook until shells open, 4 to 5 minutes. Remove using a slotted spoon and reserve.

Add the coarsely chopped onion, celery, ½ cup of the wine, and 1 bay leaf to the boiling water in the Dutch oven and reduce heat to medium-low. Cook, uncovered, for 15 minutes. Strain mixture, reserving liquid and discarding vegetables.

Sauté the finely chopped onion and garlic in oil in the Dutch oven over medium heat until onion is soft, about 5 minutes. Add reserved liquid, remaining wine, tomatoes, parsley, tomato paste, remaining bay leaf, remaining teaspoon of salt, and other seasonings. Stir. Add all seafood and fish. Heat for 5 minutes. Serve with lemon wedges.

One of my dearest friends, whom I consider to be my "kid brother" is a young man who now works for the federal government in a very important position. Nicholas Giordano was a junior in the Catholic High School where I taught twenty-three years ago.

When Nicky graduated high school in 1966, he and I went on a memorable vacation to Italy. Have you ever met someone who makes you laugh until you actually physically hurt? Well, Nicky and I had that effect on one another and continue to do so until this day.

A number of years ago, Nicky was assigned by the government to the same geographical area where I was living and working. He tracked me down and for the next few years, I, he, his lively wife, Rita, his daughter, Gina, and his son, Nicky Jr. became a family. His kitchen became our meeting place where we cooked, laughed, ate, laughed, and shared our mutual respect and love.

But during our Italian trip in 1966, Nicky and I would invariably order and enjoy this next recipe. I'm sure you will, too.

Stracciatella
(Egg Soup, Roman Style)

YIELD: *4 Servings*

6 cups beef or chicken broth
4 eggs
Salt to taste
4 tablespoons grated Parmesan cheese

2 tablespoons bread crumbs
1 teaspoon flour
Grated rind of 1/2 lemon

Warm the broth over low heat.

In a bowl beat eggs, salt, cheese, bread crumbs, and flour until mixture thickens somewhat. Add lemon rind.

Bring broth to a boil, and slowly add egg mixture by letting it drip from a fork. Let boil for 1 minute and serve hot.

Zuppa di Patate e Uova— Sicilian

(Potato and Egg Soup)

YIELD: *4 Servings*

3 tablespoons olive oil
4 medium potatoes, cubed
1 medium onion, chopped
1 quart water

¼ cup minced fresh parsley
Salt and freshly ground pepper to taste
4 eggs

In a large skillet heat oil and sauté potatoes and onion for 5 minutes. Transfer to a pot. Cover with water and add parsley, salt, and pepper. Bring to a boil, cover, and boil gently until potatoes are tender, 20 to 25 minutes. Lower heat, drop eggs, one at a time, into broth. Cover and poach for 5 minutes.

Fritteda—Sicilian

(Sweet-and-Sour Minestrone)

YIELD: *6 Servings*

2 tablespoons olive oil
1 medium onion, chopped
1 package (10 ounces) frozen artichoke hearts, thawed
1 teaspoon nutmeg
1 No. 2 can peas (1 pound 3 ounces)
1 No. 2 can fava beans (1 pound 3 ounces)

1 cup beef stock or bouillon
1 tablespoon tomato paste
3 sprigs fresh basil or 1 tablespoon dried
½ teaspoon salt
¼ teaspoon freshly ground pepper
1 teaspoon sugar
1 tablespoon red wine vinegar
2 cups cooked elbow macaroni

In a large saucepan heat oil and sauté onion until opaque, about 3 minutes. Add artichokes, sprinkle with nutmeg, and sauté for 5 minutes. Add peas and fava beans and their liquid, beef stock, tomato paste, basil, salt, pepper, sugar, and vinegar. Stir and simmer for 20 to 25 minutes. Add cooked macaroni and heat through. Correct seasoning if necessary. Let stand 20 to 25 minutes before serving or serve at room temperature.

Note: Fritteda can be served as a vegetable casserole by omitting the beef stock and macaroni.

Stracciatella con Funghi e Pomodori—Sicilian

(Egg-Drop Soup with Mushrooms and Tomatoes)

YIELD: *4 Servings*

3 tablespoons olive oil
1 medium onion, chopped
1 garlic clove, halved
½ pound mushrooms, thinly sliced
2 cups canned whole tomatoes
2 tablespoons fresh rosemary or 2
   teaspoons dried
1 teaspoon salt

¼ teaspoon freshly ground pepper
1 quart chicken stock (Mamma's Chicken
   Broth, p. 124)
2 eggs, slightly beaten
4 friselle (bread rusks)
1 cup grated caciocavallo or Romano
   cheese

Heat oil in a large skillet; sauté onion and garlic until golden. Add mushrooms and sauté for 3 minutes. Stir in tomatoes, rosemary, salt, and pepper; simmer for 10 minutes. Discard garlic and transfer mixture to a large pot.

   Pour in chicken stock and bring to a boil. Pour in eggs slowly, stirring rapidly with a whisk, until eggs coagulate. Place 1 *frisella* in each soup bowl and ladle soup over it. Sprinkle with grated cheese and serve immediately.

Minestra di Ceci—Sicilian
(Chick-pea Soup)

YIELD: *4 to 6 Servings*

2 cups chicken stock (Mamma's Chicken
    Broth, p. 124)
1 cup chopped carrots
1 large tomato, peeled, cored, and
    chopped
1 teaspoon dried or 1 tablespoon fresh
    rosemary

2 No. 2 cans chick-peas (1 pound
    3 ounces each)
Salt and freshly ground pepper
1/2 cup grated Parmesan cheese

In a pot bring chicken stock to a boil; drop in carrots, tomato, and rosemary, and boil gently until carrots are tender, 10 to 15 minutes. Add chick-peas and their liquid and cook 10 minutes longer over medium heat. Salt and pepper to taste. Sprinkle with Parmesan cheese before serving.

Noccioline di Manzo
in Brodo—Sicilian
(Meatball Soup)

YIELD: *4 to 6 Servings*

Meatballs

1 pound ground beef
1 egg
1 small onion, minced
1 small garlic clove, minced
1/4 cup minced fresh parsley
1/2 cup bread crumbs

1/3 cup grated Romano cheese
1/2 teaspoon salt
1/4 teaspoon freshly ground pepper
6 cups beef or chicken stock
8 ounces egg noodles
3/4 cup grated Romano cheese

In a bowl combine beef, egg, onion, garlic, parsley, bread crumbs, the ⅓ cup cheese, salt, and pepper. Wet hands with water and shape meat mixture into small balls 1 inch in diameter. Set aside.

Bring beef stock to a boil; drop in meatballs and simmer until meatballs are cooked, 8 to 10 minutes.

Cook egg noodles according to directions on package. Drain and add to soup.

Ladle soup into warm bowls and sprinkle generously with grated cheese.

Zuppa di Verdura—Sicilian
(Seasonal Fresh Vegetable Soup)

YIELD: *6 to 8 Servings*

1 medium onion, chopped
4 stalks celery, chopped
1 pound zucchini, sliced
¼ cup olive oil
6 cups chicken broth (Mamma's Chicken Broth, p. 124)
½ pound fresh fava beans (see Note)
½ pound fresh string beans

1 cup fresh peas
4 sprigs fresh Italian parsley
2 bay leaves
1 teaspoon salt
½ teaspoon bruised peppercorns
4 medium ripe tomatoes, peeled, cored, and chopped
1 cup grated Parmesan cheese

Brown onion, celery, and zucchini in hot olive oil for 5 to 8 minutes. Transfer to a large pot. Pour chicken broth into pot; add fava beans, string beans, peas, parsley, bay leaves, salt, and peppercorns. Bring to a boil; cover and boil gently until beans and peas are tender, 15 to 20 minutes.

Stir in tomatoes and simmer for 10 minutes. Correct seasoning if necessary. Discard parsley, bay leaves, and peppercorns. Serve hot with grated cheese.

Note: This recipe may be made with any combination of fresh vegetables in season (carrots, potatoes, squash, peppers, eggplant, leeks, turnips, etc.).

Minestra di Melanzane— Sicilian

(Eggplant Soup)

YIELD: *4 Servings*

¼ cup olive oil
1 small onion, chopped fine
2 stalks celery, chopped fine
1 large green bell pepper, cut in strips
½ pound eggplant, diced
1 cup skinned, chopped fresh or canned
  tomatoes

3 leaves fresh basil or *1 teaspoon dried*
Salt and freshly ground black pepper
1 quart beef stock or bouillon
½ cup grated Parmesan cheese
  (optional)

In a skillet heat olive oil and sauté onion, celery, bell pepper, and eggplant for 5 minutes. (Add more oil if vegetables begin to stick.) Lightly stir in tomatoes, basil, and salt and pepper; simmer for 5 minutes. Transfer mixture to a pot. Pour beef stock over vegetables and bring to a boil. Cover and boil gently for 10 minutes. Correct seasoning if necessary. Serve as is or with grated cheese.

11

MEATS WORTH THEIR PRICE

My mother had a way with steak and roast beef that turned an ordinary piece of meat into an epicurean delight. She concocted a simple marinade in which she soaked the meat for about an hour and then used to baste the meat while cooking. The resulting juices are served as a gravy with the meat to be sopped up with hefty chunks of Italian bread. Since the prices of beef today make it almost as valuable as gold, the marinade will make it taste as good as it costs.

When you use this recipe, please be sure that you use all the ingredients. I emphasize this because I have some very close friends in Pine Hill who didn't, and their supper turned out disastrously. These friends are Tony and Anne-Marie Ianucci. One day Anne-Marie bought some beautiful steak and decided that she would surprise her husband and kids by cooking the steak with the marinade she had heard me talk about. But she didn't remember the entire recipe. All she remembered was that I had said to use wine vinegar. Well, she did. About half a bottle. That night at dinnertime she produced the steak, which looked great, and her family dug in enthusiastically. *Gah!* In no time at all, the whole family had the worst case of puckered lips in Pine Hill's history. After they had recovered slightly, they tossed the rest of the steak to their dog. The poor thing took one sniff and then ran into the doghouse.

Italian Beef Marinade

⅔ cup olive oil
¼ cup red wine vinegar (here is the secret: the vinegar acts as a natural tenderizer!)
1 teaspoon oregano

3 garlic cloves, finely minced, or 1 teaspoon garlic powder
1 teaspoon salt
½ teaspoon freshly ground pepper

Shake well together and use as directed in the introduction.

Bistecca Messinese
(Steak, Messina Style)

YIELD: *Serves 4*

1 1-inch thick, boned steak (about 2 pounds)
Flour, for dredging
1 teaspoon garlic powder
Olive oil, for frying
1 large onion, thinly sliced
1 diced green bell pepper

1 cup chopped mushrooms
1 cup chopped celery
1 large diced carrot
2 diced potatoes
2 cans (8 ounces each) tomato sauce or 1½ cups basic tomato sauce

Preheat oven to 325°F. Dredge steak in flour and garlic powder, brown on both sides in small amount of olive oil. Then place in a baking pan. Add the remaining ingredients to the steak and bake 2 hours.

Steak Pizzaiola

YIELD: *Serves 3*

1 recipe Sauce Pizzaiola (page 42)
3 thin steaks

Salt and freshly ground pepper to taste
Olive oil

Prepare the sauce. Season the steaks with salt and pepper and fry in a little olive oil in a skillet until browned on each side and half cooked. Spread the sauce thickly over each steak, cover the pan, and cook over low heat for 10 minutes.

Once you've tried this it will be hard to be satisfied with steak made in any other way.

Bracciole di Manzo
(Rolled Flank Steak)

Bracciole means arms, and these tasty, filled, rolled meat dishes do remind one of pudgy arms. They can be served just as they are, or along with the recipe for Mamma Bear's Basic Tomato Sauce (page 41)—to dress up a plate of "gravy" meats that are served with macaroni or spaghetti. This can turn a poor man's dish into a king's delight. When *bracciole* are served as the meat accompaniment to a great dish of macaroni, they are taken out of the sauce, sliced into ¼-inch pieces, and arranged on a serving platter. Or they may be served as a separate meat course accompanied by vegetables and/or a crispy green salad.

Flank steak (see Note)
Italian Bread Crumbs (page 97)
Chopped Italian salami or pepperoni
  slices

Hard-boiled egg, sliced
¼ cup olive oil (optional)

Roll out the beef and cover it with a generous coating of Italian bread crumbs, chopped Italian salami, and slices of hard-boiled egg. Roll up carefully at a diagonal and fasten closed with strong toothpicks, cooking skewers, or cooking thread. Then brown in a skillet in olive oil if small, or brown in a 375°F oven if large.

Note: When you go to buy a flank steak at the supermarket, it may be designated as flank steak, steak for rolling, or *bracciola*.

Early every Sunday morning Mamma rises to make the morning coffee and begin her tomato sauce. The usual addition to her sauce is her incomparable meatballs. For a long time every Sunday morning while she was in church, some of the meatballs would disappear from the pot. This was the mystery of the "Meatball Snatcher." One Sunday morning she decided to make the beds upstairs first and go to a later Mass. She heard someone come into the kitchen through the back door and a moment later heard the lid being removed from the pot of sauce. She knew it was the mysterious "Meatball Snatcher." She quietly came down the stairs and approached the kitchen. What she saw was my oldest brother Leo standing near the pot, lid in one hand and a speared meatball in the other, sinking his teeth into the juicy morsel while his grandson Eugene (seven years old) was sitting at the table and whispering to his grandfather: "Popi, can I have one?" Finally the mystery was solved. They all broke into laughter when Eugene displayed wisdom beyond his seven years as he declared: "Grandma, you make the best meatballs in the world! Can you give my mommy the recipe?"

When you begin to make these meatballs in your own home, don't be surprised if a mysterious meatball snatcher shows up in your kitchen.

Polpetti di Mammate
(Mamma's Meatballs)

YIELD: *30 Medium Size Meatballs*

3 pounds ground chuck
1½ cups Italian Bread Crumbs (page 97)
½ cup chopped fresh parsley
3 garlic cloves, finely minced, or
   1 teaspoon garlic powder

2 eggs
¼ cup water
1 cup grated Parmesan cheese

Mix all ingredients together in bowl (with your hands of course; if you're squeamish, use a potato masher) and form into 1-inch balls. Fry in a skillet until golden brown in hot olive oil. Eat as they are, or add them to Mamma Bear's tomato sauce (page 41) and serve with spaghetti or macaroni.

Among the lists of charismatic gifts and ministries that St. Paul includes in his letters to the Corinthians, there is one that is conspicuous by its absence. I have no doubt that if Paul had been a guest in my mother's kitchen, he would have added to that list of charisms (free gifts God gives to the followers of His Son through the power of the Holy Spirit to enable them to minister to one another), the charismatic gift of good cooking. St. Paul would have learned from my mother, as I have, that what transforms these simple ingredients skillfully blended into joyous masterpieces is that they are prepared and served with a generous amount of warm human love. A simple cup of water given to another for the sake of love becomes the most magnificent wine.

I believe that the next recipe is the most "charismatic" of all because of the time and love necessary to prepare it.

Veal alla Calabrese

YIELD: *Serves 4*

2 pounds veal cutlets
1/2 cup all-purpose flour
1 1/2 teaspoons salt
1/2 teaspoon freshly ground pepper
1/4 cup olive oil

1/2 pound small fresh mushrooms, boiled for 5 minutes in salted water and drained (see Note)
1/2 cup water
2 tablespoons white distilled vinegar

Wash the cutlets under cold water and pat dry with a paper towel. Cut the meat into 2-inch strips and pound with a kitchen mallet (to tenderize the veal).

In a bowl combine the flour, 1/2 teaspoon of salt, and pepper. Dredge the veal strips in the flour mixture. Brown the strips quickly in the olive oil in a skillet. Remove the meat and set it aside.

Sauté the mushrooms in the same oil. Return the veal to the skillet and add the water and 1 teaspoon of salt. Let simmer for 1/2 hour over low heat. Then add the vinegar and simmer for another 10 minutes.

Serve over cooked rice. Once you taste this dish, the only thing that will prevent you from having it three times a week is the outrageous price of veal.

Note: Two large cans of small whole mushrooms may be used instead.

Veal Parmigiana

YIELD: *Yield will vary, but estimate one for each person being served*

Make veal cutlets according to Italian Bread Crumbs recipe on page 97. Preheat oven to 350°F. In an oven dish or pan arrange cooked cutlets on a layer of basic tomato sauce (page 41). Place slices of mozzarella (pizza cheese) on top of cutlets and cover with sauce. Bake for 10 minutes. Serve hot.

*　　　　*　　　　*

There is a story about a typical American (Anglo-Saxon) who became interested in Italian food because her next-door neighbor was a generous Italian-American who always sent samples of her cooking over. One day the Italian lady sent something over that the American family raved about. The American lady telephoned to find out what it was and to ask for the recipe. Her Italian neighbor said it was tripe and the only place it could be purchased was from a little butcher shop in the Italian section of town. If the American lady would go down there and buy a pound of it, her Italian neighbor would be happy to show her how to cook it. The poor American lady had no idea what tripe was, so she dutifully ventured down to the Italian butcher shop. What she saw nearly made her run out screaming. There in front of her on gleaming steel hooks she saw goats heads, eyes fixed in a stare; rabbits turned out of their skins; and baby calves skinned and gutted. She nervously waited her turn and asked almost in a whisper, "Do you have any tripe?"

"Sure," the butcher answered as he opened the showcase and pulled out a tray of white honey-combed substance with his blood-stained hands. "How much do you want?"

"One pound," she answered. "But first can you tell me what it is?"

The butcher looked at her for a moment. Then noticing her pale freckled complexion and light hair, he answered: "Lady, it's cow stomach!"

She couldn't speak for a moment, but then finding her voice she said, "Never mind, just give me a pound of ground meat." She took her package and left in a hurry.

She arrived home to her waiting family and said simply, "They didn't have any tripe."

This story merely points out that the Italians, like most other Europeans, eat with gusto foods that others would run away from. My advice is if you don't know what it is, ask, and if you don't think you'll like it, don't eat it. With that warning out of the way, let's make Trippa alla Calabrese.

Trippa alla Calabrese

1 pound tripe
1 teaspoon freshly ground black pepper
   or crushed hot red pepper flakes
1 bay leaf
½ teaspoon oregano
1 large onion, thinly sliced

4 peeled potatoes, diced
1 cup water
1 can (8 ounces) tomato sauce
1 cup basic tomato sauce (page 41)
¼ cup olive oil

Cut the tripe into ¼-inch strips (scissors work well). Wash well in salted water and rinse in clear water. Then put tripe in a pot and barely cover with water to which 1 tablespoon salt has been added. Add the pepper, bay leaf, and oregano. Bring to a boil, then lower heat to a simmer for ½ hour. Add the onion, potatoes, and the 1 cup water, and cook until water evaporates. Then add the tomato sauces and olive oil, bring to a boil, and lower heat and simmer for ½ hour.

Macaroni Meat Loaf

YIELD: *Serves 4*

¼ cup chopped onions
1 tablespoon chopped fresh parsley
¼ cup chopped green bell pepper
2 tablespoons olive oil
1 cup beef stock or bouillon
2 eggs, beaten

1 teaspoon salt
1 teaspoon dry mustard
1 tablespoon horseradish
¾ pound chopped beef
¼ pound chopped pork
2 cups elbow macaroni, cooked

Preheat oven to 350°F.

Sauté onion, parsley, and green pepper in olive oil until soft, then remove from heat.

In a large bowl blend together beef stock, eggs, salt, dry mustard, and horseradish. Add beef, pork, onion mixture, and elbow macaroni; mix well.

Place in a greased loaf pan. Bake in moderate oven (350°F) 1 hour, or until firm.

Beef Stew Italiana

YIELD: *Serves 6*

2 pounds stew beef, cubed
1/2 cup olive oil
4 potatoes, peeled and quartered
2 onions, thinly sliced

2 small 8 ounces each cans tomato sauce
   or 2 cups basic tomato sauce (page
   41)
Salt and freshly ground pepper

Brown meat in olive oil in a large heavy saucepan. Remove meat and brown potatoes in same saucepan. Remove potatoes and brown onions in same saucepan. Then return all ingredients to the saucepan along with the tomato sauce. Salt and pepper to taste. Simmer over low heat for 2 hours, adding water as needed.

*   *   *

It was a long-standing tradition in Italy for every little town to have an annual celebration or *festa* in honor of its patron saint. These *feste* were characterized by outdoor processions in which the statue or image of the patron saint was carried through the streets and into the village church in which the religious ceremony was held.

The origins of these traditions go back to the religion of pagan Italy and the ceremonies that the people used to honor the gods and goddesses. When Christianity came to Italy, holy men and women, the saints, were honored because they had lived in heroic sanctity. The saint was venerated not because he or she was a little god, but because during his or her life, he or she demonstrated great virtues in practicing the Christian life. When they lived they were sought after by the common people because they consistently displayed charismatic gifts, such as healing or miracles. Even today, there are men and women whose ministries the Lord honors in remarkable ways, and who point out that it is not they who heal but the Lord. The ordinary Christian understands that all good comes from the Lord, yet when he comes upon a sanctified individual, he regards that person as a special intercessor and honors him or her. Perhaps in the Roman Catholic world enthusiasm carried veneration of these saints of God almost to the point of idolatry. The saints themselves expressed justified horror at the thought and were always careful to give all the glory to their God and to strenuously teach that the sanctified life was not their special privilege but available to all who would give their lives completely to God. They would say "Don't honor me, for I am just like you, but learn from me to follow God's laws."

When the Italians immigrated to this country and gathered in "Little Italies," they brought with them their long tradition of the *festa*. One of the traditional foods served at these celebrations of the saints' lives is the almost-maddening sausage sandwich, maddening because it is so delicious. Here then is the recipe for Salcicci di Festa.

Salcicci di Festa
(Festive Sausage Sandwiches)

YIELD: *Serves 6*

1 pound sweet or hot Italian sausage, cut into 3-inch lengths
4 green bell peppers, washed and cut into ¼-inch-wide strips
3 medium potatoes, peeled and quartered

2 medium onions, sliced thick
¼ cup olive oil
1 teaspoon salt
6 Italian rolls

Brown the sausage in a heavy skillet, then remove. Add olive oil, peppers, potatoes, onions, and salt. Cook over low heat until all vegetables are tender. Place sausage in crisp Italian rolls and cover with the pepper mixture. Bite in and enjoy *una buona festa* (a good feast).

Chicken alla Waxed Paper

YIELD: *Serves 6*

This recipe is another Mamma Orsini original. It was invented in the days before aluminum foil, but amazingly the wax on the paper does not melt. When you serve it, you will be tempted to lick the paper; go ahead and lick to your heart's content; there's nothing wrong in really enjoying this delicious dish. If you were to patent it, you'd probably put the quick-chicken people out of business.

2 fryers, cut into pieces   *Olive oil*
1 recipe Italian Bread Crumbs (page 97)

Preheat oven to 375°F. Wash the chicken pieces and pat dry with a paper towel. Coat well with bread crumbs. Place each piece of chicken on a sheet of waxed paper large enough to wrap securely. Sprinkle with olive oil and wrap tightly. Place wrapped pieces in a single layer, fold side down, in a large shallow oven pan. Bake for approximately 1 hour. Serve immediately.

Pollo al Limone
(Chicken with Lemon)

YIELD: *Serves 6*

This is another interesting way to serve budget chicken.

1 large chicken, cut up   *1 teaspoon salt*
1/4 cup olive oil   *1/2 teaspoon freshly ground pepper*
Freshly squeezed juice of 3 lemons

Preheat oven to 375°F.

Wash chicken pieces thoroughly in clear cold water. Allow to dry. Place in an oven pan. Mix together remaining ingredients in a cup and pour over the chicken, saving some sauce for basting (see Note). Bake chicken for 45 minutes, basting with remaining lemon mixture. Serve hot.

Note: If you add peeled and quartered potatoes to the baking pan, and prepare a good salad, you'll have a pleasant, easy dinner.

Chicken alla Cacciatore
(Hunter's Style Chicken)

Another chicken standby in Italian-American kitchens is this dish.

3-pound roasting chicken
3 tablespoons olive oil
1 medium onion, finely chopped
1 garlic clove, crushed
⅝ cup dry white wine
¾ pound ripe tomatoes, skinned, cored, and diced, or 1 can (14 ounces) peeled tomatoes, crushed

1 teaspoon tomato paste
¼ teaspoon oregano
½ pound button mushrooms, sliced
Salt, freshly ground pepper, and sugar to taste

Divide the chicken into 8 pieces. Heat the oil in a shallow saucepan and fry the chicken over low heat for about 12 minutes, or until golden on all sides. After 5 minutes add onion and garlic and fry with the chicken, until soft. Add wine and allow to bubble briskly until reduced by half, then stir in the tomatoes, tomato paste, and oregano. Cover the pan and simmer gently for 20 minutes. Add the mushrooms and seasonings to taste. Continue cooking gently, without the lid, for another 10 minutes, or until mushrooms are cooked and tomatoes are reduced to a sauce consistency. Serve hot with good Italian bread.

Cotolette con Funghi alla Crema

(Veal Chops with Mushrooms in Cream Sauce)

YIELD: *Serves 6*

1 ounce dried porcini *mushrooms*
10 sprigs fresh Italian parsley, leaves
   only
1 small garlic cloves, peeled
6 tablespoons sweet butter
1 pound mushrooms

Salt and freshly ground pepper to taste
3 tablespoons olive oil
6 loin veal chops
1/3 cup brandy
3/4 cup heavy cream

Soak the dried *porcini* mushrooms in a bowl with 4 cups of lukewarm water for ½ hour. Drain the mushrooms, saving the soaking water. Clean the *porcini* very well, being careful that no sand remains attached to the stems. Pass the mushroom-soaking water through several layers of paper toweling in order to thoroughly strain out all the sand.

Finely chop the parsley and garlic together on a board.

Melt 4 tablespoons of the butter in a casserole over medium heat. When the butter is completely melted, add the parsley and garlic and sauté for 5 minutes.

Meanwhile, clean the mushrooms with a damp paper towel; then cut them into slices about ¼-inch thick. Add them and the *porcini* to the casserole and sauté for 5 minutes. Then add ¼ cup of the strained mushroom-soaking water and simmer for about 15 minutes, adding more mushroom water as needed. Season with salt and pepper.

Heat the oil and the remaining butter in a frying pan over medium heat. When the butter is completely melted, add the chops and sauté them for 1 minute on each side. Add porcini mushrooms. Season the chops with salt and pepper. Add the brandy to the pan and let it evaporate (about 2 minutes).

Transfer the chops to the casserole with the mushrooms and start adding the cream to the casserole, a little at a time, until all the cream is incorporated (about 10 minutes).

Transfer the meat and the mushroom sauce to a warm platter and serve immediately.

Fesa con Prosciutto

(Leg of Veal with Prosciutto)

YIELD: *Serves 4*

1 leg (2 pounds) of veal
2 carrots, cut into strips
½ pound prosciutto, cut into ¼-inch-
wide strips

2 tablespoons butter
1 tablespoon olive oil
2 sage leaves
1 cup dry white wine

Make lengthwise incisions all around the veal. Place the prosciutto and carrot strips in the incisions, and bind with kitchen string.

In a large cooking pan, heat butter and oil over a low flame. Brown veal, then add sage and wine. Cover and continue cooking for about 2½ hours. Veal should be checked during cooking to make sure it isn't drying out.

Remove string, cut veal into slices, top with sauce from pan, and serve.

Abbacchio Disossato Brodetato

(Boned Baby Lamb in Lemon and Egg Sauce)

YIELD: *8 Servings*

2 tablespoons unsalted butter
4 tablespoons extra-virgin olive oil
3½ pounds boneless leg of lamb, cut into
   2-inch cubes
2 tablespoons chopped onion
4 garlic cloves, chopped
1 tablespoon all-purpose flour
2 cups dry white wine

6 slices prosciutto, chopped
2 tablespoons chopped fresh Italian
   parsley
1 teaspoon nutmeg
3 egg yolks
Freshly squeezed juice of ½ lemon
1 tablespoon grated Parmesan cheese

Heat the butter and oil in a large skillet and sauté the lamb over very high heat until brown on all sides. Remove from pan.

Lower the flame; add onion and garlic and sauté until soft. Add the flour, wine, lamb, prosciutto, parsley, and nutmeg; cook until lamb is tender. Add water, if necessary, to prevent pan juices from drying out. Remove skillet from heat.

Beat egg yolks lightly with a fork. Slowly add the lemon juice and grated cheese to the eggs, beating all the while. Pour egg sauce over the hot lamb, mixing continually. Serve hot.

Scaloppine di Vitello alla Messinese—Sicilian

(Veal Cutlets, Messina Style)

YIELD: *6 to 8 Servings*

2 pounds ⅛-inch-thick veal cutlets
6 tablespoons olive oil
3 slices salt pork, chopped

2 cups whole canned tomatoes, chopped
2 yellow bell peppers, cut in strips
1 teaspoon sage

1 medium onion, minced
2 stalks celery, minced
1 carrot, chopped
2 slices ham, chopped

1 tablespoon minced fresh parsley
Salt and freshly ground black pepper
8 slices white bread

Preheat oven to 350°F.

In a large skillet brown cutlets lightly on each side in 2 tablespoons hot oil. Transfer to a shallow oiled baking pan. Set aside.

In the same skillet, brown salt pork for 3 minutes. Add onion, celery, and carrot, and sauté for 5 minutes. Stir in ham, tomatoes, bell peppers, sage, parsley, and salt and pepper to taste; cover and simmer for 5 minutes. Pour mixture over veal slices and bake for approximately 30 minutes.

Remove crusts from bread. Heat remaining 4 tablespoons oil in a large skillet until it begins to sizzle. Add bread and fry until lightly browned on both sides. Serve veal cutlets with vegetable topping over *pain carre* (fried bread).

Arrosto di Vitello al Latte—
Sicilian
(Rosemaried Veal Roast)

YIELD: *6 to 8 Servings*

3 to 4 pounds boneless veal roast (leg)
3 garlic cloves, halved
¼ cup butter
2 teaspoons rosemary

Salt
1 cup milk
Freshly squeezed juice of 2 lemons
Parsley

Rub veal with garlic. In a large saucepan brown veal lightly in heated butter. Sprinkle with rosemary and salt to taste. Pour milk in bottom of pan. Cover and simmer slowly until veal is tender, about 2 hours, basting occasionally.

Cool 20 minutes before slicing. Slice thinly and arrange on heated platter. Squeeze lemon juice over veal slices and garnish with parsley.

Polpettone di Manzo, Maiale, e Vitello—Sicilian

(Three-Meats Loaf)

Y I E L D : *6 to 8 Servings*

1 small eggplant (about ½ pound)
Salt
¼ cup olive oil
1 pound ground beef
½ pound ground pork
½ pound ground veal
1 cup bread crumbs

½ cup grated Parmesan cheese
1 medium onion, minced
2 garlic cloves, minced
3 eggs
2 teaspoons salt
1 teaspoon freshly ground pepper

Preheat oven to 350°F.

Remove stem and skin from eggplant and discard. Dice pulp; salt liberally and drain in colander for 15 minutes. Rinse salt off with cold water, drain, and dry with absorbent paper. Sauté eggplant in hot oil until lightly browned, 5 to 8 minutes. Set aside.

In a large bowl combine all remaining ingredients. Mix in eggplant. Pour into an oiled standard loaf pan and bake for 1½ hours at 350°F. Cool for 10 to 15 minutes before slicing.

Involtini di Manzo con Vino Rosso—Sicilian

(Beef Birds in Wine Sauce)

YIELD: *4 Servings*

1 pound beef tenderloin, thinly sliced
Flour, for dredging
1/2 cup bread crumbs
1/3 cup grated Parmesan cheese
1/4 cup chopped shallots or scallions
2 garlic cloves, minced
1/4 cup chopped celery

1/4 cup chopped parsley
1/4 teaspoon salt
1/4 teaspoon freshly ground pepper
Olive oil
2 cups beef stock
1 cup dry red wine
1 bay leaf

Pound meat slices thin using a meat mallet or the flat side of cleaver. Dredge in flour and set aside.

Combine bread crumbs, cheese, shallots, garlic, celery, parsley, salt, and pepper. Spread 1 rounded tablespoon of bread crumb mixture over each tenderloin slice. Sprinkle with olive oil to moisten bread crumbs. Roll, jelly-roll fashion, and tie with kitchen string or fasten ends with toothpicks.

Brown beef birds in 2 tablespoons hot oil. Pour in beef stock, wine, and bay leaf. Bring to a boil, lower heat, cover, and simmer until meat is tender, about 30 minutes. If sauce is too thin, raise heat to high and cook for 5 minutes to reduce liquid. Serve beef birds and sauce over buttered noodles.

Farsumagru in Salsa di Pomodoro—Sicilian

(Rolled Beef in Tomato Sauce)

YIELD: *6 to 8 Servings*

Farsumagru is an extraordinary Sicilian word meaning "false lean." It describes this dish perfectly—lean meat lined with a rich filling and cooked in a rich tomato sauce—great for a dinner party!

1 round steak (1½ pounds)
1½ pounds ground beef
1 small onion, chopped
¼ cup bread crumbs
¼ cup grated Romano cheese

1 egg
½ teaspoon salt
¼ teaspoon freshly ground pepper
2 hard-cooked eggs, cut in half
⅓ cup olive oil

Tomato Sauce

1 medium onion, chopped
2 garlic cloves, halved
3 cans (6 ounces each) tomato paste
3 cups water

1 tablespoon basil
1½ teaspoons salt
½ teaspoon freshly ground pepper

Pound steak thin using a meat mallet or the flat side of a cleaver. Combine ground beef, onion, bread crumbs, cheese, egg, salt, and pepper. Spread evenly over round steak. Place hard-cooked eggs, yolk side down, along lower end of meat. Roll, jelly-roll fashion, and tie securely with kitchen string or fasten with meat bracelets.

In a large skillet brown meat roll well in hot oil. Remove meat and set aside.

To make tomato sauce: Brown onions and garlic in same oil as for meat for 3 minutes. Stir in tomato paste, water, basil, salt, and pepper. Bring sauce to a boil, lower heat, add meat roll, and simmer slowly until meat is tender, about 2 hours. Discard garlic.

Remove meat roll from sauce and cool for 1 hour before slicing. Discard thread or remove bracelets. Cut in ½-inch slices and arrange in rows on a warm serving platter. Spoon hot sauce down middle of slices and serve. There will be enough sauce to dress 1 pound of pasta of your choice.

Bistecca alla Pizzaiola— Sicilian

(Beefsteaks in Spicy Tomato Sauce)

YIELD: *4 Servings*

1 *medium onion, chopped*
2 *garlic cloves, minced*
2 *tablespoons olive oil*
4 *1-inch-thick chuck fillet steaks*
1 *No. 2½ can whole tomatoes*
  (28 ounces)

1 *teaspoon salt*
¼ *teaspoon freshly ground black pepper*
¼ *teaspoon crushed hot red pepper flakes*
1 *tablespoon oregano*

Baked Polenta

2 *cups water*
1 *cup polenta (cornmeal)*

½ *teaspoon salt*
2 *tablespoons butter*

Preheat oven to 350°F.

In a large skillet sauté onion and garlic in hot oil for 3 minutes. Add steaks and brown for 2 minutes on each side. Pour in tomatoes and crush lightly using a fork. Stir in salt, black and red peppers, and oregano. Bring to a boil, lower heat, cover skillet, and simmer slowly until meat is tender, 1½ to 2 hours.

To make polenta: Bring water to a boil. Pour in polenta, stirring rapidly. Cook until polenta has thickened like cereal. Stir in salt and butter. Pour into a greased loaf pan and bake for 15 to 20 minutes. (Insert toothpick in center of loaf; if it comes out clean, polenta is done.) Cool; cut into ½-inch slices.

Serve steaks with sauce and slices of baked polenta.

Scaloppine di Maiale al Marsala—Sicilian
(Pork Cutlets in Marsala Wine)

YIELD: *4 to 6 Servings*

1½ pounds ⅛-inch-thick pork cutlets
Flour
Salt and freshly ground pepper
⅓ cup chopped salt pork

2 garlic cloves, halved
1 cup dry Marsala wine
8 slices prosciutto

Pound cutlets thin using a meat mallet. In a bowl combine flour, salt, and pepper. Dredge cutlets in flour mixture and set aside.

Fry salt pork in a skillet with garlic for 5 minutes. Add cutlets and fry for 5 minutes on each side. Discard excess grease. Stir in wine and simmer for 10 minutes. Cover each cutlet with 1 slice of ham; cover and simmer 5 minutes longer. Discard garlic.

Arrange meat on a warm serving platter and pour sauce down center of meat. Serve immediately.

Fettine di Vitello alla Garibaldi—Sicilian
(Veal Scallops alla Garibaldi)

YIELD: *4 to 6 Servings*

This dedication is in tribute to Giuseppe Garibaldi, a great soldier and patriot, who led one thousand Red Shirt troops in the liberation of Sicily in 1860.

2 pounds veal scallops, thinly sliced
Flour
Salt and freshly ground pepper
¼ cup olive oil
6 shallots or scallions, minced

1 No. 2 can artichoke hearts (1 pound 3 ounces), drained, cut in half
½ cup dry white wine
1 No. 2 can early peas (1 pound 3 ounces)

Combine flour, salt, and pepper. Dredge veal in flour mixture. Brown scallops lightly in hot oil in a skillet for 1 minute on each side. Set aside. In same skillet, sauté shallots and artichokes for 5 minutes. Add wine, peas, and their liquid and simmer for 5 minutes. Push vegetables aside, return veal to skillet, and simmer for 3 minutes. Arrange veal slices on a heated platter with peas and sauce over them. Place artichokes around meat.

Fettine di Vitello al Forno— Sicilian
(Veal Cutlet Pizza)

YIELD: *6 to 8 Servings*

2 pounds veal cutlets
Olive oil
¼ cup grated Romano cheese

1½ cups fresh or canned tomatoes,
  chopped
1 tablespoon oregano
Freshly ground pepper

Preheat oven to 400°F.

Pound cutlets flat using a meat mallet or the flat side of a cleaver. Pour ¼ cup olive oil into a shallow baking pan; arrange cutlets in a single layer in pan. Sprinkle with cheese, tomatoes, oregano, pepper to taste, and oil. Bake for 10 minutes. Serve with crusty bread.

Lenticchie con Salsicce Alforno—Sicilian
(Baked Sausages over Lentils)

YIELD: *6 to 8 Servings*

Lentils are an excellent base for juicy, spicy, cheesy sausages. Their combination lends an international flavor to a buffet party with a minimum of effort and expense, as befits the times.

1 recipe lentil soup (page 123)
1 1/2 cups fresh or canned tomatoes, chopped

2 garlic cloves, minced
1 1/2 pounds Italian sausage or 12 links Sausage Riccio (page 160)

Cook lentil soup as directed, but use only 6 cups warm water. Bring to a boil, cover, and simmer for 40 minutes.

Preheat oven to 400°F.

Remove lentils from heat; stir in tomatoes and garlic. Transfer to a large casserole; cover with sausages and bake until sausages are cooked, browned, and bubbling, about 20 minutes.

Bonata—Sicilian
(Stuffed Spinach and Beef Loaf)

YIELD: *6 to 8 Servings*

2 packages active dry yeast
1/4 cup lukewarm water
5 cups sifted flour

1 1/2 teaspoons salt
1 1/2 cups water
Oil or melted butter

Filling

2 packages (10 ounces each) frozen
   chopped spinach
2 large onions, chopped
2 tablespoons olive oil

1 pound ground beef
Salt and freshly ground pepper
Garlic salt

Dissolve yeast in the water; let stand in a warm place for 5 minutes.

Measure sifted flour and salt into a large bowl; make a well in center and pour in yeast-water mixture and 1½ cups water. Mix until dough cleans sides of bowl and forms a ball (add extra water if necessary). Turn onto a lightly floured board and knead 8 to 10 minutes. Place dough into a greased bowl and brush top with oil. Cover with a cloth and let rise in a warm place (85°F) free from drafts until doubled in bulk, about 1 hour.

While dough is rising, cook spinach according to directions on package. Drain and press out water. In a large skillet sauté onions in hot oil for 3 minutes. Stir in ground beef and sauté until meat is lightly browned, 5 to 8 minutes. Season with salt, pepper, and garlic salt to taste. Add drained spinach and mix well. Set aside. Preheat oven to 400°F.

After dough has doubled in bulk, punch it down and turn onto a floured board. Knead it for 5 minutes. Roll dough into a 12 × 18-inch rectangle ¼-inch thick. Brush with oil and spread meat-spinach mixture evenly over rectangle. Roll, jelly-roll fashion, and place (fold side down) on an oiled baking pan. Bake until dough is browned and cooked through, 30 to 40 minutes. Cool and cut into 1-inch slices. Serve.

Convenience Dough: Mix 4 cups Bisquick with ¾ cup milk. Turn onto a well-floured board, dust with flour, and roll into a 12 × 18-inch rectangle by ½-inch thick. Continue as directed above.

Involtini di Maiale—Sicilian
(Pork Roll-ups)

YIELD: *Serves 4*

Involtini is a term for cutlets (pork, veal, beef, or chicken) spread with a bread crumb mixture, rolled, and braised or grilled in sauce or broiled.

1 1/2 pounds pork cutlets	Salt and freshly ground pepper
1 cup bread crumbs	Garlic salt
1/3 cup chopped fresh parsley	Olive oil
1 tablespoon rosemary	1 bunch scallions, sliced lengthwise

Preheat broiler for 10 minutes.

Flatten cutlets using a meat mallet or the flat side of a cleaver.

Combine bread crumbs, parsley, rosemary, salt, pepper, and garlic salt to taste. Moisten bread crumb mixture with 2 tablespoons olive oil.

Spread 1 to 2 tablespoons of bread crumb mixture over each cutlet. Place 2 to 3 scallion slices at lower end of cutlets; roll, jelly-roll fashion, and fasten open ends with toothpicks or skewers.

Arrange pork roll-ups in a broiler pan with 2 tablespoons olive oil. Place pan 3 inches below flame and broil until meat is well done, 4 to 6 minutes on each side. (If grilling over a charcoal fire, place meat directly over fire and grill until meat is well browned and sizzling.)

Variation: Substitute beef, chicken, or veal cutlets and prepare in the same manner. If desired, use oregano, tarragon, or basil instead of rosemary.

Spiedini alla Siciliana
(Beef Roll-ups)

YIELD: *Serves 4*

1 1/2 cups bread crumbs	1 pound eye round, cut in 1/8-inch slices
1 1/2 cups grated Parmesan cheese	Olive oil
Salt and freshly ground pepper	8 bay leaves

Filling

1 large onion, chopped
2 tablespoons olive oil

1 cup canned whole tomatoes, chopped
1/3 cup minced fresh parsley

Preheat broiler for 10 minutes.

Combine bread crumbs, cheese, and salt and pepper to taste. Set aside. Pound meat slices thin using a meat mallet or the flat side of a cleaver. Brush meat with oil on both sides, dredge in bread crumb mixture, and set aside, reserving remaining crumb mixture.

To make filling: Sauté onion in 2 tablespoons olive oil until tender, about 5 minutes. Add tomatoes and parsley and sauté for 3 minutes. Remove from heat and stir in remaining bread crumb mixture.

Spread 1 to 2 tablespoons filling over each beef slice. Roll, jelly-roll fashion, and place 1 bay leaf over every open end. Secure ends and bay leaves with skewers. Arrange in a shallow broiler pan to which 2 tablespoons oil has been added. Broil 3 inches from flame until meat is cooked, 5 to 8 minutes on each side.

Scaloppine di Vitello al Marsala—Sicilian
(Veal Cutlets with Marsala Wine)

YIELD: *Serves 6*

1 1/2 pounds veal cutlets, thinly sliced
Flour
Salt and freshly ground pepper
1/2 pound mushrooms, sliced lengthwise

1/4 pound prosciutto, chopped
1/3 cup olive oil
1/2 cup dry Marsala wine

Pound cutlets thin using a meat mallet or the flat side of a cleaver. Combine flour, salt, and pepper. Dredge cutlets in the flour mixture and set aside.

Sauté mushrooms and prosciutto in 3 tablespoons of the olive oil until tender, about 5 minutes. Set aside.

Pour remaining oil into the skillet and fry cutlets lightly for 1 to 2 minutes on each side. Pour in wine and mushrooms-prosciutto mixture and cook over high heat for 3 minutes.

Arrange meat on a warm serving platter. Pour mushroom sauce over meat. Serve immediately.

Sausage Riccio

YIELD: *About 40 links*

Dominick Riccio, now an ordained Catholic Deacon and an old friend, was an excellent butcher; here is his recipe for real Italian sausage.

3½ pounds pork loin	*¾ cup coarsely grated Romano cheese*
1½ pounds beef	*¾ cup coarsely grated Parmesan cheese*
5 teaspoons salt	*1 teaspoon freshly ground pepper*
1½ cups minced fresh Italian parsley	*1 cup water*
3 tablespoons fennel seed	*½ pound sausage casings (see Note)*

Grind pork with beef using a medium blade on a grinder, or have your butcher do this for you. Combine ground meats with salt, parsley, fennel seed, Romano and Parmesan cheeses, and pepper. Mix until all ingredients are well blended. Pour in water gradually (mixture may take a little less or more) and mix until all ingredients are bound together. Correct seasoning if necessary.

Place sausage casings in a bowl of cold water. Open one end of casing and run cold water through entire casing. Cut 2 feet of casing, tie one end with kitchen thread; fit open end onto a small funnel tube (either hand or machine funnel). Push sausage mixture through funnel tube into entire casing. Tie open end and then twist filled casing into sausage links, the links should be tightly packed. Repeat process until mixture is finished.

Fry, grill, broil, bake as may be suggested in a recipe, or freeze sausage for future use.

Note: Casings may be ordered through your butcher or purchased at pork stores.

Sausage Patties: Prepare sausage mixture as directed, but do not use casings. Instead shape mixture into 2½-inch rounds and fry or grill until brown and crispy in texture. This sausage mixture makes excellent stuffing for poultry, meat rolls (*braciole*), and vegetables (peppers, zucchini, escarole).

Polpette de Carne Fritte— Sicilian

(Spicy Fried Meatballs)

YIELD: *4 to 6 Servings*

1½ pounds ground beef
1 medium onion, chopped
1 cup bread crumbs
⅓ cup grated Romano cheese
½ cup chopped fresh parsley

2 eggs
1½ teaspoons salt
1 teaspoon freshly ground pepper
3 tablespoons olive oil

Combine beef, onion, bread crumbs, cheese, parsley, eggs, salt, and pepper; blend. Shape mixture into thick 2½-inch rounds and fry in hot oil until well browned on one side, 3 to 5 minutes. Flatten meatballs slightly with a spatula; turn and fry for 3 to 5 minutes on other side.

Serve with salad and tomatoes, crusty bread, and home fries.

Polpette di Carne alla Griglia
—Sicilian
(Pine Nut Hamburgers)

YIELD: *4 to 6 Servings*

1 1/2 pounds ground beef
1 medium onion, chopped
1 large garlic clove, minced
1 cup bread crumbs
1/3 cup Romano cheese
1/4 cup pine nuts (pignoli)

1/2 cup chopped fresh parsley
2 eggs
1 1/2 teaspoons salt
1 teaspoon freshly ground pepper
Oil

Preheat broiler.

Combine beef, onion, garlic, bread crumbs, cheese, pine nuts, parsley, eggs, salt, and pepper; blend well. Shape mixture into thick 2 1/2-inch rounds.

Brush broiler pan or grill with oil, arrange hamburgers on pan, and broil 3 inches from flame until hamburgers are well browned and crispy, about 5 minutes per side.

Pollo al Marsala—Sicilian
(Chicken with Marsala Wine)

YIELD: *4 Servings*

1 frying chicken (3 1/2 pounds), quartered
Flour
Salt and freshly ground pepper
2 tablespoons olive oil
1 small onion, chopped
1 stalk celery, chopped
2 tablespoons plus 1/4 cup melted butter

1/2 cup Marsala wine
1 cup chicken stock or bouillon
1 teaspoon tomato paste
1 teaspoon rosemary
1/2 pound mushrooms, thinly sliced
1/4 cup minced fresh Italian parsley

Dredge chicken in flour; season with salt and pepper to taste. Sauté chicken in hot oil until golden, turning once. Transfer to a large saucepan.

In the same skillet brown onion and celery in 2 tablespoons melted butter for 3 minutes. Transfer to the saucepan and add wine, chicken stock, tomato paste, and rosemary. Stir well, cover, and simmer until chicken is tender, about 1 hour.

While chicken is simmering, sauté mushrooms and parsley in ¼ cup melted butter for 5 to 8 minutes. Add to saucepan 10 minutes before chicken is done.

Pollo fra Diavolo—Sicilian
(Deviled Chicken)

YIELD: *4 to 6 Servings*

Olive oil
1 broiling chicken (3½ pounds), cut into
   serving pieces
½ cup finely chopped shallots
2 garlic cloves, halved
1 No. 2½ (2 pounds 3 oz) can whole
   tomatoes in puree

1 cup dry white wine
⅓ cup chopped fresh parsley
1 teaspoon salt
¼ teaspoon freshly ground black pepper
¼ teaspoon crushed hot red pepper flakes
1 pound spinach fettuccine

Preheat oven to 350°F.

In a large skillet heat 2 tablespoons olive oil and brown chicken until golden. Transfer to a large casserole.

In the same skillet, sauté shallots and garlic for 3 minutes (add more oil if necessary). Stir in tomatoes, wine, parsley, salt, and black and red peppers. Simmer for 10 minutes. Pour sauce over chicken and bake until chicken is tender, about 1 hour.

While chicken is baking, cook fettuccine according to package directions and drain. Serve chicken and sauce over fettuccine.

Pollo con Melanzane—Sicilian
(Chicken with Eggplant)

YIELD: *4 to 6 Servings*

Salt
1 medium eggplant (about 1 pound),
peeled and chopped
1 broiling chicken (3 pounds), cut into
serving pieces
2 tablespoons plus 1/4 cup olive oil
2 cups chicken stock or bouillon

2 tablespoons tomato paste
1 tablespoon oregano
1 large onion, sliced
2 large green bell peppers, cut in strips
2 cups fresh or canned tomatoes, skinned,
cored, and chopped
Freshly ground pepper

Salt eggplant liberally and drain in a colander for 30 minutes. Rinse off salt, drain, and dry with absorbent paper.

In a large saucepan brown chicken in 2 tablespoons hot oil. Pour in chicken stock, tomato paste, and oregano and simmer for 40 minutes.

While chicken is simmering, heat 1/4 cup olive oil in a large skillet. Add onion, bell peppers, and eggplant and sauté for 10 minutes (add more oil if necessary). Add tomatoes and salt and pepper to taste and simmer for 5 minutes longer. Transfer to saucepan and simmer until chicken is tender, about 10 minutes. Correct seasoning if necessary.

Pollo in Salsa di Capperi— Sicilian
(Chicken in Caper Sauce)

YIELD: *4 to 6 Servings*

1 frying chicken (3 to 4 pounds), cut
into serving pieces
Olive oil
2 large onions, chopped
4 stalks celery, chopped
4 tablespoons tomato paste
1 cup water

1/2 teaspoon salt
1/4 teaspoon freshly ground pepper
1/3 cup capers
2 tablespoons vinegar
1 tablespoon sugar
1/2 cup pitted green Sicilian olives

In a skillet brown chicken lightly in 2 tablespoons hot olive oil. Transfer to a large saucepan.

Add 2 tablespoons oil to skillet and lightly brown onions and celery until soft, 8 to 10 minutes. Add tomato paste, the water, salt, pepper, capers, vinegar, and sugar; simmer for 5 minutes. Pour over chicken; cover saucepan and simmer until chicken is tender, about 1 hour. Add olives and simmer 10 minutes longer. Remove from heat and cool for 20 minutes before serving. (The sweet-and-sour sauce will be too piquant if served hot.)

Involtini di Pollo
(Elegant Stuffed Chicken Breasts)

YIELD: *6 Servings*

Flour
Salt and freshly ground pepper
6 chicken breasts, boned
6 slices (¼ pound) prosciutto
6 slices (8 ounces) mozzarella cheese
¼ cup plus ⅓ cup butter

1 cup chicken stock or bouillon
1 cup Marsala wine
2 tablespoons olive oil
½ pound mushrooms
⅓ cup minced fresh Italian parsley

Mix flour with salt and pepper to taste. Dredge chicken breasts in flour mixture. Layer each chicken breast with 1 slice prosciutto and 1 slice mozzarella. Roll and close ends with skewers or toothpicks.

In a large skillet brown chicken breasts lightly in ¼ cup heated butter. Then pour in chicken stock and wine. Cover skillet and simmer slowly until chicken breasts are tender, about 30 minutes.

In another skillet heat ⅓ cup butter and the olive oil. Add mushrooms and sauté until crisp, about 8 minutes. Stir in parsley and sauté 3 minutes longer. Add mushroom sauce to chicken 5 minutes before it is done. Remove skewers or toothpicks before serving. Serve over buttered noodles.

Cannelloni a la Valle dei Tempi—Sicilian

(Cannelloni from the Valley of the Temples)

YIELD: *4 to 6 Servings*

Restaurants nestled in Agrigento's famous Valley of the Temples, feature cannelloni (pasta pipes) filled with tasty spiced meat and smacked with a layer of sauce and spicy cheese.

1 recipe Quick Tomato Sauce (page 47)	*3 sprigs fresh parsley, chopped*
1 recipe Basic Pasta (page 52)	*2 stalks celery, chopped*
Water	*2 bay leaves*
Salt	*1 teaspoon salt*
1½ pounds beef round	*1 teaspoon peppercorns*
¼ pound pork	*¼ pound mortadella, chopped*
2 carrots, peeled and chopped	*½ cup grated caciocavallo cheese*

Prepare Quick Tomato Sauce. While sauce is simmering, make pasta. Cut dough in half and roll out on a floured board into two thin sheets (⅛ inch thick). Cut into 4 × 5-inch rectangles. Sprinkle lightly with flour and let dry for 1 hour on your board. Drop rectangles, a few at a time, into rapidly boiling salted water (about 4 quarts) for 5 to 8 minutes. Remove using a slotted spoon into a bowl of cold water. When pasta is cool enough to handle, drain on damp towels.

   Place beef, pork, carrots, parsley, celery, bay leaves, salt, and peppercorns in a large saucepan. Cover with water (approximately 1½ quarts). Bring to a boil, cover, and simmer until meat is tender, 1 to 1½ hours. Drain off liquid and discard peppercorns. Grind up meat and vegetables using a meat grinder or in blender. Add mortadella and blend. Preheat oven to 400°F.

   On shorter end of pasta rectangle, spread 2 tablespoons of the meat mixture. Roll, diploma style, and place cannelloni in a shallow baking dish which has been coated with a thin layer of sauce. Arrange cannelloni 1 layer deep, cover generously with sauce, and sprinkle with cheese. Bake for 10 to 15 minutes. Serve with additional sauce and cheese.

Vermicelli alla Siracusana—Sicilian

(Vermicelli, Syracuse Style)

YIELD: *4 to 6 Servings*

The Italians have facetiously named vermicelli, which means little worms! Probably because vermicelli (very fine strands of egg noodles) multiply after cooking and look like worms. Syracusians, in all seriousness, have created a colorful and snappy vegetable sauce to complement the tasty pasta.

3 yellow or green bell peppers
1 medium to large eggplant (1 to 2 pounds)
Salt
1 1/2 pounds ripe tomatoes or 2 cups canned plum tomatoes
1/4 cup olive oil
2 garlic cloves, minced
4 fresh basil leaves or 1 tablespoon dried

1/4 cup capers
8 black Sicilian olives, pitted and chopped
6 anchovies, chopped, or 1 can (6 ounces) Italian tuna
1/2 teaspoon salt
1 pound vermicelli
1/2 cup grated caciocavallo or Romano cheese

Cut peppers in half, remove and discard stems, seeds, and ribs. Rinse with cold water, dry, and broil, skin side up, for 2 minutes. Cool, peel off skins, and cut in strips.

Remove and discard peel and stem from eggplant. Dice eggplant, salt liberally, and drain in a colander for 15 minutes. Rinse off salt, dry with absorbent paper, and set aside.

If using ripe tomatoes, plunge in boiling water for 1 to 2 minutes. Remove and discard skins and stems. Chop tomatoes and set aside.

Heat oil in a large skillet; add garlic and brown lightly. Add diced eggplant and pepper strips and sauté for 10 minutes (add more oil if vegetables begin to stick). Stir in tomatoes, basil, capers, olives, anchovies, and salt. Cover skillet and simmer slowly for 5 to 10 minutes.

Cook vermicelli according to package directions and drain. Transfer to a warm serving bowl, cover with vegetable sauce, and mix well. Sprinkle with cheese and serve immediately.

Mille Foglie alla Pirandello

(Leaves of Pasta alla Pirandello)

YIELD: *8 to 10 Servings*

Luigi Pirandello, one of the greatest playwrights of the twentieth century, was born in Agrigento, Sicily. Mille Foglie alla Pirandello is dedicated to him and matches his magnificence. These light, graceful, and tender leaves of pasta are comparable in texture to the famous Napoleon pastry.

1 recipe meat and tomato sauce (page 52)
1 recipe Basic Pasta (page 49)

½ pound coarsely grated caciocavallo or Romano cheese
½ cup grated Parmesan cheese

Prepare meat and tomato sauce. While sauce is simmering, make Basic Pasta. Cut dough in half and roll out on a floured board into two very thin sheets (⅛ inch thick). Cut sheets into 2½ × 12-inch strips. Sprinkle with flour and drop a few strips at a time into boiling salted water (about 4 quarts) for 5 to 8 minutes (see Tip). Remove using a slotted spoon into a bowl of cold water. When pasta is cool enough to handle, drain on damp towels. Preheat oven to 400°F.

Into a 9 × 13-inch shallow baking pan, spread one ladle of sauce. Layer pasta strips alternately with sauce and grated caciocavallo cheese until pasta and cacciocavallo are used, ending with sauce and cheese on top. Bake for 15 minutes. Before serving, cut into large squares and top with additional sauce and grated Parmesan cheese.

Tip: When cooking large-cut macaroni, add a little olive oil to boiling water to prevent macaroni from sticking together.

Gnocculli—Sicilian

(Gnocchi with Meat Sauce)

YIELD: *6 to 8 Servings*

Gnocchi is a type of pasta made with flour and ricotta cheese or potatoes or cereal. *Gnocculli* (Sicilian dialect for *gnocchi*) resemble nuggets of gold and taste like minimorsels of heaven.

1 recipe meat and tomato sauce (page 49)

4 cups sifted flour

1 pound ricotta cheese

Salt

1 cup grated Parmesan cheese

Prepare meat and tomato sauce as directed.

In a large bowl combine flour, ricotta, and a pinch of salt. Mix until dough cleans sides of bowl and forms a ball. Turn onto a lightly floured board and knead until dough is smooth, 5 to 8 minutes.

Cut dough into 8 sections. Roll each section into long finger-shaped rolls (½ inch in diameter) and cut into ½-inch pieces. Using your index finger, press each piece in the center gently but firmly and roll slightly to form a shell-like shape. Sprinkle with flour and let stand for 15 minutes.

Shake off excess flour and drop *gnocculli* into 6 quarts rapidly boiling water to which 3 tablespoons of salt have been added. Boil until tender, 12 to 15 minutes. Drain well, cover with meat and tomato sauce, sprinkle with cheese, and serve immediately.

Pasta Fritta—Sicilian
(Fried Spaghetti)

YIELD: *4 Servings*

Pasta Fritta is traditionally served for *il cenone* (Christmas Eve supper). I think it's an unusual and tasty first course for any time of the year.

½ pound spaghettini or vermicelli
1 can (2 ounces) anchovies
¼ cup olive oil

3 eggs
3 tablespoons grated Parmesan cheese
Freshly ground pepper

Cook spaghettini following package directions. When done, drain well and set aside.

Chop anchovies, reserving 3 whole fillets for garnish.

In a large skillet heat oil and add cooked spaghettini and chopped anchovies. Fry for 8 to 10 minutes over medium heat until spaghettini is golden and crispy on bottom side.

Beat eggs slightly with cheese and pepper to taste. Pour over spaghettini and cook until eggs are set.

Cover skillet with a plate the same size as the skillet and reverse spaghettini onto plate. Slide back into skillet to cook bottom side for 2 minutes. Slide onto a warm serving plate and garnish with anchovy fillets. Cut into wedges, omelet style, and serve immediately.

Variation: Substitute a 6-ounce can of Italian-style tuna for anchovies and cook as directed above.

Spaghetti alla Carrettiera—
Sicilian

(Coachman's Spaghetti)

YIELD: *4 to 6 Servings*

Sicilian coachmen created Spaghetti alla Carrettiera to have something hot, simple, filling, and inexpensive to eat while working. Long ago, along the main thoroughfares in Sicily, it was common to see these men in their black frocks boiling water over small wooden fires for their daily pasta *sciutta* (pasta coated lightly with herbs and cheese or tomato sauce). Formerly, this specialty was considered a peasant dish, but today it is an epicurean favorite of both rich and poor alike.

1 pound spaghetti
1/4 cup olive oil
2 garlic cloves, minced

2 cups chopped fresh parsley
1/2 cup Romano cheese
Freshly ground pepper

Cook spaghetti according to package directions. While spaghetti is cooking, heat oil in a large skillet and sauté garlic for 2 or 3 minutes. Stir in cooked, drained spaghetti, parsley, and cheese, and mix well. Heat together for 2 minutes. Transfer to a warm serving bowl and season with pepper to taste.

Conchiglie con Cavolfiore— Sicilian

(Shells and Flowers)

YIELD: *4 to 6 Servings*

1 large head cauliflower (2 to 3 pounds)
  or 2 packages (10 ounces each)
  frozen cauliflower
1 tablespoon salt
1 pound pasta shells

¼ cup olive oil
2 large garlic cloves, minced
⅔ cups grated Romano cheese
Freshly ground pepper
Salt (optional)

Wash cauliflower with cold running water; remove leaves and core. Cut or break head into rosettes. Boil cauliflower rosettes in salted water and cook until tender, 15 to 20 minutes. Drain, reserving ½ cup of the liquid, and set aside.

Cook shells according to package directions and drain. Heat oil in same pot and sauté garlic until golden. Add cooked shells, cauliflower rosettes, the reserved ½ cup liquid, cheese, and pepper to taste. Toss until ingredients are thoroughly mixed. Season lightly with salt, if necessary.

Agnello in Vino Rosso

(Braised Lamb in Wine Sauce)

YIELD: *6 Servings*

2 pounds boneless lamb (shoulder or
  leg), cut into ¼-inch cubes
1 tablespoon vegetable oil
3 shallots, peeled

1 garlic clove, peeled
3 tablespoons minced fresh Italian
  parsley
½ cup dry red wine
1 tablespoon Italian seasoning

Cut all fat off lamb and flatten cubes using the flat side of a meat cleaver.

Heat vegetable oil in a large frying pan with a cover. Chop shallots into the pan and push the garlic through a press into the pan. Add the parsley and lamb and sauté over brisk heat until lamb pieces are lightly browned on both sides. Add the wine and seasoning and bring to a boil over high heat. Reduce the heat until the liquid in the pan is barely simmering. Cover the pan and braise for 8 to 10 minutes, or until the lamb is tender and done to your taste. If necessary, add more seasoning before serving.

Saltimbocca di Pollo

(Chicken Saltimbocca)

YIELD: *4 Servings*

3 large whole chicken breasts, boned, skinned, and halved lengthwise
¼ cup freshly grated Parmesan cheese
1 tablespoon finely chopped fresh sage
Freshly ground pepper to taste

12 thin slices prosciutto
4 tablespoons unsalted butter
1 tablespoon olive oil
2 tablespoons chicken broth

Halve chicken pieces crosswise, making 12 pieces. Flatten each to ⅛-inch thickness by pounding lightly between 2 sheets of waxed paper. Sprinkle each piece with 1 teaspoon cheese, ¼ teaspoon sage, and pepper. Place a slice of prosciutto over each chicken piece. (Trim excess prosciutto if desired.) Secure prosciutto to each chicken piece with a wooden toothpick.

Heat 2 tablespoons of the butter and the oil in a large skillet over medium heat. Add chicken, prosciutto-side up, and cook until golden, 4 to 5 minutes. Turn chicken over and cook until done, about 2 minutes. Place chicken on a serving platter.

Add broth and remaining butter to the skillet and cook, stirring constantly to dislodge particles from skillet bottom, until butter melts. Pour butter mixture over chicken and serve at once.

Scaloppine Martini

(Veal Martini)

YIELD: *6 Servings*

12 veal medallions
1 cup flour
2 eggs, beaten
1 cup grated Parmesan cheese

Olive oil, for frying
2 tablespoons butter
Freshly squeezed juice of 1/2 lemon
1/2 cup beef stock

Dredge veal in flour, dip into beaten eggs, then dredge in cheese.

In a skillet fry veal in olive oil until golden on both sides. Remove to a plate, cover with a warm plate, and set aside.

Discard oil from skillet. Add butter, lemon juice, and beef stock. Simmer over low heat until liquids are reduced by half, about 15 minutes. Pour sauce over veal and serve.

Polpettone al Vino Rosso
(Red Wine Meatloaf)

YIELD: *4 to 6 Servings*

Although through the years, I have almost cut red meat out of my personal diet, when I do eat meat, it's Italian style. This next recipe is Italian-style meatloaf—or as my Mamma used to say, *"lofa meat."*

1 pound ground veal or beef
½ pound good-quality Italian pork
sausage, skinned
2 eggs
2 cups red dry Italian wine

Salt and freshly ground pepper to taste
½ pound mortadella slices (see Note)
All-purpose flour
Olive oil

Preheat oven to 300°F.

In a mixing bowl, combine veal, sausage, eggs, ½ cup of the wine, and salt and pepper. Form into a loaf and cover the loaf with mortadella slices. Tie with kitchen string, flour lightly, and brown in 2 tablespoons of olive oil in a skillet. Transfer to oven loaf pan, add rest of wine, and cook for 50 minutes.

Remove from oven, let rest for 10 minutes, then slice and serve with oven juices (of course you take the string off first; string is hard to digest).

Note: If mortadella is unavailable, it may be omitted.

* 12 *

FRUITS OF THE SEA

Not too long ago in the Roman Catholic world, every Friday was fish day. Meat was not eaten on Fridays as a sacrificial reminder to Catholic Christians that on Good Friday Jesus Christ made the supreme sacrifice of His life to save us all from our sin. There were other special days selected during the year, that were also so honored, especially Christmas Eve. I have selected a few fish recipes that are favorites in Italian-American homes and are likely to become your favorites, too.

When I was a little kid during the immediate post-depression, my family lived in a modest rented second story. My mother frequently cooked Pesce Stocco O Baccala on Fridays. Because of its first stage of preparation, I could always tell when it was Thursday. Our bathroom was located at the head of the stairs leading to our front door and on Thursdays there would always be a large dried cod fish floating in the bathtub. The bathtub, fortunately for us kids who hated baths, was the only vessel large enough to contain the dried cod. One day, a friend of mine who had never been inside my house came to call me out to play. He saw two doors after he had climbed the stairs, one directly in front of him (the bathroom) and the other to his right (our front door). I was in the bathroom at the time having just washed my face and hands, and I heard a loud knock at the door. I opened the door and saw the shocked look of my little pal when he looked past me and saw the bathroom. Before I could hurry him into the other door, his swift eyes caught sight of that huge fish floating in the bathtub. His innocently sincere comment was,

"WOW! That's terrific! I bet you're the only kid on the block who can go fishing in his bathtub." Whenever I hear about Pesce Stocco o Baccala, I think about how neat it would be for a kid to go fishing in his bathtub.

Pesce Stocco o Baccala
(Codfish Stew)

YIELD: *Serves 6*

2 pounds dried cod
2 medium onions, minced coarsely
1/4 cup olive oil
2 large potatoes, peeled and quartered
1/2 teaspoon salt

1/2 teaspoon crushed hot red pepper flakes
2 fresh ripe tomatoes, washed and
   quartered
Water

Soak the dried cod in water for 24 hours, changing the water about 6 times. Remove skin from the softened cod and separate the cod flesh from any bone using a sharp knife. Cut the cod into large bite-sized pieces. Place in a colander to drain.

In a heavy saucepan sauté onion in olive oil over low heat until soft. Then slowly brown potatoes in the same pan; remove. Add the fish and sauté over medium heat for 10 minutes. Add salt, red pepper, tomatoes, and cooked potatoes. Stir gently. Add just enough cold water to cover contents of pan. Bring to a slow boil, then lower heat and allow to simmer for 1/2 hour. Serve in deep bowls with good Italian bread to soak up the gravy.

Shrimp Scampi

YIELD: *Serves 4*

¼ cup olive oil
6 large garlic cloves, diced
1 pound, medium, raw fresh or frozen
  shrimp, shelled and cleaned

¼ cup chopped fresh parsley
1 teaspoon salt
½ teaspoon freshly ground pepper

Heat olive oil in a large frying pan or saucepan. Sauté diced garlic until just turning brown. Add shrimp, salt, and pepper. Mix and sauté over medium heat for 5 minutes. Add parsley and simmer covered for 15 minutes. Serve hot with slices of Italian bread to sop up the delicious soupy gravy.

Shrimp and Macaroni Casserole

YIELD: *Serves 6*

3 cups shell macaroni #21, cooked
2 cups small cooked shrimp
1 cup diced celery
1 cup grated Parmesan cheese
2 eggs, slightly beaten

2 cups milk
½ teaspoon salt
Pinch of pepper
1 tablespoon butter

Preheat oven to 350°F.

Place one third of the macaroni in the bottom of a greased 2-quart casserole. Add half the amount of shrimp on top of the layer of shells. Sprinkle 2 tablespoons of cheese and ½ cup of celery, continue to layer all the ingredients the same. In a bowl combine remaining grated cheese, eggs, milk and seasonings. Pour over shells. Dot top of casserole with butter. Set casserole in pan of hot water. Bake until firm, about 1 hour.

Pesce alla Pizzaiola

(Fish with Tomato Sauce)

YIELD: *Serves 4*

4 portions frozen or fresh white fish,
  skinned and boned
1 bay leaf
1/2 cup chopped fresh parsley
1/2 teaspoon thyme
5 tablespoons olive oil

1 cup seasoned flour (mix 1 teaspoon salt,
  1/2 teaspoon pepper, and 1/2 teaspoon
  garlic powder into flour)
2 garlic cloves, finely minced
1 pound ripe tomatoes, peeled, cored, and
  chopped, or 1 can (14 ounces) peeled
  tomatoes
Salt, freshly ground pepper, and sugar to
  taste

Lay the fish with the bay leaf, parsley and thyme in a dish and pour the olive oil over it. Leave for 2 hours, turning the fish once. Drain the fish, reserving the marinade, then dry and coat with the seasoned flour. Strain the marinade into a frying pan and, when hot, fry the fish until golden on both sides and cooked, 8 to 12 minutes depending on thickness. Drain the fish, arrange on a serving dish and keep hot. Add the garlic to the oil remaining in the pan and cook until golden; add the tomatoes and cook over high heat until the liquid is evaporated and tomatoes are reduced to a thick pulpy sauce. Add salt, pepper, and dash of sugar. Mix well and pour over fish. Serve immediately.

Fried Shrimp Italiano

1 pound raw shrimp, shelled and
  deveined
1 recipe basic flour paste (page 120)
Oil, for frying

Dip shrimp into batter and lower into hot oil. Fry from 4 to 8 minutes (depending on size), until golden and crisp. Drain on absorbent paper and serve immediately.

Baked Fish Siciliano

YIELD: *3 Servings*

3 portions white fish, skinned and boned
2 tablespoons olive oil
1 medium onion, chopped
1 can (8 ounces) peeled tomatoes
2 garlic cloves, peeled
1 teaspoon salt

½ teaspoon freshly ground pepper
8 pitted green olives, chopped
1 tablespoon capers, drained
1 tablespoon chopped fresh parsley
1 small stalk celery, very finely chopped

Preheat oven to 375°F.

Arrange the fish in a single layer in a shallow, oiled oven casserole. Heat the olive oil in a frying pan and sauté the onion gently until soft and golden. Add the tomatoes and their juice, garlic, salt, and pepper. Cook briskly, stirring frequently, for 5 minutes.

Stir in the olives, capers, parsley, and celery and spoon sauce evenly over the fish. Cover and bake for 25 minutes. Serve hot.

Baked Fish with Almonds

YIELD: *4 Servings*

4 fresh trout (1 to 1½ pounds each),
   scaled and dressed (see Note)
1 tablespoon vegetable oil
½ cup dry white wine

¼ cup chopped fresh Italian parsley
¼ cup blanched slivered almonds
3 lemons, cut into very thin slices and
   seeded

Preheat oven to 400°F. Coat a baking dish with the oil and arrange trout in a single layer.

Mix wine and parsley and spoon the mixture over the fish. Evenly spoon almonds over the fish and arrange lemon slices on top. Bake for 20 minutes; serve immediately.

Note: Have your fish store scale and dress the trout. The heads can be removed or not, as you please.

Shrimp in Herb Sauce

YIELD: *4 Servings*

6 to 8 ripe plum tomatoes, cored
2 tablespoons vegetable oil
¼ cup chopped fresh Italian parsley
1 tablespoon Italian seasoning
2 tablespoons chopped fresh dill

1 garlic clove, crushed
Pinch of cayenne pepper
Salt and freshly ground black pepper
2 pounds medium-sized shrimp, shelled
  and deveined

Place tomatoes in boiling water. Remove from heat and let tomatoes sit in the water for 2 to 3 minutes. Transfer to a bowl of cold water and let them sit for an additional 2 to 3 minutes, or until the skins begin to pucker. Peel tomatoes and squeeze out seeds, then chop (there should be about 1 cup).

Pour oil into a large frying pan and add tomatoes, parsley, seasoning, dill, cayenne, garlic, and pepper. Cook over medium heat for 2 minutes. Add salt and pepper to taste.

Add the shrimp and cook for 6 to 8 minutes, or until the shrimp are pink and tender. Do not overcook; stir often to mix the shrimp into the sauce as they cook. Serve immediately.

Variations: Instead of tomatoes, use 1 cup sautéed chopped mushrooms, green peppers, and onions or zucchini; or use a mixture of two or more vegetables.

Substitute ½ cup dry red wine for the tomatoes.

Baccala con Olive in Umido —Sicilian

(Codfish Stew)

YIELD: *6 to 8 Servings*

Here is another popular dish that's inexpensive, savory, and so inviting. Its preparation is somewhat time-consuming, but it's well worth it.

Fish

2½ pounds dried boned codfish
Flour
Salt and freshly ground pepper

4 tablespoons olive oil
2 large onions, chopped
½ pound Italian black olives

Sauce

1 tablespoon olive oil
1 can (6 ounces) tomato paste
1 tablespoon oregano

½ teaspoon salt
¼ teaspoon freshly ground pepper
3 cans water

Cover codfish with cold water and soak for 2 days, changing water 3 or 4 times.

Drain; cover fish with warm water and bring to a boil. Simmer until fish is tender but firm, about 1 hour. Drain well and dry with absorbent paper. Dredge fish in flour; salt and pepper lightly. Brown lightly in 2 tablespoons of hot oil. Remove to a heated platter and keep warm.

Prepare the sauce.

Heat remaining 2 tablespoons olive oil and brown onions and olives for 5 minutes. Pour in tomato sauce; add fish and cover. Simmer until all flavors are blended and fish is fork-tender, about 30 minutes.

To make sauce: In a saucepan heat 1 tablespoon olive oil; add tomato paste, oregano, salt, and pepper. Stir and sauté for 3 minutes. Pour in water, stir, and simmer for 10 minutes.

Zuppa di Pesce all Siracusana —Sicilian
(Fish Stew, Syracuse Style)

YIELD: *4 to 6 Servings*

1 medium onion, minced
2 garlic cloves, crushed
2 stalks celery, minced
¼ cup olive oil
1 can (6 ounces) tomato paste
2 cans water
½ cup dry white wine
2 bay leaves

4 sprigs fresh parsley
1 teaspoon salt
¼ teaspoon freshly ground pepper
*2 pounds cuttlefish, sliced, or cleaned
  squid*
1 dozen mussels, scrubbed and debearded
1 pound bass, cut into 3-inch pieces
1 pound codfish, cut into 3-inch pieces

In a skillet brown onion, garlic, and celery in hot oil. Stir in tomato paste, water, wine, bay leaves, parsley, salt, and pepper; simmer for 10 minutes. Add cuttlefish and simmer for 30 minutes. Add mussels, bass, and codfish and simmer until fish flakes at touch of fork and looks opaque, about 15 minutes. Discard unopened mussels, garlic, parsley, and bay leaves.

Serve in soup bowls with crusty rusks of bread for soaking up the sauce.

Nasello Fritto—Sicilian
(Golden Fried Whiting)

YIELD: *4 to 6 Servings*

3 pounds whiting, drawn and cleaned
Flour
2 egg whites, slightly beaten

Olive oil
Salt and freshly ground pepper

Slice whiting into 2-inch pieces. Dredge in flour, dip in egg whites, and fry in 1 inch of oil until golden, about 3 minutes on each side. Salt and pepper to taste and serve immediately.

Calamari Ripieni di Ricotta al Forno—Sicilian

(Ricotta-Stuffed Squid Casserole)

YIELD: *4 to 6 Servings*

Sauce

1 small onion, chopped
1 tablespoon olive oil
2 cups whole tomatoes, cored and
  chopped
6 sprigs fresh parsley

1/2 cup dry white wine
1/2 teaspoon salt
1/4 teaspoon freshly ground pepper

Squid

2 eggs
1 pound ricotta cheese
1/4 cup grated Parmesan cheese

1/4 cup minced fresh parsley
2 medium squid, cleaned
2 tablespoons olive oil

Preheat oven to 350°F.

To make sauce: Brown onion in hot oil for 2 minutes. Stir in tomatoes, parsley, wine, salt, and pepper and simmer for 15 minutes.

To prepare squid: Combine ricotta with eggs, cheeses, and parsley. Fill squid cavities two-thirds full with ricotta mixture. Secure open ends with toothpicks or sew with coarse kitchen thread. Brown squid in hot oil for about 5 minutes. Transfer to casserole and pour sauce over fish. Cover and bake until squid is tender, about 45 minutes.

Insalata di Tonno—Sicilian
(Tuna Salad)

YIELD: *4 Servings*

2 cans (7 ounces each) Italian-style
   tuna packed in oil
2 medium onions, minced
4 stalks celery, chopped
Juice of 2 medium lemons

Salt and freshly ground pepper
1 head romaine lettuce, cored and
   washed
2 tomatoes, cut in wedges

Place tuna with its oil in a medium bowl and break fish up into small pieces. Add onion, celery, lemon juice, and salt and pepper to taste; mix well. Serve over crisp lettuce leaves and garnish with tomato wedges.

Nasello in Umido—Sicilian
(Stewed Whiting)

YIELD: *4 to 6 Servings*

3 pounds whiting, drawn
3 to 4 tablespoons olive oil
1 large onion, chopped
2 large ripe tomatoes, skinned, sliced,
   and seeded

1/3 cup chopped fresh parsley
1 cup clam juice
Salt and freshly ground pepper to taste

Cut whiting into 3-inch pieces. Rinse with cold water, drain, and dry with absorbent paper. In a skillet brown lightly in hot oil and set aside.

In the same skillet, sauté onion in hot oil for 3 minutes. Add tomato slices and parsley and sauté for 3 minutes. Return whiting to skillet; pour in clam juice and salt and pepper. Cover and simmer slowly until fish flesh is opaque and fork-tender, 10 to 15 minutes.

* 13 *

GOLDEN EGGS WITHOUT THE GOOSE

Most of these recipes were tested and enjoyed in the warm atmosphere of Mr. and Mrs. Dan Hughes's kitchen. That's right! Not *all* my friends are Italian. In fact, Dan and Ann Hughes and their children, Patti and Danny, were my official Pine Hill family. They were designated so by the boss, Mamma Orsini, after she met them. Danny was my disciple and traveling companion. My Italian nationality didn't have too much influence on him ... it's only coincidence that when not in school (where he has studied Italian), he worked part time at the Naples Pizzeria in Deptford Township, New Jersey. Again, it's only coincidence that the pizzeria was owned and operated by a former student of mine, Anthony Pullella.

Peppers and Eggs

YIELD: *Serves 5*

4 *large green bell peppers, washed and cut into ¼-inch strips*
¼ *cup olive oil for frying*
1 *medium onion, sliced thin*

6 *eggs*
½ *cup Parmesan cheese*
1 *teaspoon salt*
½ *teaspoon freshly ground pepper*

Sauté peppers and onion in a skillet until soft. Beat eggs, cheese, salt, and pepper together and pour over pepper mixture. Cook until eggs are set but not too firm. Spoon into split hard-crusted Italian rolls and watch as "depression" disappears.

Frittata Calabrese
(Potato Omelet)

YIELD: *Serves 5*

4 large potatoes, diced
2 garlic cloves, minced
1/2 cup olive oil
1/2 cup chopped fresh parsley

1 tablespoon salt
1 teaspoon freshly ground pepper
6 eggs, slightly beaten
3/4 cup grated Parmesan cheese

Brown potatoes and garlic in oil in a large skillet over medium heat. Lightly beat together remaining ingredients and pour over browned potatoes. Reduce heat and cook until eggs are set around edges of skillet. Place under broiler until eggs are set on top and very lightly browned.

Uova Rosati
(Red Eggs)

YIELD: *Serves 5*

4 garlic cloves, peeled
1 teaspoon salt
1/2 teaspoon crushed hot red pepper flakes
1/4 cup olive oil

4 medium ripe tomatoes
6 eggs
1/2 cup grated Parmesan cheese

Sauté garlic, salt and red pepper in oil in a skillet until garlic begins to brown. Add tomatoes and crush with a fork; mix well and simmer over low heat for 1/2 hour.

Beat eggs well with Parmesan cheese and pour over tomatoes, stirring mixture until eggs are cooked. Spoon onto plates, serve with crispy Italian bread, and enjoy.

Pasta Omelet

YIELD: *6 Servings*

5 eggs
2 cups leftover cooked spaghetti
¼ cup grated Romano cheese
1 teaspoon salt

Freshly ground pepper to taste
1 tablespoon olive oil
1 tablespoon butter

Beat the eggs well in a bowl; stir in the pasta, cheese, salt, and pepper. Fry in oil and butter in a large skillet, either folding as an omelet or just turning straight over, pancake style. Cook omelet until golden and fluffy (not rubbery or overcooked), about 3 minutes per side. Tomato sauce may be used to top this omelet.

Eggs have always been popular in Italian cookery, and they are indispensable for their nutritional and economic values. Italians have known for centuries that eggs carry in their golden hearts every food element that the human body needs. Whenever anyone in my family caught a cold, Mamma would run to the kitchen to mix two egg yolks with a little sugar and stir them into the morning coffee for *sustanza* (strength). However, if you are watching your cholesterol, go easy on whole eggs and use cholesterol free egg substitutes.

Although eggs are eaten often in Italy, they are never eaten for breakfast. But they are frequently added to soups and are the main ingredient in some entree dishes and desserts. Until recently, most religious holidays exempted meat from the diet, so eggs and fish were the usual protein alternatives.

Most Southern Italians prefer to have their eggs cooked in olive oil rather than butter. Fried eggs and omelets are the most popular types of prepared eggs in all of Italy.

Omelets, or *frittate,* are the theme of most light suppers and appear unfailingly on antipasto tables in restaurants. Substantial in composition, frittatas usually stand two to six inches high and are cooked on both sides.

Asparagus Frittata

YIELD: *5 Servings*

1 onion, finely chopped
1 garlic clove, finely chopped
¼ cup olive oil
1 pound asparagus spears, cooked

1 tablespoon lemon juice
6 eggs, slightly beaten
¼ cup grated Parmesan cheese
Salt and freshly ground pepper to taste

In a large skillet sauté onion and garlic in oil until soft; add asparagus spears, arranging like spokes of a wheel. Sprinkle asparagus with lemon juice. Combine eggs and cheese and pour over asparagus. Cook over low heat until eggs are set around edge of skillet. Place under broiler until eggs are set on top and slightly brown.

Frittatone alla Campagnola— Sicilian

(Ham Omelet Cake)

YIELD: *2 to 4 Servings*

This omelet is not a dessert, but it is as high and round as a layer cake. It's served hot as a light luncheon or supper dish. It is also served at room temperature as an appetizer.

2 tablespoons olive oil
1 small onion, minced
1 cup chopped prosciutto or ham
8 large eggs

½ cup bread crumbs
¼ cup grated Parmesan cheese
2 tablespoons minced fresh parsley
¼ teaspoon white pepper

Heat oil in an 8-inch skillet and sauté onion for 3 minutes. Add ham and brown lightly. Beat eggs slightly and combine with bread crumbs, cheese, parsley, and pepper. Pour over ham and onions and cook over low heat. Pull eggs along sides with spatula, spilling egg liquid onto bottom of skillet. Continue until eggs do not run. Slip omelet onto a plate (same size as skillet). Turn over onto another plate and slip back in skillet to cook other side for about 2 minutes. Serve hot or at room temperature.

Frittata Ripiena al Forno— Sicilian

(Ricotta Omelet in Tomato Sauce)

YIELD: *2 to 4 Servings*

1 pound ricotta, drained
4 tablespoons grated Parmesan cheese
¼ teaspoon white pepper
1 teaspoon nutmeg
8 large eggs

2 tablespoons water
Salt and freshly ground black pepper to taste
¼ cup butter
1 cup basic tomato sauce (page 41)

Combine cheeses, white pepper, and nutmeg and set aside.

Beat eggs with water, and salt and pepper.

Melt butter in a large skillet; raise heat and pour in eggs. Stir, bringing eggs from sides of pan to the center. Do this quickly and shake pan simultaneously so that eggs will not stick to the bottom. Keep on lifting and stirring the eggs until all the liquid runs under and coagulates. Remove from heat. Preheat oven to 325°F.

Spread ricotta filling over omelet. Roll, diploma style, and close open ends with toothpicks; place in a buttered casserole and pour tomato sauce over it. Bake for 10 minutes.

Frittata di Spinaci e Formaggio—Sicilian

(Spinach-Cheese Omelet)

YIELD: *2 Servings*

1 package (10 ounces) frozen spinach
6 large eggs
¼ cup plus 3 tablespoons Parmesan cheese

¼ teaspoon freshly ground black pepper
Butter

Cook spinach according to package directions. Drain well and set aside.

Beat eggs with ¼ cup grated Parmesan cheese and pepper. Melt 2 table-spoons butter, raise heat, and pour in egg mixture. Pull in sides of omelet with fork and stir in center; continue until all liquid runs to the bottom and coagulates. Place spinach over omelet and dot with butter. Fold over edge one quarter and then the other edge by one quarter, with both edges meeting at center. Turn omelet over onto heated platter and sprinkle with 3 table-spoons grated cheese.

Uova Strapazzate al Pomodoro—Sicilian

(Scrambled Eggs and Tomatoes)

YIELD: *4 Servings*

2 tablespoons olive oil
1 medium onion, minced
1½ cups canned or fresh tomatoes,
  chopped
1 teaspoon dried basil

½ teaspoon salt
¼ teaspoon freshly ground pepper
½ teaspoon sugar
8 large eggs, slightly beaten

In a large skillet heat oil and sauté onion for 2 minutes. Stir in tomatoes, basil, salt, pepper, and sugar and simmer for 8 to 10 minutes. Stir in eggs and let set for 2 minutes. Scramble and cook until eggs have coagulated. Serve over hot buttered toast.

Mozzarella Fritta con Uova
—Sicilian
(Mozzarella Omelet)

YIELD: *1 Serving*

2 large eggs
Salt and freshly ground pepper

2 tablespoons butter
1 slice mozzarella cheese

Beat eggs slightly with salt and pepper to taste. Melt butter in a small skillet. Raise heat, pour in eggs, and scramble with fork until eggs are semi-coagulated, about 30 seconds. Center cheese slice over eggs; fold one edge over one quarter and the other edge over one quarter with both edges meeting at center. Turn omelet over onto warm plate. Continue making individual omelets for as many people as are present.

Uova in Camicia al Pomodoro
—Sicilian
(Poached Eggs in Tomato Sauce)

YIELD: *4 Servings*

2 tablespoons olive oil
1 medium onion, minced
1 No. 2½ can whole tomatoes, chopped
1 teaspoon dried basil or 4 fresh leaves

1 teaspoon salt
¼ teaspoon freshly ground pepper
6 to 8 eggs
¼ cup grated Parmesan cheese

In a large skillet heat oil and sauté onion for 3 minutes. Stir in tomatoes, basil, salt, and pepper. Simmer for 10 minutes. Break eggs, one at a time, onto a saucer. Slip each egg from saucer onto tomato sauce, cover, lower heat, and poach until whites coagulate, 3 to 5 minutes. Sprinkle eggs with cheese and place under hot broiler for just long enough to toast cheese, about 1 minute.

Crocchette d'Uova—Sicilian

(Egg Croquettes)

YIELD: *4 to 6 Servings*

6 large eggs, slightly beaten
1/3 cup grated Romano cheese
1 cup bread crumbs
1/4 cup minced fresh parsley

1 small onion, minced
Salt and freshly ground pepper to taste
Olive oil

Combine eggs, cheese, bread crumbs, parsley, onion, and salt and pepper. Mix well. Heat oil, ½ inch deep, in a large skillet. Drop croquettes by round tablespoons into hot oil and fry until golden brown, turning once. Serve as an hors d'oeuvre, as a first course, or in place of potatoes.

Uova di Torino

(Eggs with Cardoons in Béchamel)

YIELD: *4 Servings*

2 cardoons
3 tablespoons butter
2 cups béchamel (page 42)

8 hard-boiled eggs, peeled and halved
1 cup grated Parmesan cheese

Clean cardoons of filaments and hard leaves. Cut into pieces and cook in salted boiling water until tender. Then drain and sauté in skillet with butter.

Prepare béchamel.

Line halved eggs in a rectangular pan, top with cardoons and béchamel, and sprinkle with cheese. Broil for 15 minutes. Serve hot.

Uova Vellutate
(Velvet Eggs)

YIELD: *4 Servings*

8 *hard-boiled eggs*
3 *ounces boiled ham, minced*

2 *cups béchamel (page 42)*
4 *tablespoons heavy cream, whipped*

Halve eggs lengthwise, remove yolks, and set whites aside. Place yolks in a mixing bowl. Add ham and 1 tablespoon of béchamel. Fill whites with yolk mixture.

Mix remaining béchamel with whipped cream and spoon over eggs. Serve cold.

Fonduta Piemontese
(Cheese Fondue, Piedmont Style, from Le ricette regionali italian *by Anna Gosetti della Salda, Editore Solares, Milan)*

YIELD: *4 Servings*

1 *pound fontina cheese, thinly sliced*
7 *tablespoons milk*
1¼ *tablespoons butter*
4 *egg yolks*

1 *white truffle, sliced (if unavailable, use*
1 large white mushroom)
4 *slices toast*

Soak cheese in milk in a bowl for at least 2 hours.

Melt butter in a saucepan and add cheese-milk mixture, stirring with a whisk until cheese is ropy. Raise the heat and continue stirring rapidly. Add egg yolks, combining well after each addition. Continue stirring until mixture is no longer ropy.

Pour fondue into individual dishes, garnish with truffles, and serve hot with toast.

Meringhe
(Meringues)

YIELD: *4 Servings*

4 egg whites
8 tablespoons confectioners' sugar

Pinch of salt
Almond extract

Beat egg whites, 4 tablespoons of sugar, salt, and a few drops of almond extract until firm. When mixture is off-white in color, add balance of sugar and continue beating until stiff.

Place mixture into a pastry bag and squeeze onto a greased cookie sheet in 3½-inch-wide candy-kiss–shaped domes. Bake at 210°F for about 1½ hours, or until golden. Cool and serve with ice cream.

Isola Fluttuante
(Floating Island)

YIELD: *4 Servings*

6 eggs, separated
9 tablespoons confectioners' sugar
Pinch of salt

1 teaspoon almond extract
1 quart milk plus 2 cups hot milk

Beat egg whites, 4 tablespoons sugar, salt, and almond extract until firm and off-white in color. Add balance of sugar and continue beating until stiff.

In a saucepan boil quart of milk over low heat. Place large spoonfuls of meringue mixture in milk. Continue cooking over low heat until meringue balls are firm. Remove them from milk, pat with paper towels, and place in a serving bowl.

In a saucepan over low heat, beat egg yolks with a whisk, and slowly add the 2 cups hot milk, stirring constantly, until mixture thickens enough to slide off the back of a spoon. Do not boil. Pour the cream around the meringues and serve either warm or cold.

Zabaglione

(From Le ricette regionali italiane by Anna Gosetti della Salda, Editore Solares, Milan)

YIELD: *4 Servings*

4 egg yolks
4 tablespoons sugar
Dry Marsala

Beat egg yolks and sugar with a whisk, preferably in a thickly plated copper bowl, until well combined. Slowly add 4 half-eggshells of Marsala, stirring constantly. Place bowl over a pot containing hot water, and heat over a low heat, stirring constantly.

When zabaglione begins to thicken, remove from heat and transfer to serving cups. Serve with dry biscuits.

Note: Zabaglione originated in Piemonte and gets its name from San Giovanni Bayon, patron of the chefs of Turin, who was revered by Duke Carlo Emanuele di Savoia. His head chef invented the creamy dessert.

Asparagi con Uova Piemontese

(Asparagus Piedmont with Eggs)

YIELD: *4 Servings*

1 pound asparagus spears, cooked
1/4 cup olive oil
1/2 cup grated provolone cheese
4 fried eggs

4 slices toasted Italian bread
1/2 cup grated Parmesan cheese
1/4 cup chopped fresh parsley, for garnish
Salt and freshly ground pepper to taste

In a skillet cook asparagus over medium heat in oil. Add provolone, reduce heat, and cover until cheese melts. Arrange toast on plates, cover with asparagus, and top with a fried egg. Sprinkle eggs with grated Parmesan and chopped parsley.

Misto di Pepe con Uova

(Mixed Peppers with Eggs)

YIELD: *6 Servings*

2 large green bell peppers
1 large red bell pepper
3 tablespoons vegetable oil
2 medium onions, chopped
3 medium zucchini, diced

2 eggs
1/4 cup chopped fresh Italian parsley
Salt and freshly ground pepper to taste
3 tablespoons freshly grated Parmesan
   cheese

Wash and halve peppers. Discard the stems, ribs, and seeds, then chop or cut into slivers.

Heat oil in a frying pan and add the peppers and onions. Sauté until onions are translucent. Add zucchini and cook for a few minutes.

Beat eggs and parsley together; add salt and pepper to taste. Pour eggs into vegetable mixture while stirring rapidly with a fork. Mix well. Cook for a few minutes, or until eggs are set. Sprinkle with cheese and serve immediately as an appetizer or as a main course accompanied by a salad, fruit, and cheese.

Frittata ai Quattro Formaggi

(Frittata with Four Cheeses)

YIELD: *4 Servings*

6 eggs
1 tablespoon grated Parmesan cheese
3 tablespoons milk
1 tablespoon plus 1 teaspoon butter

1 ounce Swiss cheese, diced
1 ounce fontina cheese, diced
2 ounces mozzarella, diced
Parsley, for garnish

In a bowl beat eggs using a fork, then beat in Parmesan and milk.

Melt 1 tablespoon butter in a skillet and pour egg mixture in slowly. When crust forms and egg is still soft, add diced cheeses.

Flip the frittata, add remaining butter to the pan, and cook until golden. Sprinkle with parsley and serve.

Frittata con la Salsiccia

(Frittata with Fresh Sausage)

YIELD: *4 Servings*

6 eggs
½ pound fresh sausage, peeled and
   crumbled
1 tablespoon butter

Beat eggs gently using a fork or whisk. Add sausage and mix well.

Heat butter in skillet until it sizzles. Add egg mixture and cook, turning once, over medium heat until golden on both sides. Serve hot.

Frittatadi Cipolle

(Frittata with Onions)

YIELD: *4 Servings*

3 onions, finely chopped
1 tablespoon olive oil
1 tablespoon butter
Pinch of salt

6 eggs
2 tablespoons chopped fresh parsley
Freshly ground pepper to taste

Sauté onions in oil and butter in a skillet over low heat, adding a pinch of salt and a little water to avoid burning. Let cool. Drain onions and reserve shortening mixture.

Beat eggs and add parsley, pepper, and drained onion.

Heat pan with reserved shortening, pour in egg mixture, and cook, flipping once, until golden on both sides. Serve hot or cold.

Frittata Gialla

(Yellow Frittata)

YIELD: *4 Servings*

1 medium onion, thinly sliced
1 tablespoon olive oil
1 tablespoon butter
Two large carrots, grated
4 egg whites

2 tablespoons flour
1 tablespoon milk
Pinch of saffron
Salt to taste

Sauté onion in oil and butter until soft. Add carrots and heat for 5 minutes.

Beat egg whites. Blend flour into milk, add saffron and salt, and fold into egg whites.

Add egg mixture to carrots and onions and cook, flipping once, until golden. Serve hot.

Frittata al Tartufo

(Frittata with Truffles)

YIELD: *4 Servings*

5 eggs
Salt and freshly ground pepper to taste
2 tablespoons Parmesan cheese
1 white truffle, sliced (if unavailable, use
   one large white mushroom)

1 teaspoon butter
1 tablespoon olive oil

Beat together eggs, salt, pepper, cheese, and two thirds of truffle.

Melt butter and oil in a skillet and add egg mixture. Stir for 1 minute, then flatten, and cook, turning once, until golden on both sides.

Garnish with remaining truffle and serve hot.

Frittata al Pane

(Bread Frittata)

YIELD: *4 Servings*

1 handful of inside portion of day-old
   loaf of Italian bread
1 cup milk

1 tablespoon butter
4 eggs, beaten
Salt and freshly ground pepper

Soak bread in milk until softened, then squeeze out excess milk.

Melt butter over low heat, add the bread, and flatten using a fork. Immediately add beaten eggs with a pinch of salt and pepper. Cook until golden on both sides, and serve hot or at room temperature.

Frittata di Spaghetti
(Spaghetti Frittata)

YIELD: *4 Servings*

4 ounces Italian sausage
1 pound spaghetti, cooked
2 tablespoons butter

1 tablespoon grated Parmesan cheese
2 tablespoons mozzarella, diced
3 eggs

Cover the bottom of a skillet with water, add sausage, and cook over low heat for 5 minutes. Crumble and set aside.

Heat spaghetti with 1 tablespoon butter in a deep casserole, and add Parmesan, mozzarella, and sausage.

Beat eggs until foamy and pour into spaghetti mixture, blending well using a wooden spoon.

Heat remaining butter in a frying pan. Add frittata mixture and cook, turning once, over low heat until golden (about 7 minutes per side). Serve hot or at room temperature.

Crocchette d'Uova
(Egg Croquettes)

YIELD: *4 Servings*

6 hard-boiled eggs
1 recipe béchamel (recipe follows)
1 raw egg yolk

Salt and freshly ground pepper to taste
2 cups bread crumbs
Butter, for frying

Chop hard-boiled eggs and mix with béchamel. Add raw yolk and blend well using a fork. Season with salt and pepper.

Shape egg mixture into small balls. Bread them and fry in hot butter. Serve with a tomato sauce or a hot sauce.

Béchamel

2 tablespoons butter
2 tablespoons flour, sifted

2 cups hot milk
Salt and freshly ground pepper to taste

Melt butter in a deep casserole over low heat. Sprinkle the flour over the butter and continue cooking for 4 seconds.

Pour hot milk slowly into casserole, stirring constantly to dissolve the flour. Cook for 15 minutes over low heat. Remove from heat. Stir in salt and pepper.

Tortino alla Toscana
(Tuscan Egg Torte)

YIELD: *4 Servings*

4 artichokes
4 eggs

2 tablespoons milk
Salt and freshly ground pepper to taste

Preheat oven to 250°F.

Cut artichokes lengthwise in wedges. Boil them for 10 minutes, then place in a well-buttered pan.

Beat eggs with milk, and salt and pepper; pour over artichokes. Bake uncovered until eggs are creamy. Serve hot.

Uova in Carpione

(Pickled Eggs)

YIELD: *4 Servings*

4 eggs
Butter, for frying, plus 4 tablespoons

2 tablespoons white vinegar
Fresh sage and parsley to taste

Fry the eggs in butter. Place on a dish.

Add 4 tablespoons butter to pan and cook over low heat until the butter is dark brown. Add vinegar, sage, and parsley and cook for 50 seconds. Pour over eggs. Let cool and serve at room temperature.

Uova con Purea di Patate

(Eggs with Potato Puree)

YIELD: *4 Servings*

2 pounds potatoes, boiled and peeled
5 tablespoons milk
3 tablespoons butter plus additional, for
    dotting

2 tablespoons grated Parmesan cheese
4 eggs

Preheat oven to 320°F.

Puree potatoes, milk, butter, and 1 tablespoon of cheese in processor. Spread the mixture into a rectangular baking dish. Make four indentations in puree and break an egg into each one. Sprinkle remaining tablespoon of cheese over potatoes and eggs, and dot with butter. Bake for about 8 minutes, until eggs are set. Serve hot.

Uova Ripiene Verdi
(Stuffed Eggs)

YIELD: *4 Servings*

*4 hard-boiled eggs, peeled and halved
    lengthwise*
4 ounces tuna packed in oil
1/2 teaspoon mustard
2 tablespoons butter
*1/2 package frozen spinach, defrosted and
    well-drained*

*1/2 cup mayonnaise plus mayonnaise for
    topping*
*1 tablespoon finely chopped Italian
    parsley*
1 tablespoon finely chopped capers
2 tablespoons finely chopped gherkins
Salt and pepper to taste

Remove yolks from hard-boiled eggs. In a blender combine egg yolks, tuna, mustard, butter, and spinach; blend well. Remove yolk mixture from blender and mix with mayonnaise, parsley, capers, and gherkins. Add salt and pepper to taste. Fill empty hard-boiled whites with mixture. Top with additional mayonnaise and refrigerate until ready to serve.

Pane con Frittata alle Erbe
(Herb Frittata Sandwiches)

YIELD: *2 Servings*

3 eggs
1 tablespoon finely chopped scallions
1 tablespoon chopped parsley
1 tablespoon chopped basil
1 tablespoon chopped mint

Salt to taste
3 tablespoons olive oil
Butter
4 slices bread

Mix eggs with scallions, parsley, basil, mint, and salt; beat well.

Warm oil and 1 teaspoon butter in a large skillet, add egg mixture, and cook, turning once, over medium heat until golden on both sides.

Toast bread, butter it, and make frittata sandwich.

14

NUNS COOK, TOO!

A s a child my first impression of Catholic nuns was that of severe-faced women dressed in long, terrifying, black dresses. They represented the dark and ominous side of Christianity and were to be treated with the greatest long-distance respect. They were to be revered because they were special supranormal women who talked to God and taught children to fear Him. Much to my delight, I later discovered that they are normal, ordinary women who have given their lives in service to God's people out of love for Jesus Christ. Nuns, or sisters, are wonderful women and so very very human, and I have been fortunate through the years to have many as my friends and associates in the Lord's vineyard.

A parish where I used to have residence was blessed enough to have seven nuns to staff its parochial school. As resident in the parish rectory, it fell to me to walk over to the convent chapel every weekday morning for 6:30 A.M. mass. To fulfill this duty I had to rise every morning at 5:50 A.M. to shower, shave, and wake up before I got there. Some mornings, especially after a long night of correcting papers and preparing for my own classes, only my body got over to the convent. But when I realized that the sisters had been in their chapel since 5:30 A.M. praying (probably for me), I tried my best not to fall asleep while I was reading the Scriptures.

I forgot to mention that every sister except one was a native-born Italian and that they belonged to the group of sisters called the Sisters of Our Lady of Mercy. Of course the priests were often invited (not often enough to suit me!) to the convent to join the sisters for wonderful Italian dinners and warm Christian fellowship. They were delightful, witty, and wise women supremely dedicated to their task.

This next group of recipes was generously given to me by Mother Grazia, their immediate superior, at my insistence. The recipes were given to me in Italian, but I've translated them for you. I wouldn't want you to miss out on these mouth-watering recipes.

Risotto in Bianco
(Rice in White Wine)

YIELD: *Serves 4*

1 onion, thinly sliced
½ stick (4 tablespoons) butter
1 cup uncooked rice

½ cup white wine
3 cups beef stock

Sauté the onion in a saucepan in which butter has been melted. When the onion is beginning to brown, add uncooked rice, sauté for 1 minute, then add white wine. When the wine has evaporated, add beef stock. Cook over low heat for 20 minutes. Serve hot.

Roasted Tomatoes

Fresh tomatoes
Italian Bread Crumbs (page 97)

Olive oil

Preheat oven to 350°F. Cut not-so-ripe tomatoes into thick slices. Place them in a shallow oven pan. Generously sprinkle with Italian bread crumbs and olive oil. Bake for 15 minutes. Serve hot or cold. Use as a sidedish for meat or fish.

Stuffed Mushrooms

Large mushrooms
1/4 cup fresh parsley
1 garlic clove, peeled
1/4 cup olive oil
Butter, 2 tablespoons

Salt and freshly ground pepper to taste
1/4 cup bread crumbs
1/8 cup grated Parmesan cheese
1 egg
Mozzarella cheese

Preheat oven to 300°F.

Wash the mushrooms, remove and mince the stems.

Chop the parsley and garlic together, and sauté both in olive oil and a pat of butter in a skillet. As soon as the parsley begins to fry, add the minced mushroom stems. Let this simmer for a minute and then add salt and pepper along with bread crumbs. Mix until you have a pasty consistency. Remove from heat.

When cool, add Parmesan and egg. Mix well. Fill the mushroom caps with the mixture. Grease a shallow oven pan with butter and place the filled mushroom caps in it. Cover each stuffed cap with a small slice of mozzarella cheese or dot of butter. Bake for 25 minutes.

Carciofi Ripieni

(Stuffed Artichokes)

YIELD: *Serves 4*

¼ cup chopped fresh parsley
2 garlic cloves, minced
4 tablespoons butter
½ pound ground beef
Salt and freshly ground pepper to taste

1 tablespoon tomato sauce (page 41)
4 artichokes
¼ cup olive oil
1 cup beef or chicken stock

Sauté parsley and garlic in 2 tablespoons butter in a skillet. Crumble in ground beef, salt and pepper, and tomato sauce. Simmer until well cooked, about 20 minutes.

Remove the outer leaves and the choke from the artichokes. Wash and drain the artichokes completely. Fill them with beef mixture and place them in a large saucepan in which olive oil and remaining butter have been heated. Cook them over low heat. Add beef stock (or enough to cover bottom 1 inch of artichokes). Cover and simmer for about ½ hour, or until leaves pull off easily.

Bocconcini Saporiti

(Tasty Mouthfuls)

YIELD: *Serves 4*

4 thin veal cutlets
1 egg, slightly beaten
Italian Bread Crumbs (page 97)
¼ cup olive oil
6 tablespoons butter

4 slices prosciutto or boiled ham, in
  2-inch strips
½ pound mozzarella cheese, in 2-inch
  strips

Dip cutlets in slightly beaten egg and then in bread crumbs.

Brown them in olive oil and 2 tablespoons butter in a medium-hot skillet.

Grease a baking dish with butter. Cut the cooked veal into 2-inch strips and place in a prepared baking dish. Place on each strip of veal a strip of prosciutto and a strip of mozzarella. Dot with butter and make another layer the same way on top. Bake in a 350°F oven for 10 minutes. Serve hot.

* 15 *

SALAD ... FOR GOOD DIGESTION!

Italians eat light salads at the end of the meal rather than at the beginning. The philosophy is that the fresh greens should follow the main course as a natural aid to good digestion. Light salads are simple affairs, perhaps torn fresh-crisp romaine or iceberg lettuce lightly tossed with a mixture of olive oil, red wine vinegar, salt, and pepper to taste. A good light salad dressing would consist of the following:

¼ cup olive oil
3 tablespoons red wine vinegar
½ teaspoon salt

Dash of freshly ground pepper
Sprinkle of oregano (optional)

In a jar shake well together all ingredients. Toss lightly with lettuce, escarole, endive, or dandelion torn into small pieces.

* * *

During the summer, a fresh salad ranging from the simple to the complex, served with thick, crisp, and crusty slices of Italian bread can make a whole, delightful meal. In this chapter we will start with the simple and go on down to the more complex with variations.

Insalata di Pomodoro
(Tomato Salad)

YIELD: *Serves 4*

4 medium, fresh vine-ripened red
  tomatoes, washed and quartered
1 large onion, thinly sliced
¼ cup olive oil

Salt, freshly ground black pepper or red
  crushed hot red pepper flakes, and
  oregano to taste

Toss lightly all ingredients together.

Insalata di Patate
(Potato Salad)

YIELD: *Serves 6*

6 large potatoes, boiled in skin
2 medium onions, thinly sliced
⅔ cup olive oil
¼ cup red wine vinegar

2 teaspoons salt
1 teaspoon freshly ground black or
  crushed hot red pepper flakes

Peel potatoes when cooled and cut into large bite-sized chunks. Toss together lightly with other ingredients.

Insalata Suprema

(Salad Supreme)

1 recipe Insalata di Patate (page 210)
1 can (1 pound 3 ounces) drained chick-
  peas
1 can (8 ounces) Italian tuna fish or
  regular tuna packed in oil

½ cup pitted black olives, sliced
½ cup pitted green olives, sliced
½ cup shredded provolone or Bel Paese
  cheese

Prepare Insalata di Patate. Toss together remaining ingredients.
    Served in large portions with good Italian bread, this makes a tasty light meal. It may also be served in smaller portions on beds of crisp lettuce (escarole or endive) to make an excellent antipasto (appetizer).

Insalata di Pasta e Ricotti Giardiniera

(Ricotta Macaroni Vegetable Salad)

YIELD: *Serves 4*

½ pound elbow macaroni, cooked and
  chilled
1 cup ricotta
½ cup cooked peas
½ cup cooked sliced carrots
2 tablespoons minced green bell pepper

1 tablespoon minced onions
1 teaspoon salt
¼ teaspoon freshly ground black pepper
½ cup Italian dressing (bottled or your
  own)

Combine macaroni with other ingredients. Mix lightly using a fork until blended.
    Serve in a bowl lined with lettuce garnished with sprigs of parsley.

Insalata di Pasta e Formaggio

(Ricotta Macaroni Salad)

YIELD: *6 Servings*

1/3 cup chopped onion
1/2 cup chopped green bell pepper
1 cup ricotta
1/4 cup milk
1 tablespoon lemon juice or cider vinegar

1 tablespoon olive oil
Salt and freshly ground black pepper to taste
Dash of paprika
1/2 pound freshly cooked elbow macaroni

Combine all ingredients except macaroni and blend well. Add to hot macaroni, mixing so that macaroni is well coated. Chill thoroughly.

Serve on a bed of lettuce garnished with sprigs of parsley.

Insalata di Pasta

(Macaroni Salad)

YIELD: *4 Servings*

1/3 cup chopped onion
1/2 cup chopped green bell pepper
1 cup ricotta
1/4 cup milk
1 tablespoon lemon juice or cider vinegar

1 tablespoon olive oil
Salt and freshly ground black pepper to taste
Dash of paprika
1/2 pound freshly cooked elbow macaroni

Combine all ingredients except macaroni, blending well.

Add to hot macaroni, mixing so that macaroni is well coated. Chill thoroughly.

Serve on a bed of lettuce garnished with sprigs of parsley.

Insalata di Aranci—Sicilian
(Orange Salad)

YIELD: *4 Servings*

6 navel oranges
1 small onion, chopped
Olive oil, for dressing

1 tablespoon fresh parsley, chopped
Salt and freshly ground pepper to taste

Peel oranges and cut into very thick rounds. Dress oranges with onion, olive oil, parsley, and salt and pepper. Marinate for at least 30 minutes and serve.

Insalata Campagnola
(Peasant Pasta-Bean Salad)

YIELD: *6 Servings*

1 pound fresh Italian green beans
1 pound fresh wax beans
1 cup canned kidney beans
2 cups cooked fresh spinach
1/2 pound ditali *or other small pasta,* cooked and drained
1 shallot, peeled

1 garlic clove, peeled
2 tablespoons vegetable oil
1 tablespoon red wine vinegar
1 teaspoon Italian seasoning (1/2 teaspoon oregano and 1/2 teaspoon dried basil)
2 tablespoons minced fresh Italian parsley

Trim and wash the green and wax beans; cut into 1-inch lengths. Steam beans over 1 1/2 cups water for 6 minutes, then plunge into cold water until cool. Drain well, then transfer to a large salad bowl. Add kidney beans, spinach, and pasta to beans and mix well.

Mince shallot into a small bowl, then put the garlic through a press into the same bowl. Add oil, vinegar, and Italian seasoning and mix well. Pour dressing over the pasta and vegetables and toss. Sprinkle with parsley and serve.

Insalata di Pasta da California

(Pasta Salad California)

YIELD: *4 Servings*

1 pound short pasta (elbows or small
   shells)
1/2 pound fresh string beans
3 tablespoons vegetable oil
1 cup fresh mushrooms

1 cup part-skim ricotta or plain yogurt
Pinch of dry mustard
1/2 cup chopped fresh dill
1/2 cup crushed walnuts

Cook pasta in lightly salted boiling water until al dente. Drain and rinse in cold water; drain again.

   Clean, dice, and steam string beans.

   In a large bowl toss the pasta with the oil and add the beans and mushrooms.

   Mix the ricotta with the mustard, dill, and walnuts and add to the vegetable-pasta mixture. Chill before serving.

Variation: Add diced pimientos or raisins.

Insalata di Legumi da Ischia

(Vegetable Salad Ischia)

YIELD: *8 Servings*

2 medium potatoes
1 1/2 pounds fresh broccoli
3/4 pound fresh string beans
4 medium zucchini
1/2 pound ripe plum tomatoes, cored and
   diced
1/2 cup chopped celery

1/2 cup chopped scallions
1/4 cup chopped fresh Italian parsley
1 tablespoon minced fresh basil
3 tablespoons red wine vinegar
3 tablespoons vegetable oil
1 tablespoon Dijon mustard

Scrub potatoes and place in a saucepan. Cover potatoes with cold water, cover the pan, and boil for 15 minutes, or until tender. Drain and cool.

While potatoes are cooking, cut off the broccoli flowerets, discarding the stalks. Wash and trim the beans and cut into 1-inch slices. In separate pans, cover the broccoli flowerets and beans with cold water, bring to a boil, and simmer for 5 minutes. Drain and cool. Scrub and trim zucchini and cut into thin round slices.

Peel the cooked potatoes and cut into thin slices. Place the potatoes, broccoli, beans, and zucchini in a large bowl. Add tomatoes, celery, scallions, parsley, and basil.

In a separate bowl mix vinegar, oil, and mustard. Pour dressing over the vegetables and toss gently. Cover and chill until ready to serve.

Insalata di Pasta con Pesce
(Seafood Pasta Salad)

YIELD: *6 Servings*

*1 pound short pasta (elbows or small
    shells)*
2 tablespoons olive oil
1½ pounds fresh or saltwater fish fillets
*½ pound ripe plum tomatoes, cored and
    chopped (about 1 cup)*
1 shallot, minced

¼ cup chopped fresh Italian parsley
2 garlic cloves, peeled
¼ cup freshly squeezed lemon juice
2 tablespoons drained capers
2 bay leaves
Salt and freshly ground pepper to taste

Cook pasta in lightly salted boiling water until al dente. Drain and rinse in
cold water; drain again. Transfer to a bowl, toss with 1 tablespoon oil and
chill.

Cut fish into 1-inch cubes and poach them in a small amount of water for
6 minutes. Drain and cool.

Place tomatoes in a large mixing bowl and add shallots and parsley. Push
garlic through a press into the bowl. Add fish cubes and remaining olive oil
and toss gently to mix. Add lemon juice, capers, bay leaves, and salt and
pepper. Cover and chill.

Toss the salad with the chilled pasta. Remove bay leaves before serving.

Variation: Heat the oil in a frying pan and push the garlic through a press
into the hot oil. Add the shallots and chopped tomatoes. Cook for 5 minutes.
Add the parsley, lemon juice, capers, bay leaves, and fish cubes. Cook for 5
minutes, or until the fish is just tender. Salt and pepper to taste. Remove the
bay leaves and serve warm.

Mushroom Salad

YIELD: *2 Servings*

*6 large unblemished fresh white
    mushrooms*
1 tablespoon olive oil
1 tablespoon white wine vinegar
1 tablespoon Dijon mustard

Freshly ground pepper to taste
2 Bibb lettuce leaves
2 teaspoons snipped fresh chives

Wash and trim mushrooms, but do not peel them. Cut off the stems and slice both stems and caps; place them in a bowl.

Mix olive oil, vinegar, and mustard. Season with pepper. Pour dressing over the mushroom slices until well coated. Spoon mushrooms onto lettuce leaves, sprinkle with chives, and serve.

Variation: Add 3 medium chopped cooked shrimp and toss.

Insalata di Pasta con Peperoni

(Spaghettini with Red Peppers, Prosciutto, and Fresh Herbs Salad)

YIELD: *12 Servings*

This recipe is a real winner. It was given to me by a very dear friend, Harry Dombrosky; don't let his Ukrainian last name fool you, his mom's side of his family hail originally from Catania, Sicily.

½ cup (1 stick) butter
¼ cup olive oil
2 large red bell peppers, cored, seeded, and cubed
10 ounces prosciutto, chopped
12 scallions, thinly sliced
12 tablespoons minced fresh basil or *3 tablespoons dried, crumbled*
12 tablespoons minced fresh parsley
4 teaspoons minced fresh oregano or *2 scant teaspoons dried*

4 garlic cloves, minced
Salt and freshly ground pepper
2 cups rich chicken stock
6 tablespoons freshly squeezed lemon juice
2 teaspoons sugar
2 pounds spaghettini pasta
Freshly grated Parmesan cheese (optional)

Melt ¼ cup butter with oil in heavy large skillet over medium heat. Add bell peppers, prosciutto, and scallions and cook until vegetables soften, stirring frequently, about 10 minutes. Add basil, parsley, oregano, and garlic and stir 2 minutes. Season with salt and pepper. Add stock, lemon juice, and sugar and bring to boil. Reduce heat and simmer until slightly thickened, about 6 minutes. Cover and let sauce stand.

Cook spaghettini in boiling salted water until tender but still firm to bite. Mix with sauce, add cheese, and serve.

Pasta Scampagnata
(Country-Style Pasta Salad)

YIELD: *6 Servings*

This dish may be prepared one day in advance.

1/4 cup white wine vinegar
2 tablespoons freshly squeezed lemon
   juice
2 tablespoons minced shallots
1 tablespoon chopped fresh tarragon or 1
   teaspoon chopped dried
1/2 teaspoon salt
1/2 teaspoon freshly ground black pepper

1 cup virgin olive oil
3 cups broccoli flowerets
1 medium-size zucchini, thinly sliced
1 pound rainbow rotelle, cooked al dente
   and drained
1 sweet red bell pepper, chopped
1/2 pound mozzarella, cut into 1/2-inch
   cubes

In a small bowl combine vinegar, lemon juice, shallots, tarragon, salt, and pepper. Slowly whisk in olive oil. Set aside.

Steam broccoli for 3 minutes. Add zucchini to broccoli and steam 3 minutes more. Remove from heat and allow to cool.

Combine cooked vegetables with pasta, bell pepper, and mozzarella and toss. Pour dressing over all and toss again. Allow salad to absorb flavors for 1 hour in the refrigerator or at a cool temperature. Serve chilled or at room temperature.

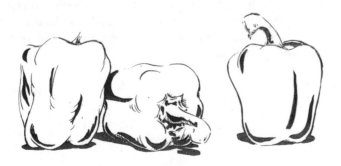

Capunatina—Sicilian

(Eggplant Salad)

YIELD: *6 to 8 Servings*

Capunatina, the internationally famous eggplant medley, combines the gems of the Sicilian vegetable kingdom into a rich sweet-and-sour salad served either warm or cold.

2 large ripe eggplants (about 3 pounds)
Salt
About 1/2 cup olive oil
2 large onions, chopped
4 stalks celery, chopped
1 can (2 pounds 3 ounces) whole tomatoes
2 fresh basil leaves or 1 teaspoon dried

1 teaspoon salt
1/2 teaspoon freshly ground pepper
1 teaspoon fennel seed
1/2 cup capers
1 cup Italian green olives, pitted and chopped
1 tablespoon sugar
1 1/2 tablespoons red wine vinegar

Remove stems from eggplants and discard. Chop unpeeled eggplant and salt liberally; drain in colander for 1 hour. (Excess water and bitter flavor will drain off.) Rinse off salt and dry with absorbent paper. Set aside.

Heat 3 tablespoons olive oil in a large skillet; add onions and celery and sauté for 5 minutes. Pour in tomatoes; add basil, salt, pepper, and fennel seed. Simmer for 10 minutes. Add capers and olives and cook sauce for 10 minutes longer. Set aside.

In another large skillet sauté eggplant in 1/3 cup hot olive oil. (Add more oil if necessary to prevent it from sticking; eggplant absorbs a lot of oil as it cooks.) Combine sautéed eggplant with sauce in a large saucepan, stirring until evenly mixed. Sprinkle sugar and vinegar over mixture and stir. Cover and simmer slowly for 10 to 15 minutes. Serve warm or cold as an appetizer, salad, or accompanying vegetable.

Variation: Add 3 tablespoons pine nuts (pignoli) and 3 tablespoons seedless black raisins to the basic recipe.

Insalata di Cetrioli e Pomodori—Sicilian

(Cucumber Salad)

YIELD: *4 to 6 Servings*

4 cucumbers, peeled and thinly sliced
1 medium onion, chopped
2 tomatoes, quartered
¼ cup fresh chopped basil or 1 teaspoon
   dried

¼ cup olive or salad oil
Freshly squeezed juice of 1 lemon
Salt and freshly ground pepper

Place cucumbers, onion, tomatoes, and basil in a salad bowl; chill. Just before serving, pour oil, lemon juice, and salt and pepper to taste over vegetables. Toss until vegetables and salad dressing are well blended.

Insalata di Finocchi e Lattuga—Sicilian

(Sweet Fennel and Lettuce Salad)

YIELD: *6 Servings*

1 head iceberg lettuce
2 stalks fennel, chopped
Leaves from 1 bunch fennel, chopped
1 No. 2 can sliced beets, drained

⅓ cup olive oil
3 tablespoons red wine vinegar
Salt and freshly ground pepper

Remove core and wash lettuce with cold water, drain, and dry. Tear iceberg leaves into bite-sized pieces and mix with fennel stalks and leaves in a salad bowl. Just before serving, add beets, oil, vinegar, and salt and pepper to taste. Toss until ingredients and dressing are blended.

Insalata di Cavolfiore— Sicilian

(Chilled Cauliflower Salad)

YIELD: *4 to 6 Servings*

1 large head cauliflower (2 to 3 pounds)
Salt
1/3 cup olive oil
Freshly squeezed juice of 1 to 2 lemons

1 garlic clove, minced
1/3 cup chopped fresh parsley
Freshly ground pepper

Remove leaves and trim base from cauliflower. Soak, head down, in cold salted water for 15 to 20 minutes. Drain. Break into flowerettes, place them in a pot, and cover with water and 1 teaspoon salt. Bring to a boil and boil gently until flowerets are tender, 10 to 15 minutes. Drain.

Combine oil, lemon juice, garlic, parsley, and salt and pepper to taste.

Place flowerets in a salad bowl; while they are still warm, pour salad dressing over them (see Tip). Chill and serve. (Excess dressing should be poured off before serving.)

Tip: Cooked vegetables absorb the full flavor of dressing the best if it is poured over them while they are still warm. Combine ingredients and toss, coating vegetables well with salad dressing. Let stand at room temperature for at least 2 hours before serving.

Insalata di Ceci—Sicilian

(Chick-pea Salad)

YIELD: *4 to 6 Servings*

2 1 pound 3 ounces cans chick-peas,
   drained
1 bunch scallions, chopped
1/4 cup chopped fresh parsley

Freshly squeezed juice of 1 lemon
1/3 cup olive or salad oil
Salt and freshly ground pepper

In a serving bowl mix ingredients together. Let stand 30 minutes before serving (always serve at room temperature).

Insalata di Lenticchie— Sicilian
(Lentil Salad)

YIELD: *6 to 8 Servings*

1 pound dried lentils
1 tablespoon salt
1 medium yellow onion, quartered
1 medium red onion, sliced and separated into rings
1 cup chopped fresh parsley

1 cup olive or salad oil
Freshly squeezed juice of 1 to 2 large lemons
Salt
Freshly ground pepper

Rinse lentils and remove bits of rock. Cover with water and soak for 30 minutes. Drain; cover with fresh water to 2 inches above lentils; add salt and onion quarters. Bring to a boil, cover, and simmer until lentils are tender but not mushy, 20 to 30 minutes. Drain, discard onions, and chill.

In a large salad bowl combine chilled lentils with onion rings, parsley, olive oil, lemon juice, and salt and pepper to taste.

Olive Condite—Sicilian

(Olive Relish)

YIELD: *6 Servings*

1 pound green Sicilian olives, pitted and crushed

2 inner stalks celery with leaves, chopped fine

1 medium onion, chopped

1/3 cup olive or salad oil

3 tablespoons red wine vinegar

Salt and freshly ground pepper

2 garlic cloves, crushed

Combine all ingredients in bowl and let stand at room temperature for one hour, then serve.

* 16 *

DESSERT IS HEAVENLY

One of the more popular feast days among Italian-Americans is the feast of St. Joseph, the foster father of Jesus. What little one reads concerning Joseph in the New Testament does inspire admiration for his courage and faith. When he took Mary to be his wife, she was already with child by the power of the Holy Spirit. Now, this was a man whose love for God overcame the natural suspicion of human nature. His faithfulness and stewardship were and are beautiful models for Christian fathers, even celibate priests called Father. This brings up an interesting question that has been asked of me by many sincere fundamentalist interpreters of the Scriptures. I am often asked, "Why do you allow yourself to be called father when the Lord said 'Call no man father upon earth, for you have one father, your heavenly Father.'" I have often been tempted to answer, "I'd rather be called father than daddy-o!" But the real answer I believe is this. When the Lord spoke those words, He wasn't speaking literally. What He meant, I believe, was that we should never forget our origin in the creative power of God the Father and to remember that our earthly fathers were not the origin of our life, but that God is the origin of life.

Zeppoli Di San Giuseppe

(St. Joseph's Cream Puffs)

YIELD: *16*

This is the traditionall dessert for the Feast of St. Joseph on March 19th.

½ cup of butter
Dash of salt
1 cup water
1 cup all purpose flour

4 eggs
1 tablespoon sugar
½ teaspoon of mango peel
½ teaspoon of grated lemon peel

Preheat oven to 400°F.

Combine butter, salt, and water in saucepan and bring to boil. Add flour all at one time, mix well until dough leaves side of pan. Remove from stove and cool 10 minutes. Add eggs one at a time and mix well after each. Add sugar and grated peels, and mix thoroughly.

Drop tablespoonfuls of mixture onto greased baking sheet leaving a 3-inch space between them. Bake in 400° oven for 10 minutes. Reduce heat to 350° and bake 30 minutes. Partially split puffs after removing from oven and let rest at room temperature for 15 minutes. Then fill with the following.

Filling

1 pound ricotta (Italian cottage cheese)
2 tablespoons chocolate chips

1 tablespoon candied orange peel
2 tablespoons sugar

Mix well and fill puffs.

Papa's Cookies

YIELD: *3 Dozen Cookies*

The fondest memories of the first six years of my life are of Papa, my father. I can remember gathering with my brothers and sister on cold winter mornings before the coal stove in our kitchen. Mamma would be pouring hot sugared coffee into bowls half-filled with *biscotti* (delicious hard cookies) that my father had baked the night before. We would each be given a steaming bowl of coffee and a handful of the cookies to be dunked whole or broken into the bowl, and would take our places before the warmth of the stove. I would take the honored position due me because I was the youngest, right on Pappa's lap. In gratitude to Almighty God we would eat our simple breakfast and prepare for the day.

Mamma always declared that Papa was the real cook of the family and that she learned all she knew from him. He was a good man and an exemplary Christian, so when he left us to go with the Lord and await the Resurrection, he left us not only his *biscotti*, but the strength of his Christian faith as an example for our lives.

It is in honor of his memory that I give you this recipe.

4 eggs
1 cup sugar
1/2 cup oil or margarine

3 cups vanilla
4 tablespoons baking powder
5 cups flour

Cream eggs and sugar; mix in shortening and vanilla.

Sift together baking powder and 2 cups of flour; add to wet ingredients and mix. Then gradually add another 2 cups of flour. Pour out onto a floured surface and knead, adding approximately 1 more cup of flour. Knead until dough doesn't stick to your hands. Take a slice of dough and roll it out to 1/2 inch thick. Cut into strips and roll with fingers into any desired shape. Place on a greased cookie sheet and bake in a 350° to 375°F oven for 12 minutes, or till golden brown.

Mostarda
(Grape Pudding)

YIELD: *Serves 12*

This is one of Mamma's special recipes. It is made in September when the backyard grapes are ripe.

Fresh Concord grapes
2 cups sugar
2 cups water
Rind from one orange, grated

3 cups Farina
1 cup chopped walnuts
1 cup semisweet chocolate bits

Stem and wash enough Concord grapes to almost fill a 3-quart saucepan. Cover with water (one cup) and allow to come to a boil over low heat. Simmer 15 to 20 minutes. Put cooked grapes into a strainer and catch juice in a bowl. Then grind grapes through a food mill into the bowl containing the juice. Set aside.

In another saucepan boil sugar in 1 cup of water. Remove from heat and add the orange rind.

To the cooled grape juice add Farina and stir to dissolve. Add this mixture to the sugar syrup. Bring to boil over low heat, stirring constantly until thick. Remove from heat and stir in the walnuts and chocolate bits. Test for sweetness. Pour into dessert dishes, allow to cool, and serve.

*   *   *

The greatest event in the history of mankind is the Resurrection of Jesus Christ that is celebrated each year on Easter Sunday. The reason why the Passion, Death, and Resurrection of Jesus were the greatest events in the Christian man's history is because through the paschal mystery men were freed from the bonds of sin and death and were enabled to become once again the Sons of God and heirs of heaven.

I have had the privilege of spending one Easter season in Rome. Although it would be ludicrous to declare Easter an exclusively Roman holiday, Easter and Rome do have a special relationship. Few will dispute the fact that watching the Pope officiate at Easter Sunday mass, amid the divinely inspired glory that is St. Peter's Basilica, can make the mortal spirit feel as if it has gotten a genuine glimpse of heaven.

For those who choose not to frequent St. Peter's for Easter services, Rome offers no fewer than 450 churches. Three of them are considered part of the Vatican: San Giovanni in Laterano, which is the cathedral of Rome; Santa

Maria Maggiore, built on the spot where the Blessed Mother told Pope Liberius snow would fall on an August day in 352; and San Paolo Fuori le Mura, built over St. Paul's tomb. Also extremely popular among pilgrims are the catacombs, especially those of San Callisto and San Sebastiano on the Via Appia Antica, and the churches of Santa Croce in Gerusalemme, built by Constantine's mother, St. Helena, to house relics of the True Cross, and San Pietro in Vincoli, which contains the chains that bound St. Peter when he was imprisoned in Rome and Michelangelo's inspiring Moses.

Easter time in Rome is a series of splendid images and gripping emotions that can humble the mighty and uplift the lowly. It is the happiness of Palm Sunday, when the Pope leads an impressive procession before throngs waving plaited fronds and olive branches sprayed silver and gold; it is the solemnity of Holy Thursday, when the Pontiff reenacts Christ's washing of His Apostles' feet beneath Bernini's magnificent baldachin; it is the sadness of Good Friday when the Holy Father leads the Via Crucis in the Colosseum and the devout wait for hours near the church of San Giovanni in Laterano for the privilege of ascending the twenty-eight steps of the Scala Santa (the stairs that Jesus is said to have climbed to meet with Pilate) on their knees; it is the relief and anticipation felt on Holy Saturday, when each church prepares for the feast that is to follow by blessing the holy water and the paschal candle and each household concerns itself with last-minute shopping and baking; and it is the unbridled joy of Easter itself, when the Pope celebrates morning mass and delivers his traditional Urbi et Orbi (To the City and to the World) message to the crowds embraced by Bernini's massive colonnade below. The atmosphere that pervades Rome at Easter is as vibrant as the colors of the azaleas that adorn the Spanish Steps at this festive time of year.

As with most holidays, food plays an integral part in a true Roman Easter celebration. After the abstinence from meat and days of individual fasting that marked Lent, Easter is a time to rejoice and enjoy the fruits of a renewed earth.

Lamb, which in the Christian tradition is a symbol of Christ and that was used during the first Passover to save the Jews from the wrath of the Almighty, is a popular main course throughout the world at Easter. For the Romans, lamb is especially appropriate, for the Latins were a sheep-herding people even before the days of the Empire. Surprisingly, the Romans can boast that even Easter eggs have a Roman connection. According to Russian tradition, Mary Magdalene gave an egg, which had turned red in her hand, as proof of the Resurrection to the Roman Emperor Tiberius. In Estonian lore, she is said to have offered it to Pilate, begging him not to have Christ put to death.

The main ingredient of the following Easter pie is wheat. Jesus himself told us the parable about the grain of wheat that must die and be buried in order for it to burst into new life. The grain of wheat was the symbol of His own death and resurrection. Wheat again was chosen by Him to be the ever-lasting memorial in the form of unleavened bread in the greatest Sacrament of His love and sacrifice, the Lord's Supper or Holy Communion.

Our recipe for wheat pie then is a fitting symbol for Easter.

Pastera
(Easter Grain Pie)

YIELD: *Serves 10*

Pie Crust

5½ cups all purpose flour
3 teaspoons baking powder
½ teaspoon salt
1 cup sugar

1 cup shortening
1 cup water
1 egg
Melted butter

Filling

3½ pounds ricotta
1 pound wheat (available from Italian stores)
1½ cups sugar
6 eggs

1 tablespoon cinnamon
1 tablespoon vanilla
½ teaspoon salt
½ cup chopped candied citrus

To make pie crust: In a bowl mix dry ingredients together; add shortening, water, and egg and mix well. Turn out onto a lightly floured surface and knead till smooth. Form into 2 balls, 1 large for lower crust, and 1 to form strips to cover top of pie. Cover and set aside.

To make filling: Mix cheese, wheat, and sugar. Fold in eggs one at a time. Add remaining ingredients and mix well. Preheat oven to 350°F.

Roll out the large ball of dough to 14 inches in diameter and ⅛ inch thick. Place in an ungreased, 12-inch springform pan and add filling.

Roll out second ball of dough to ⅛ inch thick and cut into 1-inch-wide strips. Crisscross top of pie with strips. Brush with melted butter. Bake 2½ hours, or till golden brown.

There is one acknowledged "expert" of the culinary arts in the Orsini family, and that is my brother Leo's wife, my sister-in-law Inez. She is an excellent cook, a marvelous baker, and a great hostess at holiday dinner parties. Every holiday, the Orsini clan gathers around Inez's dessert table at the end of the evening to partake of the scrumptious delicacies only she can prepare. I persuaded her to share her dessert secrets with us so that your gatherings can be as sweet and delicious as ours. We begin with an Italian wine punch that goes well with sweets.

Vino Dolce e Spumante
(Sweet and Sparkling Wine Punch)

YIELD: *Serves 12*

1 bottle (1 quart) Asti Spumanti wine, cold

1 bottle (1 quart) inexpensive rose wine, cold

1 bottle (1 quart) club soda, cold

1 bottle (1 quart) ginger ale, cold

1 package (1 quart) lemon ice, cold

1 package frozen strawberries, thawed

In a large punch bowl, pour liquid ingredients over the lemon ice; garnish with the thawed strawberries. Serve this beautiful punch with the following specialties.

Crispelle
(Fried Sweet Dough)

YIELD: *2 Dozen*

2 cups all-purpose flour
1/4 cup sugar
3 eggs

Vegetable oil
Confectioners' sugar

Place flour and sugar in a mixing bowl, mix thoroughly, and form a little well in center. Add the eggs one at a time, mixing well (use the original mixer—your hands).

Place the dough on a floured surface and knead for 10 minutes. Cut the dough in half and knead each half for another 10 minutes. Allow the dough to rest for 10 minutes, and then roll one of the halves with a rolling pin on a floured surface until very thin. With a pastry cutter, cut into 3/4 × 2-inch strips. Repeat for the second half of dough.

Fry the strips in 2 inches of very hot oil until browned. Drain on brown grocery bag paper and sprinkle with powdered sugar.

Variation: As an interesting alternative for the topping, you can bring to a boil 2 tablespoons water and 4 tablespoons honey. Then remove from heat. Once the mixture has cooled, it can be spooned over the crispelle.

Biscotti a L'Anice
(Anisette Biscuits)

YIELD: *2 Dozen Cookies*

1/2 cup shortening
1 cup sugar
3 eggs
3 cups all-purpose flour

3 teaspoons baking powder
1/2 teaspoon salt
2 tablespoons anisette

Preheat oven to 350°F.

In a large bowl cream shortening and add sugar; beat until creamy. Add eggs one at a time, beating well after each addition.

Sift together flour, baking powder, and salt. Stir into wet ingredients, and add the anisette. Mix well. Shape into 4 loaves. Place on a lightly greased cookie sheet and bake for 35 minutes until lightly browned. Lower heat. Remove from oven and place immediately on a cutting board. Cut into ½-inch slices. Place slices, cut side up, on a baking sheet and place in warm oven to toast, turning to toast both sides. Remove, cool, and serve.

Biscotti Regina
(Italian Sesame Cookies)

4 cups all-purpose flour
1 teaspoon baking powder
1 cup sugar
1 cup shortening
¼ cup orange juice

4 eggs
1½ teaspoons vanilla
1 egg, beaten
¼ cup milk
Sesame seeds

Preheat oven to 400°F.

Sift together dry ingredients; add shortening and mix very well. Add the juice, eggs, and vanilla and mix together. Turn out onto a floured surface and form into a long loaf, 2 × 14 inches.

Mix egg and milk.

Slice off 2-inch strips from the loaf and roll each strip in egg-milk mixture. Roll the strips in sesame seeds and place on a lightly greased cookie sheet. Bake for 18 to 20 minutes. Remove, cool, and serve.

Biscotti Veneziani
(Venetian Biscuits)

YIELD: *12 Biscotti*

6 eggs
1/2 cup sugar
1/4 cup oil

1 tablespoon vanilla
3 1/2 cups sifted all-purpose flour

Beat eggs until light; gradually add sugar, oil, and vanilla. Stir in enough flour to be able to work the dough with your hands.

Take enough dough for one *biscotto*; roll with hands (on a lightly floured board) into an approximately 8-inch-long cord. Make a slit with a knife, about 1/8 inch deep, from one end to the other. Press the ends together, making a circle with the slit facing outward. Make 4 additional slits perpendicular to the original slit. Repeat until dough is used up.

Drop the *biscotti* into boiling water, one at a time; let them boil until they float. Remove from water and place on a cloth to dry.

Bake the boiled biscotti in a preheated oven at 400°F for about 15 minutes on each side, or until golden. By the way, *biscotti* means *cooked twice*.

Cassata di Festa
(Holiday Delight)

YIELD: *Serves 8*

Cakes

6 eggs
2 tablespoons creme de cocoa
1 cup sugar

1 cup flour
Creme de cocoa

Filling

1 1/2 pounds ricotta
1 cup sugar
1 small jar candied fruits (5 ounces)

1 regular Hershey's almond chocolate bar, broken into bits
1/4 cup water mixed with confectioners' sugar, for icing

Preheat oven to 350°F.

To make cakes: Crack eggs into bowl of electric mixer and beat at medium speed for 20 minutes, adding 1 teaspoon of sugar at a time in the first 10 minutes until all is used. Add 1 tablespoon of flour at a time for the final 10 minutes. Pour the batter into 2 lightly greased 9-inch layer tins lined with waxed paper. Bake 20 minutes until lightly browned. Remove and cool.

To make filling: Beat cheese and sugar together and reserve 1 cup of mixture. Add the fruits and chocolate to the remainder. Mix well.

Split each baked cake into 2 layers. Place first layer on a serving dish and brush with creme de cocoa; spread ¼ of the filling over the layer and repeat the process with the remaining 3 layers. On top of the last layer, spread confectioners' sugar icing. Finally, cover the sides with the reserved cup of ricotta filling. Fit for a king!

Pignolata
(Honey Drops)

YIELD: *Serves 12*

2½ *pound box prepared biscuit flour*
   (Bisquick)
½ *cup sugar*
1 *cup milk*

2 *eggs*
2 *cups shortening*
1 *cup honey*

In a large mixing bowl, combine flour, sugar, milk, and eggs. Mix well for a dough of a thick consistency. Turn out onto a lightly floured surface and knead until dough can be rolled between the hands without falling apart. If dough is too loose, add a few drops of water to thicken. Take enough dough from the mass to fit into the palm of the hand. Roll into a long cylinder about ½ inch thick; cut off ½ inch bits from the rolled cylinder of dough. Treat all of the dough in the same way.

Melt shortening in a deep fryer and bring to high heat. Place a strainer that fits within the dimensions of the deep-fryer and drop a small handful of the dough bits into the hot grease. Fry the bits until golden brown, remove with strainer, and place on absorbent paper. Continue this frying process until all the dough bits are fried.

Arrange the fried bits in a mound on a serving dish and cover with honey. Serve by placing a large spoonful on a cake dish. These are eaten with a teaspoon. These are a Christmas-season favorite around our house.

Torta di Pane e Mele
(Apple Bread Cake)

YIELD: *6 Servings*

2 pounds red apples, peeled, cored, and
    cut into 1-inch pieces
4 tablespoons sugar
1/2 cup white wine
Rind of 1 lemon, grated
1 loaf white bread, sliced

1/4 pound of butter
2 tablespoons golden raisins, softened in
    a cup of warm water
1 tablespoon pine nuts (pignoli)
1/2 cup heavy cream

Preheat oven to 350°F.

Place apples in a pan and cover with water. Add sugar, white wine, and lemon rind; cook until apples are very soft, about 20 minutes. Let cool.

Butter bread slices on both sides. Line a round oven pan with bread and set aside.

Mix apples with raisins and pine nuts. Top bread with apple mixture, pressing well to avoid air pockets. Cover with more buttered breadslices and sprinkle with heavy cream. Bake for 1 hour, or until bread is golden.

Remove from the oven. Let stand until cold, about 30 minutes, and carefully unmold.

Crostata di Uva e Banane
(Grape and Banana Tart)

YIELD: *6 Servings*

1 egg yolk
1 tablespoon sugar
2 heaping tablespoons dry Marsala
1 pound seedless grapes, washed

3 bananas, peeled and sliced into 1-inch
    pieces
1 1/2 ounces Maraschino diluted with 1 1/2
    ounces water
1 pie crust, cooked (use frozen pie crust
    bought in the store)

Beat egg yolk and sugar with a whisk, gradually adding Marsala. Place in a double boiler and cook until foamy. Pour into a tureen and let cool.

Simmer grapes and bananas in Maraschino and water for 1 hour, tossing frequently.

Fill pie crust with cream mixture and decorate with grapes and bananas. Refrigerate until set and serve at room temperature.

Crostata di Riso
(Rice Tart)

YIELD: *6 Servings*

4 tablespoons rice boiled in milk and
   drained
Rind of 1 lemon, grated
2 tablespoons raisins, softened in water
   and rum flavoring to cover

2 tablespoons pine nuts (pignoli),
   coarsely chopped
1 whole egg, beaten
2 tablespoons sugar
1 pie crust

Preheat oven to 300°F.

Mix rice with lemon rind, softened raisins, pine nuts, egg, and sugar.

Fill pie crust with mixture and bake for 30 minutes. Serve at room temperature.

Torta Budino Caffe —Jo-Anne Gaglioti, Maywood, New Jersey

(Coffee Pudding Cake)

YIELD: *6 to 8 Servings*

1 cup flour
2 teaspoons baking powder
1/2 teaspoon salt
2/3 cup sugar
1/3 cup cocoa powder
1/2 water

2 tablespoons vegetable oil
1 cup walnuts, chopped
1 cup brown sugar, packed
2 tablespoons cocoa powder
1³/4 cups hot espresso coffee
Whipped cream (optional)

Preheat oven to 350°F.

Combine flour, baking powder, salt, sugar, and cocoa in a bowl. Add the water and oil and blend until smooth. Stir in the chopped nuts and pour into a greased 9-inch square pan. Sprinkle brown sugar and 2 tablespoons of cocoa powder evenly over the batter. Slowly pour espresso coffee over the cake. Do not stir.

Bake for 40 minutes. Test for doneness by inserting toothpick. It should be dry. Remove from oven and let stand for about 10 minutes. Scoop into dessert bowls and spoon on the sauce from the bottom of the pan. Top with whipped cream, if desired. Serve warm.

Cucciddati—Sicilian

(Fig Cookies)

YIELD: *5 Dozen*

Filling

1 ring (1 pound) dried figs, chopped
1 cup seedless raisins

1 cup honey
1/2 cup bourbon whiskey

Rind of 1 large orange, grated
1/2 pound walnut or hazelnut meats,
    roasted and chopped

1 teaspoon cinnamon

Pastry

2 1/2 cups sifted all-purpose flour
1/2 cup sugar
2 1/2 teaspoons baking powder
1/4 teaspoon salt

1/2 cup butter or margarine
2 eggs
1/2 teaspoon vanilla
1/4 cup milk

Icing

1 1/2 cups (1/2 box) confectioners' sugar
Freshly squeezed juice of 2 lemons
Multicolored cake-decorating sprinkles

Preheat oven to 400°F. Grease two baking sheets.

To make filling: Using a medium blade, grind to a coarse consistency the figs, raisins, orange rind, and walnuts together. (Add 2 tablespoons water if mixture is too thick for grinding.) Stir in honey, whiskey, and cinnamon; mix well. Set aside. (See Note.)

To make pastry: Sift flour, sugar, baking powder, and salt together. Cut in butter using a pastry blender or two knives until mixture resembles coarse cornmeal. Stir in eggs, vanilla, and milk and mix until dough is smooth. Gather up with fingers and form into a ball. Turn onto a lightly floured board and roll out to 1/4 inch thick. Cut dough into 4 × 2-inch strips.

On one half of strip, spread filling 1 inch thick. Fold over dough half to cover filling. With fingers or fork, press edges together to seal in filling. Slicing on a slant, cut filled strip into 1-inch-wide slices. Repeat process until dough and filling are finished.

Place slices on greased baking sheets 1 inch apart and bake until slices are lightly browned, 15 to 20 minutes. Remove from oven and cool on wire racks.

To make icing: Combine confectioners' sugar and lemon juice; mix into a smooth glaze. Glaze cookies with icing and decorate with multicolored sprinkles.

Note: Cucciddati store well for weeks in an airtight container. Filling and dough may be made in advance and stored in refrigerator for a week.

Variation: Cut dough into star, round, or crescent shapes using cookie cutters. Place 1 rounded tablespoon of filling in center of dough; cover with same dough shape and press edges together using a fork. Cut small slits, crisscross fashion, on top of each cookie. Bake and ice as directed above.

Riso Nero
(Black Rice)

YIELD: *4 Servings*

5 tablespoons rice
Pinch of salt
2 tablespoons semisweet chocolate, grated

1½ tablespoons superfine sugar
1 cinnamon stick, ground

Bring a large pot of water to a boil. Add rice and salt and cook until rice is soft. Drain and add chocolate, stirring until chocolate melts and rice becomes black. Transfer rice to a serving dish, sprinkle with sugar and cinnamon, and let cool. Serve cold.

Crema di Arancio
(Orange Cream Custard)

YIELD: *4 Servings*

2 tablespoons fine egg noodles
⅓ cup sugar
3 tablespoons cornstarch
¼ teaspoon salt

1 cup orange juice
1 teaspoon grated orange rinds
2 eggs, separated
1 cup rich hot milk

Cook and drain noodles.

Blend together sugar, cornstarch, and salt. Stir in orange juice and grated orange rind. Beat yolks well and add to other mixed ingredients.

Cook mixture in a double boiler until it begins to thicken. Add milk and stir well. Cook 10 minutes, stirring occasionally. Add noodles and stir thoroughly. Remove from heat and cool to lukewarm.

Beat egg whites until stiff, not dry. Fold into cooled mixture. Pour into individual custard cups. Cool covered before serving.

17

CALABRIA MIA

During my most recent trip to Italy, I spent one entire week with my relatives and friends in Reggio Calabria, an area of Italy well known for its delicious foods. The recipes that follow were generously given to me and enjoyed with liters of the excellent red home-made wines of the region where my mother and father lived, married, and had two children before immigrating to the United States. One word of warning: Don't travel to southern Italy in January if you expect warm weather. It was cold, nasty, and rainy—but sitting before the small electric space heaters in the homes of relatives and friends brought us closer together to share the common human experiences of love and an intensely lived family life.

While staying in Reggio Calabria, I spent one day with the family of Pina Gaglioti. Her brother Anthony is a successful businessman in Maywood, New Jersey. I have had the honor of knowing Tony Gaglioti and his wonderful family for many years. He is a warm, congenial, and thoroughly Italian gentleman. Our relationship is as close as if he were one of my brothers. His wife, Joanne, is a cook of distinction; in fact, I have included one of her prize-winning recipes in this book. It is a dessert that, once tasted, is addictive. Their beautiful children, Peter, Joseph, Matthew, and Carmelino, are extraordinary Italian-Americans destined to become exceptional men in a world of mediocrity.

For those in search of the taste of experiences that are all the more incredible because they seem so irrevocably a part of the past, the moment will come to stop and look around. Immersed in the perfume of earthy essences, in the strange light between magic and reality, you will discover this handful of earth and granite: Calabria! Its strong and harsh aspect, of unexpected loveliness at times, induces those who speak of it to do so in a hushed voice. Its countenance, though maintaining the aristocratic features of those that for centuries have not humiliated themselves, bears the signs of long inner suffering and is all the more beautiful for it. There are the eternal movement of the sea with its infinite shades of turquoise and blue and purple; sharp cliffs; velvety sands; the fragrance of oranges and jasmine—stunning and evocative of past loves; sharp rocks; dense woods that open onto small lakes like a maiden opening her shy eyes; fresh and evergreen citrus orchards with their golden fruit; haughty olive trees, evocative, in the silver of their foliage, of those grandfathers who still know the stories of olden times. Calabria! Once you have visited there, there is no chance you will forget its earthy charm.

Risotto alla Puttanesca
(Lady of the Night Rice)

YIELD: *Serves 6*

1 cup water
1 can (16 ounces) tomato puree or *2 cups basic tomato sauce (page 41)*
1/2 cup olive oil
2 beef bouillon cubes

2 cups long-grain rice
1 pound oil-cured black olives, pitted
1 pound Swiss cheese, grated
Parmesan or Romano cheese
1/2 teaspoon hot red pepper flakes

In a large saucepan bring to a boil the water, tomato puree, olive oil, and bouillon cubes. Add rice. Lower heat to moderate and cook for 20 minutes, stirring constantly. Add more water if needed. Set aside for 2 minutes. Mix in olives and Swiss cheese. Serve hot sprinkled with grated Parmesan or Romano cheese and red pepper flakes.

Spaghetti al Limone
(Spaghetti with Lemon)

YIELD: *Serves 4*

1 pound spaghetti
Freshly squeezed juice of 4 small lemons
1/2 cup olive oil
3 garlic cloves, minced

2 cups chopped fresh Italian parsley
1 cup grated Parmesan or Romano
   cheese
1 cup plain bread crumbs

Cook and drain spaghetti. Add all other ingredients, toss together well, and serve.

Spaghetti alla Marsala
(Spaghetti with Marsala Sauce)

YIELD: *Serves 4*

2 pounds lean beef, cut into chunks (lean
   beef stew will do)
1/2 cup olive oil
2 cups dry Marsala
1 cup water

Salt and freshly ground pepper to taste
1 pound spaghetti
1 cup grated Parmesan or Romano
   cheese

In a large saucepan brown the beef chunks well in olive oil. Add Marsala and bring to a boil. Boil for 3 minutes until alcohol evaporates. Add the water (there should be enough liquid to cover meat) and salt and pepper. Cover pan and simmer for two hours.

Cook and drain the pasta, mix with meat sauce, then serve sprinkled generously with grated Parmesan or Romano cheese.

Salsa di Carciofi

(Artichoke Sauce)

YIELD: *Serves 4*

4 garlic cloves, minced
½ cup olive oil
2 12-ounce cans artichoke hearts packed
   in water (reserve 1 can of artichoke
   water)

½ cup chopped fresh Italian parsley

Sauté the garlic in olive oil in a skillet until just soft. Cut artichoke hearts in quarters, add to skillet, and sauté for 5 minutes. Add 1 can of artichoke water. Bring to boil. Add parsley, lower heat, cover, and simmer for ½ hour. Serve with cooked drained pasta of your choice. I recommend spaghetti or linguini. 1 pound of pasta will serve four.

Polpettone Ripieno

(Stuffed Meat Loaf)

YIELD: *Serves 6*

3 pounds ground chuck beef
3 cups plain bread crumbs
1 cup grated Parmesan or Romano
   cheese
1 cup chopped fresh Italian parsley
3 eggs
1 tablespoon each *salt and freshly
   ground pepper*
1 cup milk
1 pound thinly sliced mortadella or
   boiled ham

1 pound thinly sliced domestic provolone
   cheese
6 hard-boiled eggs, sliced
1 tablespoon capers washed under cold
   water
3 pounds chopped spinach, cooked and
   drained
Olive oil
6 large potatoes, peeled, washed and cut
   into quarters

Preheat oven to 400°F.

In a large mixing bowl, combine ground meat, bread crumbs, grated cheese, parsley, fresh eggs, salt and pepper, and milk. After well mixed, form into a large ½-inch-thick patty on waxed paper.

Line with mortadella slices, provolone slices, and hard-boiled eggs. Spoon on capers and spinach. Roll jelly-roll style. Place meat loaf into an oven pan well greased with olive oil. Surround with potato slices and drizzle olive oil over all. Bake for ½ hour. Remove from heat, let rest a few minutes, slice, and serve hot with potatoes.

Tortiera di Carciofi con Patate

(Artichoke Casserole)

YIELD: *Serves 6*

½ cup olive oil plus oil for drizzling
1 cup Italian Bread Crumbs (page 97)
5 pounds potatoes, peeled and boiled for 10 minutes, in ¼-inch slices
2 12 ounce cans artichoke hearts, drained and marinated with freshly squeezed juice of 1 lemon

4 hard-boiled eggs, sliced
1 pound mozzarella, grated
¼ pound butter, sliced
½ cup grated Parmesan or Romano cheese
½ pound mortadella or boiled ham, sliced

Preheat oven to 350°F. Pour ¼ cup of the olive oil into a wide baking pan or an ovenproof glass pan. Sprinkle 2 tablespoons bread crumbs and cover them with half of the potato slices.

Then evenly spread the artichokes, egg slices, mozzarella, butter slices, ¼ cup of grated Parmesan, mortadella slices, 2 tablespoons bread crumbs, and ¼ cup olive oil. Press down. Cover with a layer of remaining potato slices. Press down and sprinkle with remaining bread crumbs and Parmesan. Drizzle with olive oil.

Bake for 20 minutes. Remove from oven and let rest for 5 minutes. Slice and serve hot.

Polpetti di Carciofi

(Artichoke Fritters)

YIELD: *Serves 6*

2 12 ounce cans artichoke hearts,
  drained (reserve artichoke water)
1/2 cup olive oil plus oil for frying
2 eggs
1/2 cup grated Parmesan or Romano
  cheese

1 cup plain bread crumbs
3 garlic cloves, minced
1 cup chopped fresh Italian parsley
Salt and freshly ground pepper to taste
1 cup cooked rice

Quarter drained artichokes and sauté in olive oil. Add enough artichoke water to cover and simmer for 10 minutes. Remove from heat. When artichokes are cool, mix in all other ingredients. Shape into balls (if too wet to shape into balls, add some more bread crumbs) and fry until very brown in hot olive oil. Place on a paper towel–lined dish and serve as hot appetizers or a side dish.

Cudduraci cu L'Uova

(Easter Egg Baskets)

YIELD: *1 Dozen*

5 cups sifted all-purpose flour
1 cup granulated sugar
5 teaspoons baking powder
1/2 teaspoon salt
1 1/4 cups shortening
4 eggs

1 teaspoon vanilla
1/2 cup milk
1 dozen eggs, raw and colored
1 box (1 pound) confectioners' sugar
1 teaspoon almond extract
Multicolored cake-decorating sprinkles

Preheat oven to 375°F. Grease a 12-cup muffin pan.

In a large bowl sift together flour, granulated sugar, baking powder, and salt. Cut in 1 cup shortening using a pastry blender or 2 knives until mixture resembles coarse cornmeal. Make a well in the center; drop in the 4 eggs, vanilla, almond extract, and milk. Mix until dough is smooth and cleans sides of bowl. Gather up with fingers and form into a ball.

Turn dough onto a lightly floured board; roll out one large sheet, ½ inch thick. Cut dough in 12 rounds to fit muffin cups (about 3 inches in diameter). Cut 24 3-inch strips from remaining dough (for basket handles). Line cups with rounds, pressing gently with fingers to fit. Place one raw colored egg in center of each cup. Place 2 strips, crisscross fashion, over each egg, pressing strip ends over rounds to seal edges. Bake until lightly browned, 15 to 20 minutes. Cool 5 to 10 minutes before removing from muffin pan.

Combine confectioners' sugar with ¼ cup shortening and enough water or milk to make a smooth paste. Frost baskets, and decorate with sprinkles. With remaining frosting, pipe names of family and friends on baskets using a pastry tube and decorator's writing tip.

Pizza Rustica
(Rustic Pie)

YIELD: *Serves 8*

1 pound all-purpose flour
Pinch of salt
½ pound butter
4 eggs, separated
2 pounds fresh ricotta

½ pound bacon, minced and fried crisp
1 pound Italian sausage, skinned and browned well
1 pound spinach, cooked and drained
1 egg, slightly beaten

Preheat oven to 400°F.

Mix flour with a little lukewarm water, salt, and butter. Let it rest.

Beat egg whites until stiff. Combine with ricotta, bacon, sausage, yolks, and spinach.

Roll out pastry for crust and topping. Line a deep oiled pie pan with the pastry. Add all the other ingredients. Top with other layer of pastry. Brush with one beaten egg. Bake for ½ hour. Serve hot.

Pasta alla Puttanesca

(Lady of the Night Spaghetti)

YIELD: *Serves 4*

1 pound spaghetti, cooked and drained
2 garlic cloves, minced
1/2 cup minced fresh parsley
2 anchovies
1/2 cup olive oil

1 cup pitted black olives
1 cup plain bread crumbs
1 teaspoon red hot pepper flakes
1 cup grated Parmesan cheese

In a skillet sauté garlic, parsley, and anchovies in hot oil until garlic begins to brown. Add along with other ingredients to spaghetti and toss. Cover with grated Parmesan and serve.

Stomatico

(Easter biscuit)

YIELD: *3 Dozen Cookies*

2 pounds all-purpose flour
1 cinnamon stick, grated
1 cup sugar
1/2 cup sugar syrup, caramelized

1 teaspoon baking soda
1/2 pound softened butter
Vegetable oil

Preheat oven to 300°F.

Mix together well all the ingredients except oil into a very stiff dough. Coat your hands with oil and press dough into an oiled baking pan. Bake for 20 to 25 minutes, until lightly browned. Remove, slice, and allow to harden.

Maccheroni alla Pastora
(Shepherd's Pasta)

YIELD: *Serves 4*

1 pound spaghetti
1/2 cup grated Parmesan
1 cup ricotta

1 tablespoon butter
Salt and freshly ground pepper to taste

Cook the pasta, reserving 1 tablespoon of the cooking water. Drain pasta and mix with all the other ingredients including the tablespoon of hot water. Toss and serve.

Melanzane al Forno
(Baked Eggplant)

YIELD: *Serves 6*

1 large eggplant (2 pounds)
Olive oil, for frying
1 pound mozzarella, sliced

1/2 pound prosciutto or boiled domestic
   ham
1 recipe tomato sauce (page 41)

Slice the eggplant in 1/4 inch slices. Soak in salted lukewarm water for 1 hour. Squeeze slices dry and brown them well on both sides in hot olive oil. Drain on paper towels.

Preheat oven to 350°F.

Place slices of fried eggplant in an oiled baking dish. Cover each with a slice of prosciutto and a slice of mozzarella. Cover with tomato sauce. Bake for 20 minutes.

Bucatini al Funghi

(Perciatelli with Mushroom Sauce)

YIELD: *Serves 6*

4 garlic cloves, minced
1/2 cup olive oil
1 pound mushrooms, washed and sliced
1 1/2 cups chopped fresh parsley

2 cups chopped peeled tomatoes
1 teaspoon heavy cream
1 pound perciatelli
1 cup grated Parmesan

Sauté garlic lightly in oil in a skillet. Add mushrooms and 1 cup parsley. Sauté for another 10 minutes on low heat. Add tomatoes. Cook for 1 hour on low heat. Remove from heat, add cream, and mix well.

Cook the *perciatelli* until al dente, drain well, mix with sauce, and serve hot. Add remaining 1/2 cup of fresh chopped parsley and sprinkle with grated cheese.

Sformato di Patate

(Potato Casserole)

YIELD: *Serves 6*

2 1/2 pounds potatoes, peeled and boiled in
   lightly salted water for 20 minutes
   (reserve 1/2 cup cooking water)
1 cup Italian Bread Crumbs (page 97)

2 cups Béchamel Sauce (page 42)
1/2 pound boiled ham, minced
1 pound mozzarella, grated
2 tablespoons olive oil

Preheat oven to 300°F. Grease an oven pan with oil.

Slice potatoes thinly.

Cover baking pan with 1/2 cup bread crumbs. Add 1 cup of béchamel. Cover with half the potatoes, 1/4 cup béchamel, ham, and mozzarella. Cover with remaining potatoes, remaining 1/2 cup béchamel, and olive oil. Sprinkle with remaining bread crumbs. Sprinkle with 1/2 cup of potato-cooking water. Bake for 25 minutes. Remove from oven and let rest for 5 minutes before slicing and serving.

* 18 *

WHAT ABOUT ITALIAN BREAD?

I have a very dear friend, Anna Conti, who urged me to write this cookbook. I heard somewhere that 95 percent of human beings are addicted to something. Anna's self-admitted addiction is to bread, Italian bread. I include this chapter for all the "breadaholics" in our human family.

For many Italians, bread is not what you eat with food; food is what you eat with bread. More than just a nutritional staple, bread is rich in history, legend, tradition, variety, and flavor. Its place of honor on the table has been assured since pre-Roman times. Fortunately, it is still prepared in many twentieth-century kitchens, having withstood the ravages of an industrial revolution that produces masses of white doughy squares, puts them into plastic bags, places them on supermarket shelves, and labels them "bread." The Romans would have shuddered.

For all the diehards who prefer to do it themselves, I offer this paean to *pane.*

Like most foods in Italy—pasta, sauces, sweets—there is no one "Italian" bread. Each region has its own distinctive version, often enhanced by the local touch of the local baker, who in turn got the recipe from a grandmother and her mother before her. From region to region, the fragrant aromas emanating from local *panetterie* (bread bakeries) vary, reflecting the individual character and creativity of the people.

Laden with each region's favorite ingredients—with variations in the texture of the dough in northern and southern flat breads—*focaccie* and *pizze* remain the most popular breads enjoyed throughout Italy. Food historians are not quite sure about the origins of the flat dough. The Etruscans had it well mastered in the North by the fifth century; at the same time, southern Italians were already eating flat breads covered with herbs.

The country bread from Tuscany is probably the most well-known loaf bread in Italy. Some like it for its light, airy center and hard crust; others prefer it because it contains no salt. Modern-day Tuscans claim they leave out the salt so the bread's natural flavor can complement—and not interfere with—the rich, tasty regional fare. Others say early bakers omitted salt because it was scarce, and that people grew accustomed to its salt-free taste. Speculation aside, the distinctive smooth bland flavor of *il pane toscano* makes it the most versatile of the loaf breads: Sprinkled with olive oil, crushed garlic, and salt, it makes a fabulous appetizer; when the dough is wrapped around a whole chicken and baked with aromatics and vegetables, it makes a wonderful special-occasion dish; when it is a few days old and cubed, the bread becomes one of the main ingredients with fresh vegetables in the traditional Tuscan *panzanella* (bread soup).

Pane all 'olio, olive oil bread from the North, and *pane siciliano*, Sicilian bread with sesame seeds from the South, are regional specialties that were probably inspired from the rich ingredients in their natural environments. These flavorful breads—with their firm crusts and soft centers—are ideal for sandwiches and good enough to stand on their own.

Pane Toscano
(Tuscan Bread)

YIELD: *12 Servings*

Starter

2 packages active dry yeast
½ cup warm water

½ cup all-purpose unbleached flour

Dough

5 cups all-purpose unbleached flour
1 cup whole-wheat flour
Approximately 2 cups warm water

2 tablespoons olive oil
Cornmeal, for baking

To make starter: Combine ingredients and mix well. Allow to sit for at least 3 to 4 hours.

To make dough: Combine flours in a large bowl. Make a well in the center and add the prepared starter. Slowly add the water and, using a wooden spoon, gradually mix until a soft pliable dough is formed.

Turn the dough out onto a floured surface and knead vigorously for 10 minutes. Place dough in a large bowl, top lightly with oil and spread with your fingers over entire surface. Cover loosely with a towel and allow to rise in a warm spot until double in bulk.

Punch down dough and divide in half. Form round or oval loaves and place on a baking sheet sprinkled with cornmeal. Allow to rise until double in bulk. Just before baking, make ½-inch slashes with a razor on top of each loaf. Bake in a preheated 450°F oven for approximately 30 minutes, or until very brown.

Pizza Conti

YIELD: *6 to 8 Servings*

Pizza Dough

1¼ cups sifted all-purpose flour
½ teaspoon salt
1 teaspoon sugar
1 tablespoon shortening

½ cup hot water
½ package (1½ teaspoons) active dry
  yeast
Olive oil

Pizza Sauce

2 to 4 tablespoons olive oil
1 large onion, chopped
4 large ripe tomatos, skinned, cored,
  chopped, and seeded

¼ cup minced fresh parsley
½ teaspoon salt

To make dough: In a large bowl sift flour, salt, and sugar together. Melt shortening in the hot water; cool to lukewarm. Add yeast to lukewarm liquid and let stand for 5 minutes. Add liquid to dry ingredients (except olive oil); mix until dough cleans sides of bowl and is smooth. Gather up with fingers and form a ball. Place in an oiled bowl; turn to oil top. Cover with cloth; let rise in a warm place (85° to 90°F) free from drafts until doubled in bulk, 35 to 45 minutes. Prepare pizza sauce while dough is rising.

When dough has doubled, punch down and turn onto a lightly floured board. Roll out and flatten into a well-oiled 10×15-inch rectangular baking pan. Brush with olive oil. Preheat oven to 450°F.

To make sauce: In a saucepan heat oil and sauté onion for 3 minutes. Stir in tomatoes, parsley, and salt; simmer for 5 to 8 minutes. Spread sauce over pizza dough. Immediately place in 450° oven and bake for 20 minutes. Remove, let cool for 5 minutes. Slice and serve.

Pollo in Pane
(Chicken Baked in Bread)

YIELD: *12 Servings*

2 tablespoons olive oil
2 tablespoons unsalted butter
1 roasting chicken (3 to 4 pounds)
2 large white onions, sliced
2 large red onions, sliced
1 whole head garlic, peeled

3 stalks celery, sliced
2 carrots, peeled and sliced
6 slices pancetta, cut in slivers
Salt and freshly ground pepper to taste
Dough for Pane Toscano (page 254)

In a large casserole heat the olive oil and butter; add the chicken, turning often until brown on all sides. Remove chicken and reserve. To same pan add vegetables and pancetta; cook until vegetables are soft. Season with salt and pepper.

Place half the vegetable mixture inside the cavity of the chicken. On a floured work surface, roll out dough into a large (approximately 18-inch) circle. Place circle on a lightly buttered roasting pan.

Spoon remaining vegetables onto bread dough; place whole chicken on top. Wrap chicken with dough, being careful not to make holes in the dough. If necessary, use water to seal dough. Bake in a 375°F oven for 1 hour, or until very golden.

Cut hole through top to allow steam to escape. Cool slightly before serving.

Pane all'Olio
(Olive Oil Bread)

YIELD: *12 Servings*

1 package (1 tablespoon) active dry
   yeast
Approximately 1 1/2 cups warm water
1/2 cup olive oil
3 teaspoons salt

2 1/2 cups all-purpose unbleached white
   flour
1 cup whole-wheat flour
Cornmeal, for baking

In a large bowl combine yeast, water, oil, and salt. Mix well and let sit for 10 minutes. Slowly add the flours and mix well until a pliable dough is formed. Turn dough out onto a floured surface and knead vigorously for 10 minutes. Place dough in an oiled bowl and cover loosely. Allow to rise in a warm spot until double in bulk.

Divide dough in half and form two oblong loaves. Place loaves on a baking sheet sprinkled with cornmeal. Cover loaves loosely with a towel and allow to rise until double in bulk.

Preheat oven to 400°F. Just before baking, slash tops of loaves with a razor. Bake for 40 minutes, or until golden.

Focaccia con Cipolle e Salvia
(Focaccia *with Onions and Sage*)

YIELD: *12 Servings*

Starter

3 cups unbleached flour
2 packages (2 tablespoons) active dry
   yeast

1 1/2 cups warm water

Dough

3 cups unbleached flour
2 teaspoons salt

½ cup olive oil
Approximately 1 cup warm water

Topping

3 onions, sliced and sautéed in olive oil
½ cup chopped fresh sage (or another
    fresh herb)

2 tablespoons coarse salt
½ cup olive oil

To make starter: Combine all ingredients and mix well. Allow to sit in a bowl for 3 to 4 hours.

To make dough: Place flour and salt in a large bowl. Make a well in the center and add the starter and olive oil. Slowly add the water by mixing the dough with a wooden spoon. Add enough water to form a pliable dough.

Turn dough out onto a floured surface and knead vigorously for 10 minutes. Place in an oiled bowl, cover loosely with a clean towel, and allow to rise until double in bulk.

Divide dough in half, form into flat discs, and place on an oiled baking sheet. Allow the dough to rise for about 40 minutes, or until it begins to appear puffy.

Using your finger, make indentations all over the surface of the dough.

To make topping: Combine all ingredients. Sprinkle on dough.

Bake in a preheated 400°F oven for about 25 minutes, until dough is golden.

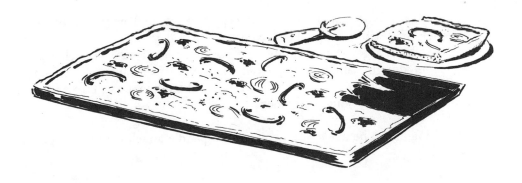

Pane Dolce Gubana

(Sweet Bread)

YIELD: *10 to 12 Servings*

Dough

1 package (1 tablespoon) active dry
  yeast
¼ cup warm water
¼ cup warm milk
½ teaspoon salt

1 tablespoon sugar
1 cup sifted unbleached flour
2 eggs
½ cup soft butter, cut into small pieces

Filling

⅓ cup each *chopped walnuts, almonds,*
  and hazelnuts
½ cup raisins
⅓ cup pine nuts (pignoli)
⅓ cup dried candied fruit
1 tablespoon sugar
Grated rind of 1 orange

Grated rind of 1 lemon
Freshly squeezed juices of 1 lemon and 1
  orange
Grappa as needed to soak (about ½
  cup)
1 egg, beaten
1 tablespoon olive oil

To make dough: In a mixing bowl combine yeast, water, milk, salt, and sugar. Allow to sit for 30 minutes (see Note). Add the flour and eggs and mix at low speed for about 3 to 4 minutes. Add butter and mix until it is worked into the dough. Cover the mixing bowl with a clean towel and allow dough to rise until double in bulk. (This dough will take longer than usual to rise.)

To make filling: Place all ingredients except Grappa and egg in a bowl. Cover generously with Grappa. Let mixture sit for 2 days.

Place dough on a generously floured surface and form a 12 × 18-inch rectangle. Cover dough with filling and oil. Place in a well-buttered 10-inch round cake pan. Brush the top with beaten egg and bake in a 350°F oven for 45 to 50 minutes, until dough is golden.

Note: This dough can be made in the mixer with paddle attachment or dough-hook.

Pane Siciliano

(Sicilian Bread)

YIELD: *12 servings*

Starter

1 package (1 tablespoon) active yeast
1 cup water

½ cup all-purpose unbleached white flour

Dough

1 cup all-purpose unbleached white flour
2 cups durum wheat flour (available in
  health food stores)
3 teaspoons salt

Approximately ½ cup warm water
Approximately ½ cup sesame seeds, for
  baking
Cornmeal, for baking

To make starter: Combine ingredients in a large bowl and let sit for several hours.

To make dough: Add the flours and salt to the starter. Slowly add more warm water if necessary. Mix well until a pliable dough is formed.

Turn dough out onto a floured work surface and knead vigorously for 10 minutes.

Place dough in an oiled bowl and cover loosely with a clean towel. Allow to rise in a warm spot until double in bulk.

Form two loaves and place on a baking sheet sprinkled with sesame seeds (see Note). Roll each loaf over the seeds, gathering as many seeds on the loaves as possible. Place prepared loaves on a baking sheet sprinkled with cornmeal. Preheat oven to 400°F. Before baking, make ½-inch-deep slashes with a razor blade along the tops of the loaves. Bake for 30 to 40 minutes, or until golden.

Note: For the authentic Sicilian *mafalda*, form each loaf by making a long snake shape with the dough. Then turn the dough back on itself, like an *S*, several times. Sprinkle each loaf generously with sesame seeds before baking.

Focaccia Calabrese

(Calabrian Vegetable Pizza)

I usually try to spend some time in Italy every year, and invariably I find my way down to Reggio Calabria to visit with my relatives. This next recipe is a Calabrian version of *focaccia*. A healthy slice of this accompanied with a glass of good red Italian wine, and Heaven can wait—at least for a little while longer!

1 recipe focaccia *dough (page 256)*

Topping

1 large head escarole, cleaned, chopped, and dried

1 recipe Pizzaiolo tomato sauce (page 00)

1 tablespoon capers, washed under cold water and dried

½ cup Spanish salad olives, drained

½ pound Italian ham or mortadella, chopped

1 cup grated Italian provolone cheese

1 cup grated mozzarella

Sprinkling of grated Parmesan or Romano cheese

Prepare dough.

Simmer escarole in tomato sauce for 20 minutes, then set aside.

Roll out dough and top with escarole sauce and other topping ingredients. Bake in a preheated 400°F oven for 25 minutes.

Grissini
(Bread Sticks)

YIELD: *5 Dozen*

Dough from focaccia *(page 256)* or   *¼ cup cornmeal*
   Pane Siciliano *(page 259)*

After dough has risen once, roll out two 12 × 18-inch rectangles. Place rectangles on a floured surface and cover loosely with a clean towel. Allow to rise again until puffy, about 40 minutes.

Using a very sharp knife or pizza cutter, cut dough in half lengthwise. Then cut into strips about ⅓-inch wide. Stretch each small strip slightly and place on a baking sheet sprinkled with cornmeal. Bake in a 400°F oven for 20 minutes, or until golden.

ABOUT THE AUTHOR

Father Joseph E. Orsini was born in Bayonne, New Jersey, on June 1, 1937, to Giuseppe and Carmela Amore Orsini, immigrants from Reggio Calabria, Italy. The last of seven children, Father Orsini attended public grammar school in Bayonne, Catholic high school in Jersey City, and Don Bosco College. He won his B.A. in Classical Language in 1960 from Seton Hall University and was awarded the Cross and Crescent for academic excellence.

He studied Theology at St. John's Home Missions Seminary in Little Rock, Arkansas, where he taught Latin and Italian; he was ordained in Camden, New Jersey, on May 16, 1964. He went on to earn the M.A. degree in Secondary Education at Seton Hall University magna cum laude and the Doctor's degree in the Philosophy of Education at Rutgers University.

Since ordination, Father Orsini has served many parishes in the Diocese of Camden and taught in three Catholic high schools. He has been involved in the Charismatic Renewal and the Cursillo and Marriage Encounter movements on many levels.

He has been serving UNICO National, a service organization of Italian-American business and professional men, since 1965 as national chaplain, and was then awarded for distinguished service. Marquis Who's Who, Inc. selected him to be a biographee for the fifteenth edition of *Who's Who in the East*.

He is the author of *Hear My Confession*, a personal testimony of his life, *Papa Bear's Favorite Italian Dishes*, and *The Cost in Pentecost*. He has appeared on national television on the "Mike Douglas Show" (it was novel that a priest be the author of a cookbook). It was on this show that Father Joe first met Dom DeLuise, who was guest co-host that week. This meeting was preordained and the friendship born of it has lasted over the years and been nurtured with love.

Father Orsini was the Catholic campus minister at Stockton State College and at Atlantic County Community College, and past chaplain of Rutgers University in Camden, New Jersey. He is the founder of The Word of God Fellowship, a work inspired by the Holy Spirit. This Catholic organization is devoted to bringing the Good News of Jesus Christ and His saving message, so that many will experience His Love and His healing touch.

On March 9, 1986, Knighthood in the Royal Order of Cyprus was conferred on Father Orsini and entertainer Dom DeLuise, in recognition of their contributions to the Catholic faith and propagation of their Italian heritage.

INDEX